_____ GARRISON COMMUNITY

contributions in sociology series editor:

_____ DON MARTINDALE

Department of Sociology, University of Minnesota

contributions in sociology 2

Charlotte Wolf

Department of Sociology, Temple Buell College

GARRISON COMMUNITY

A STUDY OF AN OVERSEAS AMERICAN MILITARY COLONY

Greenwood Publishing Corporation

Westport, Connecticut

Library of Congress Catalog Card Number: 70-81523
SBN: 8371-1853-0

Greenwood Publishing Corporation
51 Riverside Avenue, Westport, Conn. 06880
Greenwood Publishers Ltd., 42 Hanway Street, London, W.1., England
Printed in the United States of America

Designed by Joan Stoliar

To René

CONTENTS

viii
___

CONTENTS

TABLES

TABLES

PREFACE

This book is a study of an American military community in Ankara, Turkey, and its relationships with the external Turkish society. It was undertaken in the belief that if overseas military people and their actions were to be understood, they would have to be viewed as embedded in a community context. The social world of the American military community in Ankara was dominated by a single system of power, the one-dimensional reality of the military institution serving as reference point for other institutional and group claims.

The peculiarities of this overseas community were to a great extent attributable to the way in which military dominance and ethnic position had contributed to its formation. It was hypothesized that both of these aspects would be reflected in the highly structured military web of individual relationships. Thus, if it was within the compelling crucible of time and place in the community that the transient member's ways of seeing or not seeing were tempered, then only by reference to these could an explanation of his cross-cultural behavior be made.

Although the military community is studied in this volume primarily as a subtype of community, it constitutes a significant subject for examination in a number of other ways as well. As a form of the total institution,[1] the diffuseness or restrictiveness of its social boundaries might be more discerningly perceived as influenced by the social climate and the cultural characteristics of the external milieu. That is, the extent of closure both within the community and manifested toward the outside might be roughly measured as a response to its foreign situation. One could hypothesize, for example, that Turkey as an environment would be likely to have a less ameliorating effect upon the strictures of the military community than would a Western European country. The military community could also be studied as a historical phenomenon, sharing with other such historical communities typical traits and relationships. And, finally, this military community is interesting as a unique product of cold-war America.

It is in the spirit of the last that the title *Garrison Community* was chosen. Of course, this is a variation on Harold Lasswell's theme of "the garrison-state."[2] Although his hypothesis is not applicable here, nonetheless, this garrison community might exemplify a small and total societal arrangement which "tends to subordinate all social values and institutions to considerations of military potential."[3] The heuristic possibilities should not be overlooked, since the implications for the viability of democratic institutions in the heart of an armed camp might prove instructive. Who knows? In today's world the garrison community might be a microcosmic prophecy: the shambling shape of things to come.

CHARLOTTE WOLF
Boulder, Colorado
March, 1969

NOTES

1. For a discussion of his concept of total institutions, see Erving Goffman's essay, "The Characteristics of Total Institutions," in *Complex Organizations: A Sociological Reader,* ed. Amitai Etzioni (New York: Holt, Rinehart and Winston, 1964), pp. 312–340.

2. Harold D. Lasswell, "The Garrison-State Hypothesis Today," in *Changing Patterns of Military Politics,* ed. Samuel P. Huntington (New York: Free Press, 1962), pp. 51–70.

3. Ibid., pp. 62–63.

ACKNOWLEDGMENTS

I would like to express my appreciation to all those who assisted me in the conception and preparation of this study. Above all, I am profoundly grateful to Professor Don Martindale for his never-failing encouragement and advice. To acknowledge his example as a great teacher and scholar is to recognize the most forceful influence reflected in this book.

Beyond this stellar support, I owe much to the many American military people in Ankara who gave so freely and generously of their time and effort. While it is impossible to mention them separately, I wish to thank them all.

Permission to study the community was granted through the Headquarters of the United States Air Force in Washington, D.C., and by the various American military commanders in Ankara. Considerable assistance was lent to me in these negotiations by members of the American Embassy in Turkey. To those involved I wish to express my special indebtedness.

I also want to thank Mrs. Helen Keefe, who so ably and cheerfully typed the original manuscript. And last, I wish to thank my husband René. His thought and interest, courage and imagination are deeply woven into every part of this book.

C.W.

——————————————————————— GARRISON COMMUNITY

1

THE MILITARY COMMUNITY OVERSEAS: PROBLEMS AND CONCEPTS

Since the end of World War II, as the world commitments and political responsibilities of the United States have been expanded, American military personnel have gone overseas in ever-increasing numbers.[1] As these Americans have been transported, so have their institutions, their culture, and many of their material accouterments. With such social and economic self-sufficiency, ethnic communal enclaves have developed within the foreign milieus. And the everyday routine of American children going to American schools, American fathers going to American jobs, American mothers shopping at American stores goes on in places as distant as Tokyo and Heidelberg, Izmir and Naha, Reykjavik and Manila.[2] Like small alien islands in seas of foreign culture, these communities tenaciously maintain their distinctive way of life.

Although many observers, both American and foreign, have noted that these overseas Americans live relatively isolated from the local inhabitants, seldom venturing beyond the invisible American surround, and that their participation with the local inhabitants is usually limited in scope and attenuated in depth, little research or commentary has been directed toward their community arrangements as such. Rather, the main thrust of criticism and analysis has been concerned with the effectiveness of Americans in carrying out their overseas missions, their representative roles in contact with native populations, and the enhancement or tarnishing of the United States's "image" by reflections from such interpersonal contacts. Occasionally, criticism has become caustic when leveled at the arrogance and superiority displayed by these dwellers of "little Americas" or "golden ghettos."[3] Yet on the whole, few writers have evinced more than passing interest in overseas Americans *within* the context of their specialized communities and in how such communities affect the individual American in his attitudes and responses to the external situation.[4]

The problem area explored here is that of an overseas American military community and its dimensions and patterns of extra-community participation and closure. It is the argument of this book that such patterns are community-mediated, and that the effect of this mediation is internally

2
———

differentiated in respect to structural groups. In a broad sense, therefore, it is suggested that by *structure alone* individual and group patterns of extra-community participation and closure are to a great extent shaped and delimited.

Although the scope of this study is restricted to a contemporary military community, it should be noted that transplanted military communities are hardly unique. Foreign military encampments are an historical phenomenon which has appeared in many places and at many times. Of course such phenomena have had their local and temporal peculiarities wherever and whenever they have occurred. But a cursory review of the literature indicates that tensions between members of the ethnic enclave and the native population have developed with great frequency.[5] It is possible, therefore, that extra-community closure and strained relations with native peoples are endemic to the military community situation; and it is also against the possibility of this generalization that a specific study of this type must be viewed.

THEORETICAL FRAMEWORK: THE COMMUNITY

The problem of the relationship between community structure and extra-community participation and closure in an overseas American military setting was explored within the framework of the community theory developed by Don Martindale. His theory emphasizes process and change in this integrated system of social life. Such an approach is comparatively recent, and therefore its value is better delineated perhaps when compared with divergent theories and definitions of community.

The concept of community has had a long and turbid history. Since Aristotle stressed that the nature of man was intrinsically social and that his political and social arrangements—family, village, state—could be subsumed under the category of community, the conceptual meaning and its range of applicability have undergone great variation. At times the term has been used synonymously with those of commonwealth, state, and society; at times it has been posed as an antithetical counterpart to that of society; at times it has been used to denote subunits within the encompassing unit of society. The matrix of ideas in which notions of community have been rooted has more often than not been representative of main trends in the history of social thought —for whenever man and his social arrangements have been a matter of inquiry, ideas concerning community have been involved.

Considering the rich diversity of its past, it is small wonder that in sociology today there are numerous analytical approaches to the study of a community. Although these approaches have been variously classified, for our purposes here they will be roughly divided according to their *predominant* perspective as follows: concepts emphasizing the social-psychological or biological bases of community; typological definitions of community; definitions specifying the spatial and numerical dimensions of community; concepts stressing community processes and change.

4

Concepts Emphasizing Social-Psychological or Biological Bases of Community

The question implicitly invoked in concepts that primarily emphasize the social-psychological or biological bonds of community has to do with *why* men have been brought together or held together in communal association. If it is to be answered at all, the nature of the question requires an assertive answer—and as such has been fertile ground for a myriad of controversial guesses.

Such thinkers as Aristotle and Grotius assumed that man was *naturally* social (natural as opposed to conventional or artificial); and a community, having its roots in man's nature, was as a consequence also natural. Secondary ties of custom and advantageous exchange ever tightened these bonds. Other thinkers analogically employed the idea of social organism to underline the natural aspects of community. Plato, Livy, and St. Paul used this analogy on the level of literary metaphor. The idea of community as mind or soul, for example, can be traced from Plato to Durkheim and McDougal. It is possible that the organic model reached its descriptive apogee with Herbert Spencer's application. Robert M. MacIver, who elegantly describes the organic analogy as "that fruitful mother of social misconception,"[6] traces the idea of community as organism through Aristotle, St. Paul, Nicolas of Cusa, Hobbes, Spencer, and Schäffle. Regardless, it is important to note that this approach not only pointed up the social-psychological bases of integration but also provided a philosophical rationale for whatever political system being espoused.

5

In the long run the social and political implications of this idea did not go uncontested. Commencing with Althusius and Pufendorf,[7] social contract theorists on the whole denied the instinctive sociability of man. Community was seen as resultantly emerging from a deliberately conceived compact for collective security. Man's original condition, that existing before his communal association, was on the one hand starkly described as a hideous world of "all against all" by Hobbes, or on the other hand as a kind of elysium of innocence and delight by Rousseau.

Although the main thrust of social contract theory ceased to be important after David Hume's destructive critique, attendant ideas can still be found in modern concepts of community. It is interesting in this regard how much is owed to Rousseau. He perhaps more than anyone else idealized, romanticized, and sanctified the community. He saw it as an outgrowth of consensus, achieving a corporate and moral personality of its own *(moi commun),* superior to that of any of its parts. It became the source and repository of all human virtues; and, in contradistinction to any of its more creative or dissenting members, it was always right: it represented the general will. The reification of the community as a moral and autonomous organism *sui generis* is an idea that Émile Durkheim borrowed from Rousseau and developed as central to his thought.[8] Moreover, the nostalgia that Rousseau felt for the idealized simple community now lingers on in the penumbra of sentimentality adhering to such contemporary ideas as those of G. D. H. Cole or Robert A. Nisbet.[9]

Those who have stressed the biological bases for community have seen it in terms of either kinship or of symbiosis.

6

When blood ties and blood fiction have been utilized as explanation for the origin of communities, it has often been within the context of a typology—the community based on kinship posed as a polar type, prior in time and simpler in organization than its opposing type. Anthropologists have also stressed that kinship is a basic integrating factor of nonliterate tribal communities. Sociologists like Robert E. Park, Ernest Burgess, Roderick McKenzie, and E. C. Hughes have believed that symbiosis, as an ecological mechanism, helped to account for man's relationships within the community and to the general environment.[10]

While most sociologists today acknowledge, of course, the importance of social-psychological factors, and to a much lesser degree biological factors, it is those for whom solidarity, common interests, consciousness of unity, interidentification, consensus, and sentiment are sovereign in their total appraisal of the community whose ideas can be included under this classification.

Typological Definitions of Community

Man, with his passionate desire for order in a seemingly chaotic world, has generalized his knowledge and imposed his order on history when he has viewed it as a succession of chronological stages. Embedded in this world view has been the judgment that ultimately history is a matter of decline or of progress or of cyclical recurrence. From the time of Auguste Comte some sociologists have fashioned this approach to their own purposes by typing social living as either one kind of community or another, usually within a time context.

7

On the whole, most of the typologies of community have been dichotomous: the community (or tribal group or peasant village or rural settlement) has been posed at one pole of the spectrum, and the society (or the urban, secular, industrialized mode of living) posed as its antithesis. Examples of such typologies are those of Auguste Comte, Herbert Spencer, Sir Henry Maine, Émile Durkheim, Ferdinand Tonnies, Robert E. Park and Ernest Burgess, Robert Redfield, Louis Wirth, Howard Becker, and Talcott Parsons. The continuum between the two types has usually been seen on a time basis, hence unidirectional, progressing from the simplicity of the community to the complexity of urbanized life.

With Comte and Spencer this transition was optimistically interpreted as progressive improvement. Later, such triumphant confidence in the goodness and inevitability of the evolutionary process faltered, and the time-bound march toward size and complexity was looked on with growing disenchantment.

Sir Henry Maine believed the community had evolved from one based on the status of family membership and coresidence to one of individual, contractual relationships.[11] Ferdinand Tönnies, incorporating many of Maine's ideas into his book *Gemeinschaft und Gesellschaft,* introduced the idea of psychological differences characteristic of each of these two types, springing from the two kinds of human will. In the *gemeinschaftlichen* type of community *Wesenwille* (temperament or natural will) predominated; in the *gesellschaftlichen* type of society *Kurwille* (rational will) was in the ascendant. Therefore the transition from *Gemeinschaft* to *Gesellschaft* was one of increasing extrusion from

8

the warm nest of intense human relationships to the cold impersonality of a public world dominated by the objective considerations of contractual relationships: "All intimate, private and exclusive living together, so we discover, is understood as life in *Gemeinschaft. . . . Gesellschaft* is public life—it is the world itself."[12] Although these were conceived as ideal types and an existent community could manifest aspects of both, undertones of value involvement subtly penetrated the weave.[13]

The spirit of this dichotomy has been carried on in the contemporary idea of the rural-urban continuum. In recent years controversy has raged over whether such distinctions were in fact applicable or so blurred as to be irrelevant.[14]

Definitions Specifying the Spatial and Numerical Dimensions of Community

Campanilismo,[15] the term Robert H. Lowie used in delimiting the boundaries of the community to the range of its church bell, might be an abbreviated way of designating the concepts of community which are restricted in regard to number of members or to territorial size. If one or both of these requirements is not met by an existent social system, then, by definition, this social system is *not* a community. To a degree, of course, both kinds of restrictions are interrelated and even coexist in some conceptual approaches.[16]

In the case of concepts which specify population size, perhaps a few examples will suffice to illustrate the main direction they have taken. For instance, Baker Brownell states that "a community is a group of neighbors who know one another face to face."[17] G. P. Murdock and his colleagues

9

define the community as "the maximal group of persons who normally reside together in face-to-face association."[18] Robert H. Lowie believes that " 'community' in the fullest sense is connected with a narrow circle of kindred and neighbors; by way of contrast, nationalism, let alone cosmopolitanism, is invariably an artificial growth."[19] In one of the most highly specific definitions of this type, W. H. Goodenough explicitly restricts the size of the community, with few exceptions, from 1,000 up to 1,200 people, since this is his derived estimate of how many can maintain face-to-face relationships.[20]

Conrad Arensberg, in a rare burst of exasperation, criticizes this approach as a sociological failure insofar as it is a "semantic confusion between community as organization and community as an individual's maximum range of face-to-face acquaintance." Whimsically he adds: "It is in fact as if a zoologist should require of a beehive that it not be one unless he knew every bee to brush wings with every other bee."[21]

The territorial concept of community is certainly not new. In the recent past the idea can be traced from Sir Henry Maine's argument that territoriality was historically substituted for kinship as a basis for community to its adaptation by Ferdinand Tönnies to the generalized ecological approach of the Chicago school. Today cartographic delineation is championed as the *sine qua non* of community by such sociologists as Marvin B. Sussman, Carl C. Zimmerman, Roland L. Warren, B. E. Mercer, Jesse Frederick Steiner, James Coleman, and Irwin T. Sanders.[22] Perhaps the classic sociological statement in this line is that of Talcott Parsons: "A community is that collectivity the members of which share a common territorial area as their base of operations for daily activities."[23]

There is a neatness, of course, about mechanically mapping out a community. But there are problems, too. What is one to do with Znaniecki's "territorial outsiders"[24]—who might in all other ways appear to be community members? And worse, what can be done about the community, as so defined, when on all sides it is proclaimed to be eroding or even on the point of demise? This makes the concept, like a saurian remnant surfacing from the lamented past, an embarrassment—for it becomes applicable only to the archaic or to tiny pockets of agricultural or nondeveloped bliss, due to disappear within the moment.

In short, this type of definition becomes somewhat of a curiosity. Is it not as Arnold Green, who defines a community as a "local territorial group,"[25] dolefully concludes? "Modern social organization is moving away from community, toward participation in and control by, bureaucracies which transcend community, which have no definite spatial location."[26]

Concepts Stressing Community Processes and Change

All of the preceding ideas on community have had value and have lent illumination in the struggle for conceptual clarity. But it has become increasingly apparent in recent years that only when the community *qua* community is treated as a viable social arrangement of a set of integrated groups, capable of protean adjustment to changing social conditions, can it escape classification as a doomed survival of a nostalgically cosy agrarian past. Only by emancipation from the iron maidens of geographical delimitation, sentiment, and rigid either-or classifications can a theory be sufficiently comprehensive in scope to *explain* the wide varieties of communities, past and present, *including* those geographically delineated and consensually integrated.

This emancipation from parochial prescriptions commenced some time ago. In 1911 C. J. Galpin found, in plotting the boundaries of several rural communities, that the variety of services (e.g., paper routes, milk routes, shopping centers) defied cartographic representations. The social network of communal relationships simply did not remain neatly within the lines.[27]

Not long after this Robert M. MacIver in his book *Community* emphasized that territorial boundaries were not fundamental to community existence.

> [A]ll community is a question of degree. For instance, the English residents in a foreign capital often live in an intimate community of their own, as well as in the wider community of the capital. It is a question of the degree and intensity of the common life. The one extreme is the whole world of man, one great but vague and incoherent common life. The other extreme is the small intense community within which the life of an ordinary individual is lived, a tiny nucleus of common life with a sometimes larger, sometimes smaller, and always varying fringe. . . .[28]

E. C. Lindeman later continued with this line of thought, stating that community boundaries could not be accurately designated. Improved communication and transportation methods had vastly increased the possibilities for social interaction. As a result, not just one but a number of centers would exist in a community, and spatial lines would

12

be blurred, ragged, often radiating out in many directions. He suggested that only if attention was directed toward process and change could community analysis be profitable and comprehensive.[29]

This newer conception of community has been systematically developed by Don Martindale,[30] and subsequently has been tested in a number of empirical studies at the University of Minnesota.[31]

The Social Behaviorist Theory of Community

To Martindale the community is a complete social system, a total interhuman way of life, composed of the institutions and groups which make a normal life for a person or for a plurality of persons possible. These institutions are the collective solutions to the basic problems of social existence: the mastery of the material environment, socialization, and social control. Mastery of the material environment requires an adequate social and economic strategy for dominating or coming to terms with the exigent demands of the physical world. Socialization is defined as a set of means or procedures for transforming presocial materials into social forms—procedures that cut through all areas of collective and individual life. Social control necessitates the establishment and maintenance of order—an order that is more or less dependent upon the centralization of decision making and enforcement.

The principal processes operative in solving these problems and in the formation of a community are those of stabilization, consistency, and completeness. The collective response to these problems must become sufficiently fixed and dependable in order to root itself in individual habit and community custom; at the same time, such institutions, or solutions if you will, must be more or less consistent with one another so that conflicts do not arise between them (or, more precisely, between the resultant sets of behavior) and destroy the very fabric of social life; finally, the institutionalized answers as achieved and lived by these groups must be adequately integrated as to present a total system of social life. Ultimately therefore the core of the community consists of its institutions; and community life can be described processually as the continuing flux and change in the balance and integration of its institutional characteristics and relationships. Moreover, communities are analytically distinguishable from one another on this same basis—the differences in institutional nature and integration.

Secondary processes arising from the intersection of these basic processes are those of closure and innovation. On the one hand, from the coalescent action of the principles of stability and consistency, community closure is manifested as a response to external threat and internal dissension. It represents a tendency toward the crystallization of the community forms and way of life as superior to and exclusive of all others. In essence, community closure is the pivotal process which leads to conservatism and traditionalism. On the other hand, the conjoining of completeness and closure produce the counteractive process of innovation. Innovation refers not only to the creation and acceptance of new products within the community but also to the acceptance of products and human relationships penetrating from outside the community. "The established solutions of any given in-

stitutional area define both the circumstance of socially significant innovation in a particular society and the areas of
resistance to innovation."[32]

Tensions between the secondary principles of closure
and innovation will invariably exist to some degree, and the
uneasy balance achieved between these forces will serve to
describe the community in terms of liberalism and conservatism, of plasticity and rigidity. Of course, in order for a
community to have a viable social system some flexibility
and openness will, of necessity, be lost; thus individual
spontaneity and creativity within the community and the
acceptance of the desirable items and relationships external
to the community must be controlled to some degree.

In studying the extent of closure and of innovation one is
also in fact studying the intensity of the community processes and of the limitations placed upon the development
of the individual community member.

> The shell that a community forms around itself operates
> like a field force: it presses its members in and excludes
> the outsider. The more completely developed a community,
> the more it operates like a kind of pressure cooker, making
> its members in some special ways more alike and isolating
> them as a whole from outside influences.[33]

The Ethnic Community

> The fundamental principles of community formation are
> the same for the most primitive tribe as for the most
> advanced mass society. While varying without end in de-
> tail, the numbers of human communities that have been
> formed are relatively few in basic types.[34]

The ethnic community is a subcommunity, for it owes

15

its peculiarities to its situational context. It is formed by a plurality of aliens, seeking to maintain their identity and to provide for themselves the security of the old rituals and routines, played out in the shared communal circle. Thus it is, in effect, an alien community, torn from its familiar world and set down within strange, possibly unintelligible,[35] cultural surroundings. This passage from the known to the unfamiliar is not one of simple transplantation: institutional adjustments to the new conditions must be made for it to survive as a distinct entity defending its uniqueness against the overwhelming encroachment and envelopment by the majority community. The collective response to the new surroundings makes for a particular kind of community, its distinctiveness inextricably tied to its relationship with the larger setting.

It is necessary, therefore, to consider two critical aspects of the ethnic community response to its position as a "guest" in a majority community.

1. A change in institutional emphasis will occur. One of the institutions which had previously been peripheral will become central in the institutional arrangement. This new core institution will now provide the point of integration for the whole, thus setting the characteristic mode of the other institutions ranging about it and, of course, of the community itself.

2. Intensification of community processes will occur, with a resultant increase in closure. In reaction to the outer community, collective defense of the community formula will be primary—for, as Martindale succinctly puts it, "the conflict between the ethnic community, its goal-value system, and the majority community is unavoidable."[36] Moreover, it

16

is frequently the case that the majority community itself will manifest closure toward the ethnic community, more or less effectively barring the assimilation of ethnic community members. Thus an analysis of the processes of closure and innovation, their related extensiveness and their conflictual points of intersection, takes on heightened importance in the study of an ethnic community.

In summary, the ethnic community is one which is formed by a plurality of aliens within a larger, majority community. As with other communities, it represents a complete way of life for its members. However, it is not a duplicate of the old communities of its cultural origin, no matter how hard its members might try to recreate this, for the conditions under which it forms tend to produce two crucial effects: (1) the institutional point of synthesis will change; (2) the secondary principles of innovation and closure are of critical importance respectively in enriching and preserving the narrowness of the ethnic community life.

DERIVATION OF HYPOTHESIS

Problem

The present work is a study of the American military community in Ankara, Turkey, during the years 1965 to 1967. Analyzed within the framework of Martindale's theory of ethnic community, its primary focus is upon the processes of closure and innovation. As defined here, this colony of

American military personnel and dependents is an ethnic community existing within but still separate from the Turkish majority community. Its institutional point of integration is the military organization; and its other institutions—family, economics, education, and the like—reflect their peripherality to and dependence on this core institution.[37] It was conjectured that the lines of community encapsulation produced by its distinct ethnicity in a foreign country might be drawn even more tightly because of the highly organized authoritarian nature of its core institution; and a test of the principles of closure and innovation internally operative in this particular milieu might thus reveal theoretically relevant variables.

In applying this type of analysis to the military community in Ankara, certain questions become pertinent: (1) How is it possible for an ethnic community to maintain its integrity and distinctiveness? That is, *what barriers or inhibitions* against penetration and assimilation exist or are set up as community-system defenses? What are the community-mediated *ways* open to individuals or groups for extra-community innovation, and do these differ according to strata? (2) Are closure or innovation as community phenomena differentially manifested by structural groups? In other words, is there a differential relationship between structure and patterns of extra-community closure and innovation, so that certain types of behavior and attitudes are characteristic of and considered appropriate to different strata? And if this relationship between structure and process exists, is it sufficiently distinct as to permit specification of marginal and core areas of either closure or innovation?

Investigation of the first series of questions by means

GARRISON COMMUNITY

of participant observation and interviews resulted in a descriptive study of the community and of the community conditions which seemed to generate greater or lesser degrees of extra-community closure and innovation. The second series of questions became the central research propositions by which an analytical survey was oriented.

Hypothesis

From the matrix of ethnic community theory a general hypothesis was derived:

> Closure and innovation as community processes are related to comunity structure: differential patterns of closure and innovation are manifested by structural groups.

The structural variables considered relevant in this context were those of rank, age, formal education, marital status, time in the community, and career commitment. Proceeding from this, the subhypotheses are:

> 1. Core areas of extra-community innovation are composed of those groups which have the highest rank, are oldest, are married, have the most years of formal education, have lived in the community for the longest period of time, and are committed to a military career.
> 2. Marginal areas of extra-community innovation are composed of those groups which have the lowest rank, are youngest, are single, have the fewest years of formal education, have lived in the community for the shortest period of time, and are not committed to a military career.

In converse order these hypotheses are applicable to the principle of closure:

> 1. Core areas of extra-community closure are composed of those groups which have the lowest rank, are youngest, are

single, have the fewest years of formal education, have lived in the community for the shortest period of time, and are not committed to a military career.

2. Marginal areas of extra-community closure are composed of those groups which have the highest rank, are oldest, are married, have the most years of formal education, have lived in the community for the longest period of time, and are committed to a military career.

One further hypothesis was added to the above for control purposes:

3. Extra-community innovation is related to inner-community innovation. Those structural groups which manifest the greatest amount of extra-community innovation will also demonstrate the greatest amount of inner-community innovation.

Definition and Operational Specification of Terms

Before going further, it is necessary to nominally define and to operationally specify what is meant by key terms in these hypotheses—terms which will be used, of course, throughout the body of this book.

Extra-community innovation is defined herein as social participation by ethnic community members in the external majority community. Operationally, such innovation or participation is ascertained by reference to a questionnaire scale score, based on the individual American military respondent's association membership, general knowledge about and participation in the Turkish community, acquisition of the Turkish language, neighboring and friendship patterns, and general attitudes toward Turks.

Extra-community closure is defined negatively as a relative lack of social participation by ethnic community members in the external majority community. Operationally, it is represented as a score on the questionnaire scale mentioned above.

The term *core structural areas* refers, unless otherwise specified, to those structural groups in a community which are central in terms of extra- or inner-community participation. *Marginal structural areas* are understood to consist of those groups in a community which are peripheral in terms of extra- or inner-community participation. Operationally, those groups which with the greatest frequency receive comparatively high scores are considered core groups; and, conversely, those whose scores are comparatively low are considered marginal in regard to extra- or inner-community participation.

Inner-community innovation as defined herein is social participation within the ethnic community by ethnic community members. Operationally specified, such innovation or participation is measured on the basis of a scale score within the questionnaire, obtained by reference to the association membership, formal and informal social activities, neighboring and friendship patterns of the individual American military respondent.

Assumptions

Several assumptions are implied in the questions and hypotheses and must be duly noted.

In discussing ethnic community means of defense and innovation, the presupposition is one that is sociological in nature: that is, the individual community member is not a fragmented atom, independent in attitude and behavior of community influence. Of course, the military person going overseas takes his particular cultural and individual baggage of traits, attitudes, and perspectives. However, upon becoming a member of the community, his ways of seeing or not seeing become grounded in the community milieu: to a great extent his perception of reality becomes a reflection of community-defined reality. Without this assumption it would be impossible to propose an association between structure and attitude. Hence the hypothesis that the values of the total collectivity as mediated through structural groups constitute behaviorally relevant expectations toward which the individual orients himself is based here. That is, the community structure specifies the limits; the *average* individual innovates *within* these limits, according to his personal proclivities.[38]

A reciprocal relationship between closure and innovation is implied in the subhypotheses. For the purpose of this book it is assumed that the more closure manifested in any one area, the less innovation is possible, and therefore those structural groups which demonstrate the greatest extra-community participation conversely demonstrate the least extra-community closure. Whether this in fact is the case or not will be considered a moot point. Certainly participation and nonparticipation are better conceived in terms of *degrees* than by a trichotomous classification of marginal, medium, and core, as is the case in this book. There is, of course, great variation in intensity and type of involvement, and within the area of individual behavior there are overlappings and contradictions. How homogeneous is a group in regard to these particular attitudes? Where is the line drawn in the community between innovation and deviation and between

22

closure and deviation? Is this line—if it is sufficiently distinct as to say it exists—differently interpreted *for* and *by* each structural group? Such questions as these must be posed, but for the purpose of exploration and incipient understanding they have been temporarily subdued.

It is assumed that certain of the structural variables will intersect (for example, rank and education), and that rank will predominate as an indicator of structural effect, being directly derived from the central institution. However, all of the structural variables have been treated singly in order to more aptly discriminate relative effect.

DISCUSSION AND SUMMARY

When one deals with limited aspects of human situations, a caveat must be issued. A community is never an isolated phenomenon to be studied in vacuo. Certain aspects of a community can and usually must be analytically isolated for examination. But in the long run cognizance must be taken of the total context and of the situational components which in different degrees affect the area of investigation.

In studying a community there are three possible levels of approach: one can study individuals within the community; one can study the community itself—its groups, its processual and structural relationships, and the like; and one can study the contextual milieu.[39] On the whole, the external components of the community situation in Ankara

23

have been treated in a cursory fashion. But their importance cannot be denied. These components consist not only of the majority community in which the ethnic community is located, but also of the international scene and the relations between Turkey and the United States which have greatly influenced the way cultural differences and the immediate communities are viewed by the respective ethnic and majority community members. Though these wider relationships have been more or less treated as given, the interplay between these components is always in flux, the patterns of involvement and response are continually shifting. And ultimately all of these elements in all of their complexity must be recognized as inextricable parts of the whole.

In this work the approach is primarily one of studying the relationship of group members to the community. The *conceptual* gap between the individual and the social unit is bridged by a study of the dynamics of structure.[40] At this crucial point of contact it is hypothesized that community mediation takes place, and that the intensity of this community mediation will vary depending on the individual's and group's positional relationship to it. In summary, therefore, the problem is one of studying structural effects in order to permit at least tentative specifications of the conditions under which certain structural variables produce the relevant characteristics of an individual's or of a group's social environment in the American military community of Ankara, Turkey.

24

1. Although the specific number is classified information, David W. Tarr estimates that well over a million military personnel and half a million dependents are stationed overseas ("The Military Abroad," *The Annals* 368 [November, 1966]:32).

2. Tarr states that American military dependents are scattered over 105 foreign countries (ibid., p. 37).

3. The book that has become the classic statement in this regard is, of course, *The Ugly American* by William J. Lederer and Eugene Burdick. For other comments concerning overseas Americans, see, for example, the following: Harland Cleveland, Gerald J. Mangone, and John Clark Adams, *The Overseas Americans* (New York: McGraw-Hill Book Company, 1960), p. 6; Clancy Sigal, "The American G.I. in Britain," *Encounter* (February, 1960), pp. 30–47; Jack Raymond, *Power at the Pentagon* (New York: Harper & Row, 1964), Chapter VI, "America's Military Outposts"; "The Everywhere Generation," *Newsweek* (November 28, 1966), pp. 29–36; Paul C. Davis and William T. R. Fox, "American Military Representation Abroad," in *The Representation of the United States Abroad,* ed. Vincent M. Barnett, Jr. (New York: Frederick A. Praeger, 1965), pp. 129–183; "From Le Monde," *The Family* (June 16, 1967), p. 3.

4. Exceptions to this are the writings on overseas British colonies by E. M. Forster in *Passage to India,* George Orwell in *Burmese Days* and the short story "Shooting an Elephant," and Leonard Woolf in *Growing: An Autobiography of the Years 1904 to 1911.* In giving the full, qualitative meaning of enclave living these are certainly among the most cogent and sensitive portrayals. Sociologically oriented studies that are helpful are as follows: "Americans Abroad," *The Annals,* Vol. 368 (November, 1966); Milton Jacobs and Louis Schatz, *Some Effects of Overseas Duty on the Attitudes of American Troops toward Host Populations,*

25

Human Resources Office, The George Washington University, 1954; Daniel Glaser, "The Sentiments of American Soldiers Abroad toward Europeans," *American Journal of Sociology* 51 (March, 1946):433–438.

5. To take but one example of this, the history of the relationships of the Roman Army and indigenous populations is extremely illuminating. Although data are scarce, it appears possible that the closure manifested by the Roman garrisons varied in accordance with recruitment policy. If the legionnaires and auxilia were recruited locally from the provinces in which they were to serve, as became increasingly the case during the period of Empire, there was little tension. However, when Roman soldiers were sent to distant provinces, tensions were frequently manifest. The distinction between *civis* and *peregrinus* was enforced by regulation (until A.D. 212), and such diverse writers as Cicero, Josephus, and Tacitus have recorded that this distinction was demonstrated in legionary behavior toward the indigenous peoples, as well. Cicero mentions that derogatory remarks about people of the Asian hinterlands were heard so frequently as to become clichés. Interesting in this regard is Tacitus' account of the uprising in Britain against Roman troops: "The [Roman] veterans were the special object of their hatred. These men, recently settled at Camulodunum, had been turning them out of their homes, taking away their lands, and calling them captives and slaves. The soldiers did nothing to check the insolence of the veterans, for they were men of the same stamp and hoped for similar license when their own time came." Boadicea, Queen of the Iceni, who led the uprising against the Romans, called upon "the great crowd before her to fight to the last drop of their blood for victory and freedom for liberty against men who are insolent, unjust, insatiable, and impious—if indeed these can be called men who bathe in warm water, eat dainties, drink wine and anoint themselves, sleep on soft couches and indulge themselves in unnatural vices." (Tacitus, *Annals*, XIV, § 29–39.)

26

6.   Robert M. MacIver, *Community* (New York: Macmillan Company, 1917), p. 90.

7.   The idea of social contract is really much older than this. For example, Cicero, always cautious, had a tentative foot in both doors. See *De Republica,* III, § 13.

8.   This debt to Rousseau is acknowledged by Durkheim in his book *Montesquieu and Rousseau: Forerunners of Sociology* (Ann Arbor: University of Michigan Press, 1960). For example, Rousseau was quoted by Durkheim to have said: "A society is a moral entity having specific qualities distinct from those of the individual beings which compose it, somewhat as chemical compounds have properties that they owe to none of their elements" (p. 82). Rousseau, of course, was in turn indebted to Plato.

9.   G. D. H. Cole makes paramount the idea that the community "is essentially a center of feeling" (*Social Theory* [London: Methuen & Co., 1920], p. 25). Robert A. Nisbet's definition of community is rather ambiguous, but it seems to be more or less thought of as synonymous with society. He sees history as a decline of community and, therefore, of a "sense of belonging." He notes the result is an increase of impersonality and alienation in the world, which has led to the coming of the masses: "Within the mass all ordinary relationships and authorities seem devoid of institutional function and psychological meaning" (*Community and Power* [formerly *The Quest for Community*] [New York: Oxford University Press, 1962], p. 199).

10.   See, for example, the following: Robert E. Park, Ernest W. Burgess, and Roderick D. McKenzie, *The City* (Chicago: University of Chicago Press, 1925); and E. C. Hughes, "Institutions and the Community," in *An Outline of the Principles of Sociology,* ed. Robert E. Park (New York: Barnes & Noble, 1939), p. 310.

11.   Henry Sumner Maine, *Ancient Law* (Boston: Beacon Press, 1963).

27

The Military Community Overseas: Problems and Concepts

12.   Ferdinand Tonnies, *Community and Society (Gemeinschaft und Gesellschaft)*, ed. and trans. Charles P. Loomis (New York: Harper Torchbooks, 1957), p. 33.

13.   Rudolph Heberle insists that: "Though he [Tönnies] sometimes designates the family or the village as a *Gemeinschaft* and the city or state as a *Gesellschaft*, this is only a paradigm. To him *Gemeinschaft* and *Gesellschaft* are pure concepts of ideal types which do not exist as such in the empirical world" ("The Sociological System of Ferdinand Tönnies: 'Community' and 'Society,'" in *An Introduction to the History of Sociology*, ed. Harry Elmer Barnes [Chicago: University of Chicago Press, 1948], p. 234). However, Raymond Aron comments that in this typology there is "an ambiguity of value: Tonnies, like many German sociologists, suggests, though perhaps without intending to do so, the superior value of the community. He prefers the affective to the rational, organic harmony to legal order" (*German Sociology*, trans. Mary and Thomas Bottomore [New York: Free Press, 1964], p. 17).

14.   For criticisms of the rural-urban continuum concept, see, for example, the following: Richard Dewey, "The Rural-Urban Continuum: Real but Relatively Unimportant," *American Journal of Sociology* 56 (July, 1960):60–66; Horace Miner, "The Folk-Urban Continuum," *American Sociological Review* 17 (October, 1952): 529–536; Oscar Lewis, "Tepoztlan Restudied," *Rural Sociology* 18 (June, 1953):130–131.

15.   Robert H. Lowie, *Social Organization* (New York: Holt, Rinehart & Company, 1948), pp. 15–18.

16.   For example, Florian Znaniecki states: "We call a community any human collectivity which has the following characteristics: (a) The people who compose it live within a separate area, large enough to include a considerable number of inhabitants, but not too large to prevent each one from meeting at least occasionally every other inhabitant and identifying him personally. Such an area is the common *habitat* of these people"

28

(*Social Relations and Social Roles* [San Francisco: Chandler Publishing Company, 1965], p. 28).

17. Baker Brownell, *The Human Community* (New York: Harper & Brothers, 1950), p. 198.

18. G. P. Murdock et al., "Outline of Cultural Materials," *Yale Anthropological Studies* 2 (New Haven: Yale University Press, 1945):29.

19. Lowie, *Social Organization,* p. 15.

20. W. H. Goodenough, "Basic Economy in the Community," (monograph, 1941). Quoted in George A. Lundberg, Clarence C. Schrag, and Otto N. Larsen, *Sociology,* 3rd ed. (New York: Harper & Row, 1963), p. 477.

21. Conrad M. Arensberg, "The Community-Study Method," *American Journal of Sociology* 55 (September, 1954):124.

22. Marvin B. Sussman, "General Introduction," in *Community Structure and Analysis,* ed. Marvin B. Sussman (New York: Thomas Y. Crowell Company, 1959), p. 2; Carl C. Zimmerman *The Changing Community* (New York: Harper & Brothers, 1938), p. 29; Roland L. Warren, *The Community in America* (Chicago: Rand McNally & Company, 1963), p. 9; B. E. Mercer, *The American Community* (New York: Random House, 1956), p. 27; Jesse Frederick Steiner, *Community Organization* (New York: D. Appleton-Century Company, 1930), p. 20; James Coleman, "Community Disorganization," in *Contemporary Social Problems,* ed. Robert K. Merton and Robert A. Nisbet (New York: Harcourt, Brace & World, 1961), pp. 553–604; Irwin T. Sanders, *The Community. An Introduction to a Social System* (New York: Ronald Press Company, 1958), p. 120.

23. Talcott Parsons, *The Social System* (New York: Free Press, 1951), p. 91.

24. Znaniecki, *Social Relations,* p. 28.

25. Arnold W. Green, *Sociology. An Analysis of Life in*

29

Modern Society (New York: McGraw-Hill Book Company, 1956), p. 250.

26. Ibid., p. 269.

27. C. J. Galpin, "The Social Anatomy of an Agricultural Village," *Research Bulletin* 34, Agricultural Experiment Station of the University of Wisconsin, Madison, May, 1915.

28. MacIver, *Community,* p. 23. It should be noted that in a later article MacIver, with his coauthor Charles H. Page, seems to deny his previous proposition and states the following: "The bases of community are locality and community sentiment" ("Society: Primary Concepts," in *Society Today and Tomorrow,* ed. Elgin F. Hunt and Jules Karlin [New York: Macmillan Company, 1961], p. 27).

29. E. C. Lindeman, "Community," *Encyclopedia of the Social Sciences* 3–4 (New York: Macmillan Company, 1935):102–105.

30. Although in the following pages this theory will be briefly outlined, for a complete presentation, see these books and articles by Don Martindale: *American Social Structure* (New York: Appleton-Century-Crofts, 1960); *American Society* (Princeton, N. J.: D. Van Nostrand Company, 1960); *Social Life and Cultural Change* (Princeton, N. J.: D. Van Nostrand Company, 1962); *Community, Character and Civilization* (New York: Free Press, 1963); "The Formation and Destruction of Communities," in *Explorations in Social Change,* ed. George K. Zollschan and Walter Hirsch (Boston: Houghton Mifflin Company, 1964), pp. 61–87; *Institutions, Organizations, and Mass Society* (Boston: Houghton Mifflin Company, 1965). For a discussion of the relationship of this theory to that of Max Weber's theory of the city, see Martindale's "Prefatory Remarks: The Theory of the City," in Max Weber, *The City,* trans. and ed. Don Martindale and Gertrud Neuwirth (New York: Collier Books, 1962), pp. 9–67.

30

31. See, for example, the following: Norman S. Goldner, *The Mexican in a Northern Urban Area: A Profile of an Ethnic Community* (master's thesis, University of Minnesota, 1960); Judith R. Kramer and Seymour Leventman, *Children of the Gilded Ghetto* (New Haven: Yale University Press, 1961); Alex Simirenko, *Pilgrims, Colonists, and Frontiersmen: An Ethnic Community in Transition* (New York: Free Press, 1964); Noel Iverson, *Germania, U.S.A.* (St. Paul: University of Minnesota Press, 1966).

32. Martindale, *Social Life and Cultural Change,* p. 44.

33. Martindale, *American Society,* p. 106.

34. Ibid.

35. Max Weber's discussion of ethnic groups is interesting in this regard: "The community of language and, along with it, the identity of the 'ritual regimentation of life,' as determined by shared religious beliefs, obviously are universal elements of feelings of ethnic affinity *(ethnische Verwandtschaftsgefuehle),* especially since the meaningful 'intelligibility' *(sinnhafte Verstaendlichkeit)* of the behavior of others is the most fundamental presupposition of communal relationship" ("Ethnic Groups," in *Theories of Society,* ed. Talcott Parsons et al. [New York: Free Press, 1961] 1:307).

36. Martindale, *Community, Character and Civilization,* p. 311.

37. This contention is discussed and defended at greater length later in the book.

38. Nowhere is this more trenchantly illustrated than in the classic work *The Polish Peasant in Europe and America* by William I. Thomas and Florian Znaniecki.

39. In regard to these levels of analysis, obviously it is necessary to keep personality variation, structural position, and external contextual relationships analytically separate, for only then

can a problem be stated with precision and without unjustifiable assumptions about the concurrence of event and response, personality type, and strata.

40.   This gap is conceptual only for it is believed that in the existential world this cleavage does not exist. One cannot discuss man without reference to his society, for he is a social being. Nor can one attempt to discuss society without reference to its human components.

2

SITUATIONAL PERSPECTIVES: IMPRESSIONS, POLITICS, AND HISTORY

IMPRESSIONS OF ANKARA

The travel brochures, consulted by military people and travelers alike, never quite prepare one for the first impact of Ankara. Facts are served out like tasteless eatables at a bus cafe; and the touch, smell, the feeling—the gallimaufry of differences—are drained or glazed into sameness by the market banality of travel clichés. As the pamphlets state: Ankara has grown from a small provincial town of

20,000 people in 1919 to a city of almost a million.[1] Located in the western portion of the central Anatolian Plateau at an altitude of just under 3,000 feet, it is at about the same latitude as Reno, Denver, Indianapolis, and Philadelphia. This center of Turkish business and government activities lies in a natural bowl formed by rugged hills. But the experience of approaching Ankara over the dusky stillness of the steppes—treeless, empty, bleak, stretching to all horizons—is unlike any the American is likely to encounter in his own country half a world away.

From the airport one drives a long and desolate twenty-nine kilometers to the fringy, unkempt outskirts of the city. The main street, for the most part called Ataturk Boulevard, runs north and south, crossing from the old part of the city with its cacophonous melée of throbbing street life to the orderly new section of Westernized shops and banks, foreign embassies, and fancy apartment buildings. Driving the entire length of the boulevard can be, in a way, a study of contrasts, of old Turkey and new Turkey,[2] of the changes that have taken place since Ataturk made it his center for resistance against the Sultan in 1919.

The old section, spreading out from the broad boulevard with its proper buildings, quickly dissolves into labyrinthine disarray and the wild helter-skelter of bazaars, lean-to shops selling shoelaces and combs and cheap assorted items; antique stores, mosques, crumbling houses of tiny flats without electricity or water, and a frenetic traffic of crowds, cars, trucks, and horse-drawn carts. For the fastidious traveler who prefers a world of Hilton Hotel sterility, a walk through this section can become a nightmare of weird and unintelligible exotica, of apprehension, of cultural disorientation:

34

the heavyset men with great mustaches, women swathed in shawls and long skirts and pantaloons, discordant sounds, an array of barbaric colors, and the sight and smell of strange foods and products and of poverty. Here the rawness and austerity of life do not keep their distance, have not been schooled in the Western amenities, but with sickening insistency penetrate all one's senses.

The new area is drab in contrast, but in its very drabness perhaps connotes safety to the insecure. It has the sweep of broad streets and large gray concrete blocks of buildings. The newness, the ugliness of superimposed modernity is here, yet old Ankara has a way of seeping in along the edges and animating the Westernized version with Turkish flavor. This new area is the center of Turkish pride in what was willfully wrought from the ancient clay of Anatolia; this is the center where the foreigners shop and live; and this is where the American military community members live out their tours of duty, distinct and insulated from much of that which is really Turkish.

POLITICAL BACKGROUND

Although the United States had technically maintained diplomatic relations with Turkey since 1830, for most Americans Turkey was a little-known and faraway place until World War II. Even during the war the political and military role of the United States in this part of the world was

Situational Perspectives: Impressions, Politics, and History

subordinate to that of her other allies, being one of backing up British interests. It was not until February 1947, when England notified the United States that she was no longer economically or militarily able to give aid to Greece, that the problem of active involvement became acute. Shortly after this Turkey requested assistance from the United States in dealing with the pressure Russia was exerting upon her for control of the Dardanelles and of the Bosphorus.

At that time the administration in the United States was gradually tending toward acceptance of a "strategy of containment" in regard to Russian communism: it was believed that the defense of the United States and her allies depended on halting communist aggression by means of building up positions of strength around the Soviet Union, thus supporting resistance to its efforts of expansion. This being accepted as a premise, the political justification for arming and training Turkish military forces followed. Not only, it was reasoned, could an armed Turkey provide an outer bastion for Western European and American security (to say nothing of keeping access routes for Middle Eastern oil open), but in the event of attack, if Turkey was capable of holding off the Russians in this part of the world, a number of American military divisions would be freed for duty elsewhere.[3]

Given the global implications of this point of view, it was to be expected that President Truman's request for aid to Turkey and Greece in his message to Congress on March 12, 1947, would be couched in very general terms:

> I believe that it must be the foreign policy of the United States to support free people who are resisting attempted subjugation by armed minorities or by outside pressures.

36

The free peoples of the world look to us for support in maintaining their freedom. If we falter in our leadership, we may endanger the peace of the world, and we shall surely endanger the welfare of our nation.[4]

This vision of America's future role in the world political scene became known as the "Truman Doctrine." Criticism of the policy was primarily directed at its general implications: that if the United States foreign policy was oriented this way, interference in the internal affairs of other nations would be inevitable; that the so-called "free world" to be supported by American funds and arms included a number of highly reactionary governments; that the United States was being asked to emulate British imperialism; that such statements and consequent actions would be construed as aggressively anti-Soviet and possibly lead to war.[5] Furthermore, it was specifically recognized that military aid to Turkey would be, in effect, a very costly and entangling long-term commitment. Turkey at that time was incapable of providing herself with modern weapons; indeed, even in the foreseeable future she could not be expected to attain the technological development to replace those given her previously, much less to produce new equipment.

Although the issue was highly controversial, after two months of discussion the Eightieth Congress ratified Public Law 75 on May 22, 1947,[6] providing military and economic assistance to Greece and Turkey. The President, who had been named by Congress to supervise the law, issued Executive Order 9857 on May 22, 1947, delegating authority to the Secretary of State to carry out its provisions. From the beginning, therefore, the State Department was responsible for the administration of both economic and military aid[7]

37

to Turkey; and the "Country Team" notion, whereby the American Ambassador was considered the authoritative head of all American agencies and forces in any one country, can be seen as a continuation of this policy. Late in 1947 the implementation of this law was commenced by the transfer of some military goods and a small number of American military personnel to Turkey.

From 1947 to 1963 the relations between Turkey and the United States were characterized, on the whole, by extraordinary warmth and Turkey's foreign policy was one of cooperation with the Western powers. For example, in 1950 Turkey was the first United Nations member to send a brigade of troops to Korea. In February 1952, she joined the North Atlantic Treaty Organization and thus became officially associated with the Western democracies. In 1955 she became one of the signatory nations of the Baghdad Pact, later to become the Central Treaty Organization.[8] On March 5, 1959, the Bilateral Agreements of Cooperation were signed in Ankara by the United States with Turkey, Iran, and Pakistan.

However, in 1963 and 1964 the Cyprus crisis involving Turkey and Greece precipitated a kind of turning point, a commencement of disenchantment for Turkey with the United States.[9] Whether the Cyprus situation was the cause or the occasion of Turkish resentment toward what she began to view as a patron-client relationship is difficult to ascertain. Certainly the crisis is considered by many Turkish and American officials as signalling an attenuation of respect and loyalty toward the United States. The Cyprus problem has continued in great measure to dominate Turkish political life and foreign policy; and it is no overstatement to say

GARRISON COMMUNITY

that Turkey's announced position of providing protection for the rights and lives of Turkish Cypriots is advocated by most political parties and is a cornerstone of her foreign policy. In this light it is understandable why President Johnson's strongly worded letter of 1963, cautioning moderation to Turkey, has been remembered and is still angrily interpreted as a meddling in Turkey's internal affairs, as "regrettable,"[10] as "threatening,"[11] as destructive of "the old spring-like atmosphere between Turkey and the United States."[12] This wound rankles, and even in such a comparatively pro-American English-language newspaper as the *Ankara Daily News* statements like the following can be found:

> It has occurred to us after the Cyprus problem to assess Turkish-American friendship. Until that time, in the spirit of friendship and alliance the character that even the American called ugly American seemed to us beautiful. America's stand concerning the Cyprus crisis has been an event that uncovered this mask.[13]

Criticism of the United States—its foreign policies and particularly its military presence in Turkey—has become commonplace. Some American officials cavalierly attribute this to the "leftist" sentiments of a very narrow, vocal segment of the urban population (i.e., student groups and communists), and their dismissal of the Turkish press as sensational and untrustworthy has become almost axiomatic.[14] Regardless, criticism does appear to be quite prevalent, and the Turkish press, quite possibly anti-American, nevertheless articulates and influences the opinions of some segments of the literate population. Thus it can be seen that the American "presence" is a formidable issue in Turkish political life; and "get tough with the United States" platforms

39

have become almost indispensable talismans for political parties. Censorious comments, while not always as incendiary as the following, are frequent.

Yashar Kemal, one of Turkey's best known novelists, wrote an open letter in the Socialist weekly *Ant* to American novelists, enlisting their aid in saving America "from the disgust of other nations," for if the present situation continues "you will be faced with another Vietnam." He accused Americans of coming to Turkey as friends yet "entering our hearts like a traitor's dagger. . . . You have created slaves and compradors in Turkey. . . . Your soldiers can bring into the streets tens of thousands of Turks by being disrespectful to Turkish women. Your soldiers constantly tear down and trample Turkish flags. They run over people in the streets and are not even tried in Turkish courts."[15]

Sadi Kocas, in an editorial in the *Ankara Daily News,* stated:

> Americans should give up their outdated imperialist methods. . . . They should not forget they are guests. They should refrain from clandestine activities which should not even be carried out in enemy lands. At any rate, they should refrain from interfering into our domestic affairs and from interfering into political struggles between parties. And finally, the old type of imperialism that settles with its army, flag, and governor-generals in underdeveloped lands are out of date.[16]

Ziya Kayla, a former director of Turkey's Central Bank, said in an interview that he had felt for some time that the United States was pursuing only its own narrow interests, and in giving economic and military aid to Turkey, the United States had given little for the gain of turning Turkey into a satellite nation.[17]

40

It is obvious, of course, that some of these accusations are untrue. However, they do reflect the emotional tenor of Turkish attitudes toward Americans.

Though Turkish foreign policy lines have not completely changed, there is a growing movement toward improving relations with the Soviet bloc, toward neutralism in foreign affairs, disengagement from foreign commitments, and the abolishment of foreign military bases on her soil.[18] Riots and demonstrations against American forces in Turkey have become more frequent.[19] And the problems connected with bilateral agreements concerning these forces have culminated in a very hard request by the Turkish government for their review and revision.[20]

On the diplomatic scene, fence-mending has been commenced to counteract these tendencies. Particularly productive toward this goal were the talks between President Johnson and President Sunay, during the latter's visit to Washington, D.C., in April 1967. During these talks, along with the promises of lasting friendship, President Johnson pledged continuing assistance in strengthening Turkey's defense capabilities.[21]

High-level talks notwithstanding, there does seem to be a certain eagerness on the part of the Turks, not only in the streets and in the newspapers but in official circles as well, for the Americans to be gone.[22] This climate of opinion has its ambivalent aspects, to be sure. On the one hand it is recognized that the American economic and military aid has helped Turkey defend and maintain her independence and integrity against Russia, but on the other hand, there is the palpable fear that they have been saved from one threat only to be engulfed by another.

41

Official organizational histories in Ankara are usually expressed in terms of troop movements and military missions. Although they tell little of community processes, they provide an outline of the struts within which a community forms. Tables of organization and manpower authorization sheets reveal the varying size and composition of unit membership over time. Lists of community facilities and of military real estate rentals might suggest tendencies toward completeness and centralization. These bare bones, fleshed out with the remembrances of a few "old timers" and of second- or third-tour returnees, are the only witnesses that remain of the formation and growth of the American military community in the past.[23]

The Military Units and Their Missions

Late in 1947 the Army, Navy, and Air Force commenced sending personnel to Turkey to set up the Joint American Military Mission for Aid to Turkey (JAMMAT). These people were to serve as military advisors to the Turkish forces, supervising and instructing in the use of American military equipment and giving specialized training to Turkish officers and men. The goal of JAMMAT, in conjunction with the quantities of material that were beginning to arrive, was to transform the old Turkish military establishment into an up-to-date professional organization.[24] Since 1947 three changes have occurred which probably have affected in one way or another the efficacy of the means toward this end. In 1949 the position of Chief of Mission ceased to be filled by the American Ambassador to Turkey and was henceforth filled by an American general. Coincidentally and unimportantly, the name of the mission was changed from JAMMAT to JUSMMAT, or Joint United States Military Mission for Aid to Turkey. Another change that has occurred has been one of continuing expansion: from a handful of people in 1947 it grew to 245 officers and men in 1948, to 410 in 1949,[25] and by the middle of 1951 JUSMMAT "was the largest military advisory group the United States maintained abroad, counting 1,250 officers, enlisted men, and civilians.[26] The third change, noted by American military personnel and old employees in JUSMMAT, has been nebulous but increasing in impact. It is that of a cooling of the once-warm relationships between Turkish military men and their American counterparts. The atmosphere of once-eager cooperation has subtly changed to one of elusive resistance to American military advice, and it has been frequently difficult for American personnel to see, much less to advise, their Turkish counterparts.[27]

The second American unit to be stationed in Ankara was The United States Engineer Group (TUSEG).[28] It was activated in 1950, under the jurisdiction of the Chief of Engineers, Department of Army, to supervise the Military Defense Assistance Program (MDAP). It has been the unit's job to oversee American military construction—the construction of American airfields, bases, and base housing in Turkey, as well as maintaining the necessary liaison between

43

Turkish and local American authorities to make such construction possible. From 1950 to 1967 this unit supervised a total of $130 million worth of military construction for the United States Army, Navy, Air Force, and for the United States Agency for International Development (AID).[29] The size of the unit has waxed and waned, dependent upon the money available for construction from the United States and upon Turkish cooperation. Employees sadly remember the "good old years," 1950 to 1962, when a Turkish detachment of soldiers was assigned to them by the Turkish General Staff to help solve problems with right-of-ways, customs, roads, lands, and people. In 1962 TUSEG moved again[30] because of a change in work load. There was no space or facilities for the Turkish soldiers in the new offices, so they had been reassigned elsewhere—and since 1962 the difficulties in getting Turkish approval for new construction and in procuring the customs release of incoming American materials have become almost insurmountable. Although construction has been planned through 1968 and 1969, prognostications are that operations will be phased down and probably closed out before that time.

The third unit to be moved to Turkey was The United States Logistics Group (TUSLOG) with its buzzing bevy of subunits, or detachments. Negotiations for this move were commenced during the Korean War with the idea that, in the event the war widened, masses of people and materiel would be sent to Turkey and would have to be controlled and directed upon arrival. Arriving in 1955,[31] TUSLOG, under the auspices of the United States Air Force, has had the mission of providing logistical support for all the United States Armed Forces and United States government repre-

44

sentatives and activities throughout Turkey, Greece, and Crete. Although it went through one contraction,[32] on the whole its history has been one of continuing and ballooning expansion, both of personnel and of the services it provides. For example, its largest detachment in Ankara was authorized one officer and two airmen on May 15, 1956. Today this detachment has been reliably estimated as having 1,500 officers and enlisted men.[33] Because of the less technical or cross-cultural nature of many of its jobs, TUSLOG brought in a high proportion of enlisted men, changing the overall rank composition of the community. Starting out modestly, TUSLOG and its detachments now handle all of the American money in Turkey, control all of the real estate, supervise the exchange and commissary services, recreational facilities, hospital and dental services, veterinary services, unit supplies, intelligence groups, all means of communication, the dependent schools, transportation, security and law enforcement, the American Post Office, legal services, weather services, chaplain services, mortuary services, and so on and on. Indeed, one might say that, from birth to death, life is regulated here by a hovering TUSLOG: it is the very center of bureaucratic omnicompetence.

In 1958, when the Central Treaty Organization moved from Baghdad to Ankara, its contingent of American officers and enlisted men was also transferred. The number of American military personnel working in the Combined Military Planning Staff is controlled by the CENTO charter. Having only a total of fourteen American officers, twelve enlisted men, and seventy dependents (1967) in both the Combined Military Planning Staff and in the United States Element of CENTO, it is one of the smallest units in Ankara.

45

Other than these units, the military attachés, Embassy Marine guards, and so on can be considered as members of the military community. In practice, they and the ranking officers of the military units constitute a kind of informal liaison group between American government agencies and the military community.

Changing Conditions of Life in Ankara

The first American military people to come to Ankara were pioneers, in a way. Thrust into a strange cultural environment, individual and group adjustments, attitudes, and responses toward living in Turkey were comparatively pliant. It was a time of experimentation and exploration in cross-cultural exchange. To many Turks[34] these early Americans were seen as delicious curiosities, wonderfully endearing in their cultural peculiarities; and for a Turk to know a few Americans meant that he had become a prestigious authority on them in his own circle, could interpret and explain how really unique and fascinating these representatives of the industrialized world were.[35] At this time, from 1947 to 1955,[36] if one lived in the vicinity of the Americans and spoke some English, getting to know them was thought to be quite easy. They lived almost completely "on the economy": that is, they bought most of their food at the local markets, their water from the Turkish water wagons; they lived all over Ankara—wherever they could find an apartment or house that offered a modicum of modern features; they sought their entertainment and recreation in Turkish clubs and restaurants; and they "mingled freely with the Turks"—if not by choice, at least by necessity. Several Turks

46

have said—improbably, but in a highly complimentary way —that these Americans "just blended in."

Of course, one discovers in studying this early period that Americans did in fact tend to huddle together, that American military life, even in off-duty time, was group life, and that most improvisation was group-determined rather than a product of individual innovation. Almost from the beginning much American energy was directed toward the development and institutionalization of activities similar to those at home. Yet the American community was still, in many ways, too insufficiently organized, too incomplete to provide a full life for many of its members; and, any-way, a certain involvement in the Turkish community was unavoidable, if one was to live at all. As the number of Americans increased and the facilities became more extensive and the community life became more organized, the routine of buying most of one's daily items in the Turkish market, of making Turkish friends, of seeking a place in the circle of Turkish life ceased to have the practical value it had had before.

For the first two years practically all of the food American military families consumed was bought at the local markets and bazaars. However, in 1949 a small post ex-change was opened in the basement of the JUSMMAT building, and a year later a small commissary was added. Even then, due to lack of space and the difficulty of importing American products, the supply and variety of the items sold were very limited—and limited, for that matter, to a curious selection. Old residents recall with exceptional exactness the number and kind of items that were for sale: bean and bacon soup, sauerkraut, canned bacon, canned butter, flour, coffee, sugar, and canned milk for babies. It is also recalled that although a tour in Turkey was notable because one could save money, the post exchange and commissary merchandise was "terribly expensive." In addition to these sources, a special plane was dispatched to Athens once a week to bring in supplies and specially ordered items. On Sundays these things were distributed, and the anticipated day took on a festive air. During the holidays, Thanksgiving turkeys and Christmas trees were flown in for those who had gotten their names on the list in time. Once a year American families made up their liquor order; these orders were consolidated, and two months later the annual supply would arrive. This, too, was expensive, since transportation for the order had to be paid by the military families. In 1956 a downtown area was leased from the Turkish government as a center for the post exchange and commissary. The use of American road equipment—graders, loaders, bulldozers—was given to the Turks in exchange for the use of the land. In 1966 these facilities were moved (and in the process enlarged) four miles out of town to Balgat Air Station, the new Air Force center for American facilities.

Obtaining pure drinking water has always been a problem in Ankara. Although Cubuk Dam was built in the early 1930's to provide potable water for Ankara, somehow in its course from the dam to the city the water often becomes polluted.[37] Many Americans bought their drinking water from the Turkish water men, who went from door to door in horse-drawn wagons. At that time, instead of having metal caps over the openings, the bottle tops were stuffed with rags, often of dubious origin and cleanliness. After buying the water it was necessary to boil it. As one might surmise, a fairly large family could consume a considerable amount of drinking water each day; and one aspect of the American modus vivendi became the endless pots of water boiling away on kitchen stoves. Obtaining a sufficient supply of piped water for household use was also a problem. From 1948 to 1951, for example, water was extremely scarce, and pressure was available for only two hours in the morning, two hours in the afternoon, and four hours at night. The water tank in the attic or on the roof and the hum of the pump remained familiar aspects of daily life.

Medical and dental facilities were also extremely limited. At first, most Americans went to Turkish doctors, searching out those who had been educated in the United States and who spoke English (the names were passed on to newcomers). After a while, one floor of the Turkish Army Hospital was temporarily given over to an American Army Clinic. Having but a few hospital beds, three American doctors, a few hired Turkish doctors, and one nurse, only emergency operations, the delivery of babies, and outpatient treatment could be handled. The critically ill were flown to Germany or to the United States. The diet kitchen was one of the most memorable things about the one-floor hospital, for over it presided a jocular Turkish woman who firmly believed that every portion of food was improved by generous dollops of olive oil. Regardless of the ailment— hepatitis or a broken leg—inevitably the patient received fried potatoes, fried meat, and fried vegetables on his tray. At times the diagnoses were interesting, also. One American woman recalls that the spots on her child were judged to be "just fleabites." Anxiously, having rushed out and bought insecticides, she powdered, patted, and sprayed the

Situational Perspectives: Impressions, Politics, and History

young one from head to foot. The next day her relief was immense when the spots became recognizable as "only chickenpox." All this came to an end in 1957 when a fifty-bed, fully staffed Air Force hospital, housed in an entire apartment building, was opened. In 1960 the apartment building across the street was also rented for hospital use, thus greatly expanding the facilities.

Schools for the children constituted a major problem for some time. Several of the dependent children were sent to foreign embassy schools, a few went to Turkish schools; but most of the children went to a joint-cooperative American school, sponsored by all of the American and civilian units in Ankara. In comparison with the sleek, modern dependent schools that were opened at the Balgat Air Station in 1963 and 1964, these schools were makeshift affairs. Before 1956 classrooms were located all over Ankara, wherever an adequate room could be rented. The parents did almost everything for the schools from planning curriculum, buying books, aranging for bus travel, and raising support money to actually teaching. In 1956 a rented automobile garage was converted into a junior and senior high school, its roof utilized as a playground. For eight years this served until the new consolidated buildings were completed at Balgat.[38]

There has never been an American housing area as such in Ankara. In 1950 a guest house was opened for the new arrivals, since hotel rooms were at a premium. After spending a few weeks here, however, families were expected to find their own apartments and houses to rent. There were, and are, a few exceptions to this: with the influx of young, single enlisted men from TUSLOG, a large building was

50

rented in the central part of the new area of the city and converted into an airmen's billets. This still remains, but a new billet is slated to be built out of town at Balgat Air Station in the next few years. Three apartment buildings were rented in their entirety for American CENTO personnel and their families, when they were transferred to Ankara. And, of course, several houses are retained for high-ranking generals (major generals and above). Other than these, selection of housing by Americans has been and is a personal matter. But even from the first, a bunching tendency was clearly apparent. The only change in the settlement pattern over the years has been a gradual moving out to the more peripheral areas of the city, to the relatively smog-free hillsides. Since the Air Station at Balgat has opened, it has become more popular to live as closely to it as Turkish housing permits.

At first, Americans went to the embassies for religious services, Protestants going to the British Embassy church, Catholics to the Italian Embassy chapel. Jews went to the Turkish Jewish Synagogue. After TUSLOG brought in chaplains and set aside places for religious activities in American buildings, the number of those going to the embassies greatly dwindled.

Other than small, informal officers' and enlisted men's clubs and the American movies shown nightly at a conference room in JUSMMAT headquarters, the entertainment and recreational facilities available to Americans were Turkish. On the whole, Ankara offers the usual kinds, if not the number, of these possibilities: nightclubs, restaurants, sporting events, parks, swimming pools, tennis clubs, and so on. In 1950 a Turkish-American country club was started by the

51

American Ambassador, George Wadsworth,[39] and a Turkish group. The customary golf course, tennis courts, clubhouse, and swimming pool (fed by cold mountain springs) were built. Membership in this club was open to all Americans who could afford the initiation fees and the monthly dues; however, no one has been able to remember that any enlisted people ever joined. Free horseback riding was permitted to Americans at the Turkish Cavalry post at Balgat and at the President's Palace.[40] After the arrival of TUSLOG, recreation became organized and new facilities were made available. Although recreational opportunities had not been lacking before, the new rash of facilities was considered necessary for morale and as an important means of keeping Americans off the streets and out of trouble. When Balgat Air Station was opened many of the recreational facilities were moved there, as well as new ones constructed.

To conjecture on the quality and content of the relations between American military people and Turks in the first years is difficult. The more dramatic occasions are remembered, but the day-to-day relations often are not. More Americans seemed to personally know more Turks well than is the case today; and most of the warm friendships between Turks and Americans that one occasionally hears about seem to have had their beginnings during those years—1947 to 1955. Difficulties between individual Turks and Americans were apparently few—or, at least, sufficiently minimal not to attain the proportions of an "incident." From 1955 "incidents" became more frequent, possibly due to such factors as the following: an increased number of people made an increase in problems more likely; the coming of large numbers of young, single men, interested in getting away from

52

the billets and from military discipline during their off-duty time, looking for entertainment and excitement in a still traditional society, provided the ingredients for potential skirmishes.

The first demonstration against American forces that can be recalled by informants occurred in 1963. It was during the Cyprus crisis, and the atmosphere had become quite tense. A city-wide curfew from midnight until the early morning hours had been imposed. One afternoon a massive demonstration outside of one of the TUSLOG detachment buildings erupted, with masses of people milling about, shouting, and throwing stones. No one was hurt, and the damage was negligible. One American secretary, who lived across the street from the beseiged building, remembers her worried Turkish landlord rushing into her apartment to save her by placing a Turkish flag in the window.

The most memorable series of demonstrations in Ankara during that period took place in August 1964. Following a day of demonstrations outside the United States Embassy, the Turkish police cordoned off the main street leading to the building. Regardless, the already gathering crowds headed for the Embassy by taking a circuitous route, which also happened to lead past the airmen's billets. As the street in front of the billets began filling with demonstrators, young airmen hooted and called from upper-story windows. This angered the demonstrators, and they turned and commenced raining rocks on the billet windows. About the time the crowd was rushing the building, trying to force entry, the Turkish police arrived and dispersed them.[41] All of the lower-story windows were broken; but the next day Turkish workmen appeared and replaced them. According

53

to those Americans there at the time, there was no mention whatsoever of this demonstration in any of the Turkish newspapers. But the news by word of mouth spread rapidly through the American community; and many responded fearfully by staying home during off-duty hours.[42]

SUMMARY

The history of the American military people in Ankara, then, can be viewed as one of the formation and growth of community life. Corresponding to the augmentation of personnel has been the increase, expansion, and embellishment of community facilities and services—both providing the conditions of social and economic self-sufficiency. The advent of a logistical support unit in 1955 brought about a change in the rank-age composition of the community; and the military population became more heavily weighted with young, single enlisted men. A tendency toward spatial concentration and centralization of facilities and military buildings can be noted through the years. None of the buildings or facilities is any longer in the old section of the city. Particularly since the construction of a main center at Balgat Air Station has this trend become manifest.

As the ethnic community has become more organized and elaborated, it has also become more isolated from the mainstream of Turkish life. It is not that sheer numbers of people and facilities automatically produce a community,

GARRISON COMMUNITY

but they provide some of the conditions in which a community can form and grow. It is notable that attitudes and responses toward the majority community have lost much of the flexibility that it is reported they once had. In the main, Turks and Turkish culture became more defined for the individual by the shorthand of community-held stereotypes. As there has been a marking-off of the community and a gathering-in of its members, so there has been an attenuation of relationships with the majority community.

NOTES

1. In the Turkish Census of 1965 the population of Ankara was 902,216.

2. For a historical and descriptive guide to Ankara and its immediate environs, see Charlotte Wolf, "In and Around Ankara," *Cen-Topics Magazine* (December, 1965–October, 1966).

3. See, for example, the following: Harold A. Hovey, *United States Military Assistance* (New York: Frederick A. Praeger, 1965), pp. 4–6, 95, 240–241; John C. Campbell, *Defense of the Middle East* (New York: Frederick A. Praeger, 1960), pp. 31–41, 284–285, 348; Alfred Vagts, *Defense and Diplomacy. The Soldier and the Conduct of Foreign Relations* (New York: King's Crown Press, 1956), pp. 215, 493; Lewis V. Thomas and Richard N. Frye, *The United States and Turkey and Iran* (Cambridge, Mass.: Harvard University Press, 1951), pp. 139–149;

The Joint Military Mission for Aid to Turkey (Washington, D.C.: Public Relations Office, 1950), pp. 1–8; Ambassador Parker T. Hart, "Americans in Turkey" (speech given to AID Orientation Meeting, October 31, 1966).

4. Quoted by Harold A. Hovey, *U.S. Military Assistance,* p. 4.

5. A criticism condemning the *"obiter dictum"* aspect of this doctrine was set forth by Walter Lippmann in an article entitled "Policy or Crusade?" *The Washington Post,* March 15, 1947. This article was reprinted in the April 7, 1967, issue of *New York Herald Tribune/Washington Post* (International Edition), as a rebuttal to President Johnson's criticism.

6. Even before congressional ratification of this law, a survey group departed for Turkey on May 19, 1947, to estimate Turkish requirements and to recommend a program to the American Ambassador in Turkey.

7. Congress did not make explicit how the money appropriated was to be divided between military and economic aid. Hovey (*U.S. Military Assistance,* p. 5) states that an initial appropriation of $400 million and a second appropriation of $225 million were made in 1947. Of this amount, $345.3 million were used for military assistance to Greece and $152.5 million were used for military assistance to Turkey. The remainder was used for economic assistance. Since 1947, according to the *New York Times* (International Edition, April 6, 1967, p. 3), the United States has provided Turkey with slightly more than $5 billion in economic and military aid in equal proportions; and, at present, aid is costing roughly $200 million per year. It is likely, the *New York Times* reports, that economic aid will decline as the Turkish economy strengthens; however, "military aid will continue indefinitely." John M. Swomley, Jr. (*The Military Establishment* [Boston: Beacon Press, 1964], p. 144) states that military aid to Turkey has been, as of 1964, even more extensive than that which appears in official figures. The American military establishment has managed to pour into Turkey an addi-

tional unauthorized billion dollars' worth of arms, munitions, and supplies for its own vast reserves. This material was written off as surplus goods by the service branches concerned. Added to this, of course, has been the money spent by Americans stationed in Turkey. For the year of 1966, for example, "Exclusive of military and economic aid, the American presence in Turkey put 381,864,682 Turkish lira in counterpart funds into the Turkish economy last year. This is the money spent personally by U.S. civilian and military families here, the payroll of Turkish employees at American installations, and contracts for services and construction at American installations. . . . Of the 381,864,682 Turkish lira spent, 316 million was spent by military families or installations and 65 million by civilians" (*Ankara Daily News,* February 24, 1967, p. 1). At this time the exchange value was approximately 9 Turkish lira to the dollar.

8. In 1955 when the Baghdad Pact was initiated, its signatories were Turkey, Iran, Pakistan, Iraq, and the United Kingdom, with headquarters in Baghdad. After the overthrow of the Hashemite regime in July, 1958, Iraq renounced its membership, and the organization was renamed CENTO, with its headquarters moved to Ankara. The United States has never become a full-fledged member, and her participation has been from the beginning on the official basis of an "observer." This subsidiary role is not apparent in practice, however, either in the high positions held by American military men and civilians in the permanent organization or in the funds and facilities made available from United States sources for its operation.

9. It should be noted that during the Lebanon crisis of 1957 the United States was accused by Turkey of using the NATO airbase at Adana, Turkey, as a U.S. troop-transport stopover. Turkey objected to this as an arbitrary and illegitimate use of NATO-leased facilities. Turkey still remembers this event.

10. *Outlook* (English-language weekly newsmagazine in Ankara), December 19, 1966, p. 1.

11. Quoted from *Aksham* by *The Week,* January 21, 1966, p. 2.

12. *Hurriyet,* April 5, 1967.

13. Sadi Kocas, "Editorial," *Ankara Daily News,* October 17, 1966, p. 2.

14. For example, the following appears in a brochure that goes out to all American State Department personnel and to some military personnel going to Turkey: "The Turkish daily press has been more noted for its sensationalism than for objective news reporting" (*Country Study, Republic of Turkey* [Washington, D.C.: Military Assistance Institute, February 1963], p. 43).

15. Yashar Kemal, "Open Letter," *Ant,* January 18, 1967, p. 1.

16. Sadi Kocas, "Editorial," *Ankara Daily News,* October 19, 1966, p. 2.

17. Ziya Kayla, *Milliyet,* March 29, 1967.

18. In his "New Year, 1967, Message," the Turkish Labor Party Chairman, Mehmet Ali Aybar, said: "I wish the Turkish people will have an independent Turkey rid of military bases, American soldiers, American experts, and Peace Corps. Today I wish success to the brave Viet Nam People who are fighting against American Imperialists" (reprinted in the *Ankara Daily News,* January 3, 1967). In *Outlook* (December 19, 1966, p. 3) it was reported that Secretary of State Dean Rusk was going to request NATO countries to send forces to Vietnam. A Foreign Ministry spokesman said in reply to this: "The United States has always asked her NATO partners, and Turkey among them, for military aid to the war in Vietnam. . . . However, according to the Turkish Government's already declared view, our Government wants the solution of the Vietnam problem through peaceful negotiations among the parties concerned by an immediate termination of the mutual attacks before a gradual race

starts towards a world nuclear war. Under the light of this view, it is out of the question for Turkey to send troops to Vietnam."

19.   This will be discussed at greater length in later sections of this study.

20.   There are some fifty-four bilateral agreements, both written and verbal, between the United States and Turkey covering the status of American forces and facilities in Turkey. Although a great deal of criticism of these has been previously voiced by the Turks, the official request for negotiations was not made until early 1966, and proposals for changes were not submitted until late in that year. In these proposals the Turks requested that the American Postal System (A.P.O.) be abolished, that goods imported into the country duty-free for Post Exchange sales be limited, that the legal status of American servicemen, even while on duty, be put under the jurisdiction of Turkish authorities, that American and NATO bases and nuclear weapons stored anywhere in the country be completely under the control of Turkey. Negotiations on these proposals officially commenced in January, 1967, but they have not gone with impressive smoothness. According to the *Ankara Daily News* (March 25, 1967): "Officials in charge of conducting the talks on Turkish-American bilateral agreements express disappointment. They reportedly said that the talks are not progressing due to American unwillingness to consider any change in the present status."

21.   When President Sunay went to Washington to visit President Johnson, the Turkish press avidly followed each move. With a great deal of watchful sensitivity, the treatment accorded Sunay by the Americans was carefully weighed. For example, the newspaper *Aksham* on April 5, 1967, ran a front-page editorial bitterly complaining that President Johnson had failed to meet President Sunay at the airport. Johnson had met both the President of Iraq and Emperor Haile Selassie at the airport, the newspaper asserted, so why not the President of Turkey? American officials in response stated that since the middle of the

Kennedy administration no American president had met any foreign visitor at the airport. The procedure now followed was for the American president to meet the visitor on the White House lawn. The American officials also mentioned, *en passant,* that the President of Iraq had never visited the United States.

22.   This eagerness applies not only to the American military community, but to civilian representatives of government agencies in Ankara, as well. For example, in a speech given to the Turkish National Assembly the American Director of AID "promised that his organization would leave Turkey in 1975, but his hearers did not know whether to be relieved at the promise or appalled at the delay" (*Outlook,* December 19, 1966, p. 15).

23.   It is difficult to write a history of the American military community in Ankara. Not only are data scarce, but that which does exist is frequently inaccessible to the independent researcher. Some unit histories are classified as secret documents for a period of time, some have been destroyed, and some are sent to the archives in St. Louis every two years. The potential historian is not alone with this problem, for often the organization people themselves must come to grips with it. One officer, newly in charge of a detachment, complained that in trying to track down the official justification for certain procedures he had found great gaps in the records: "Everything is so classified that some things haven't even been written down." Continuity and completeness are scarce commodities. There are a handful of "old timers" scattered about—both Turkish and American civilians who have worked for a number of years with the military forces—and occasionally one can find a military person who has returned to Turkey on his second or third tour of duty. Unfortunately, some of these remembrances when compared are contradictory or questionable—and quite difficult to check. Hence, a history of the American military community, as such, must of necessity be limited and tentative.

24.   See, for example, the following: *The Joint Military Mis-*

60

sion for Aid to Turkey. History, 1947–30 June 1950 (Washington, D.C.: Public Relations Office, 1950).

25. Swomley, *The Military Establishment,* p. 144.

26. Vagts, *Defense and Diplomacy,* p. 228.

27. There have been examples of this at all levels in JUSMMAT —even the highest level. For example, the Chief of Mission, who was scheduled to give a talk to an American group in 1966, was unable to attend at the last moment. The top general of the Turkish Army, whom he had been trying to see for several weeks, had finally called him for a meeting; and, although he had been scheduled to speak for over a month and a half, this meeting was of overriding importance.

28. The group was first called the Turkey and United States Engineer Group, then TUSEG, then in 1954 it was changed to the Southern Area of Joint Construction (JCA). In 1957 it was changed back again to TUSEG. The different names reflect changes in jurisdictional commands.

29. Much of this information has come from "Historical Summary," a history written and mimeographed by TUSEG personnel, 1967.

30. TUSEG has moved five times since 1950.

31. It is needless to point out, of course, that the Korean War was over by this time. However, it is the policy of the United States military establishment to provide complete logistical support, as far as possible, to its people overseas. The extensiveness of this support is apparently dependent on the size of the community and the aggressiveness of the logistical unit.

32. Called "Operation Wring-Out," the TUSLOG office was reduced to a liaison office of thirteen men in 1958. It was reinstated one year later during a major reorganization of United States Air Force, Europe.

61

33. This was Detachment 1, which later became Detachment 30.

34. The Turkish attitudes toward Americans reported here are based on interviews with long-time Turkish employees of several of the military installations and with other Turkish residents.

35. Of course, through the years as the middle-class urban Turks have become more "Westernized" in dress, education, and attitude, this fascination with Americans and American products has greatly lessened, and critical attitudes have become far more prevalent. Before this occurred, however, the enchantment, at least in retrospect, was amazingly complete. For example, the possession of a used American refrigerator was an unbelievable joy and a symbol of status for the middle-class Turk. I have been told that frequently the painfully acquired refrigerator was placed in the front hall or in the middle of the living room, disconnected and unused, to reign in silent white magnificence, the cynosure of all eyes.

36. The year 1955 has acquired unusual significance to many Turks. It represents the dividing period "before TUSLOG" and "after TUSLOG." When TUSLOG arrived with its contingent of "young, unmarried, wild enlisted men," it is thought that the situation of intergroup goodwill rapidly deteriorated. The "before" period has been highly idealized as a halcyon period of warm relations between Turks and Americans. Thus the increased numbers and change in composition of the American Forces in Turkey were seen by Turks as signaling a threatening situation. Therefore, a chronological division might be as follows: 1947–1954, the early years of the military community; 1955 to the present, the years of expansion and deteriorating relationships.

37. Sometimes the tap water in Ankara tests out as potable, sometimes not. The reasons given for this variation are several: the pipes are of Byzantine origin and impurities from the surrounding area can easily penetrate; or the sewer and water pipes

62

were laid in close proximity, and residue from the former penetrates the latter, etc.

38.   The school at Balgat is unique insofar as it is the only military dependent school that has been constructed with funds from agencies other than the Defense Department. In 1963 the United States Agency for International Development and the Department of Defense allocated approximately $1,275,000 to construct and equip the high school, with dormitory facilities for two hundred boarding students. It is bruited about that the enterprise had to be a joint one in order that the "image" of the school be civilian and hence acceptable to the Turkish government and people.

39.   Ambassador George Wadsworth eventually gained a reputation for himself of doing for country clubs what Johnny Appleseed did for apples. It is reported that at several other Middle-Eastern posts he helped establish similar country clubs.

40.   The opportunity for riding was not seized as frequently or as gratefully as one might suppose. If one were somewhat less than an accomplished rider, trying to sit the wildly spirited, rambunctious cavalry horses, inured to all but cavalry commands and a hard rein, could make for an interesting, possibly unforgettable, afternoon.

41.   If the Turkish police had not arrived when they had, the situation might have become quite serious. The American Air Police headquarters was on the first floor of the billets; and it would have been necessary, I have been told, for them to have used weapons to block the demonstrators from the upper floors in order to protect the unarmed airmen living there.

42.   One of the most striking examples of this is reflected in the enrollment for the University of Maryland off-duty classes— for that term it dropped two-thirds of what it was normally. Of course, it should be mentioned that the classrooms and administrative offices were on the first floor of the billets. Moreover, the demonstration occurred during registration week for classes.

63

3

THE
NATURE
OF THE
MILITARY
ETHNIC
COMMUNITY:
AN OVERVIEW

S tone walls do not a prison make"—nor do lack of walls
constitute freedom from community restraint. The
American military community in Ankara has no spatial
boundaries, no housing turf that can be called specifically
American. Yet on the American's arrival, a complete and
total way of life envelops him as finally and inevitably as
if a gate had clicked closed. From the moment he is met at
the airport he is drawn ineluctably into the web of military
community life: he is assigned a job in the military organi-

zation; both formal and informal military groups interpret his new situation to him; the material necessities for the "American way of life" are provided for him; military operated schools educate his children; military religious services exist for his participation; order and correct behavior are prescribed by military norms and regulations and enforced by security units. Who he is and what he is and how he is to behave for the next two to three years are institutionally defined for him—not by the copious military regulations alone, but also by the far more awesome spectacle of structural and social relationships which give the community its highly corporate quality.

Several authorities in the field of military sociology have commented that the military community in the United States is like a "company town."[1] Assuming this is the case, then it can only be said that the "company town" transported to the Turkish milieu is even more closed and isolated from the mainstream of life about it. Among the contributory factors to this phenomenon are two which will be discussed here: the military establishment in Ankara is the *profoundly* dominant institution, pervading and integrating all of the other institutions; the distinct ethnicity of community members—manifested in language, custom, dress, function, life patterns and attitudes—tends to set them apart not only in the eyes of the Turks but, more importantly for the purposes of this study, in their own eyes.

The Nature of the Military Ethnic Community: An Overview

DOMINANCE OF THE
MILITARY INSTITUTION

The military institution sets the style and quite rigorously dominates all other community institutions. There are no other effective contenders for institutional dominance; and even some of the standards associated in the United States with these other institutions are met with resistance or are shaped to conform to military requirements. The military organization is the primary referent for community, group, and individual existence. The other institutions, while not supplanted, are ancillary. Therefore one finds that the most salient characteristics of the military institution—its structure of authority and privileges, its regulations, its ideology—are reflected in all areas of community life, giving to it a monolithic quality.

Economically, the military occupation is the *one* occupation and represents for most community members the primary source of monetary income and of life opportunities. All of the facilities—places to buy goods, places to meet and to be entertained, places for religious services, and so on—are operated and directed by the military establishment. There is not a plurality of authorities and enforcement agencies in the military community of Ankara. There is only one: the military. School administrators, working in schools financed, directed, and operated by the military, often (not surprisingly) defer to and even utilize military authority. Voluntary associations are bound up with the military estab-

66

lishment: permission to exist, type of organization, time and place of meetings are dependent upon military requirements. Religious services take place in military installations and are officiated by military chaplains. Family life provides no special sanctuary from this incursion. Individual and family identities and autonomy are caught under the cloak of rank and duty. Rank becomes the chief classifier of persons; and much of the family's life in Ankara is circumscribed by the father's niche in the hierarchy.

Thus the military institutionalization of all facets of community life is quite total;[2] and there are few alternatives to conformity in the authoritarian, hierarchical system. The penetrating contentiousness of discordant points of view issuing from organizations in the United States is muffled here. Of course, this is not to say that resistance or dissent to military interpretations does not—cannot—occur; but when it does, it is, as it must be, an address to the military establishment.

In the United States the larger local or national influence is felt on a military base; the rigidity of authority and deference patterns are somewhat mediated and softened by the wider culture; appeals to wider and more various interpretations can be more effectively made. Inequalities as defined and enforced by the military establishment are alleviated by the American world just outside. In the military community in Ankara, separated by time and distance from its cultural roots, the natural diversity of democratic institutions and pluralistic influences is to a great extent swept away; and the organizing principles become centralized and singular. The military community, for all practical purposes, becomes the world.

The Nature of the Military Ethnic Community: An Overview

In these respects, therefore, the community in Ankara is not a microcosmic duplication of American life as lived in the United States, it is not a miniature of American society. It is not only alien to the Turkish world outside of it, but in many ways it is alien to the American society, as well. With the subordination of institutions and social values to military considerations, its ethos is that of the garrison community.[3]

Military Organization

It is well to have a brief look at this institution, and in so doing help to clarify the nature of the community in Ankara. In general, there are two schools of thought regarding the classification of the military establishment as a social structure. On the one hand, there is what can now be called the Morris Janowitz school,[4] the members of which argue that the military organization is bureaucratic in nature with tendencies toward increasing rationality; it is losing its traditional aspects and now has properties "typical of any large-scale nonmilitary bureaucracy."[5]

On the other hand, there is the point of view that the military establishment is an authoritarian organization, its most basic characteristics being those of rigid stratification, hierarchy, adherence to tradition, and a corporative solidarity and mystique.[6] The following statement by Felton D. Freeman might be considered representative of this group: "The military grade structure, eminently serviceable to the special purposes of an army, is more than anything else decisive in the creation of a virtual absolutist, authoritarian social system in the body of a democratic society."[7]

Before continuing, it should be pointed out that there are often two strands of argument mixed into this discourse —which, when confused, obfuscate the conceptual problems: discussing bureaucracy vis-à-vis tradition as a mode of administrative organization is quite a different thing from discussing bureaucracy (or tradition) vis-à-vis democracy.[8] Bureaucratic and traditional aspects of an institution might very well have grave implications for the viability of democratic processes, but for the moment a discussion of the institution on the basis of rationalization and efficiency obviates democratic concerns.

If the contemporary military establishment is compared with Max Weber's ideal type of bureaucracy,[9] it appears that it is, in this conceptual sense, a mélange of bureaucratic and traditional elements, an amalgam of the rational and the nonrational.[10] When one uses Weber's simplified list of ideal typical bureaucratic characteristics—technical expertise as a basis for selection to a bureaucratic office, a hierarchy of authority, a system of rules, and impersonality in the relationships between superordinate and subordinate position-holders and in the application of those rules and norms[11] —it would seem that the military organization is more or less bureaucratic in form *but* with important qualifications. Custom and tradition inhere in and pervade the structure, often deflecting tendencies toward efficiency and rationalization.

Let us first take up the question of technical qualifications as a prerequisite for appointment to a bureaucratic position. Although there is an overall functional specialization in terms of groups of men trained for a certain range of jobs in the military organization, this is not specified in terms of individuals. Expertise is far from the sole criterion in the assignment of military personnel. The official approach is still directed toward the creation of "generalists" as against the creation of "specialists." Not for nothing are General officers called Generals. The military operates within branches and within ranks on the principle of the interchangeability of personnel. Howard Brotz and Everett Wilson illustrate this principle when they mention that "it is not uncommon to see a battlefield officer transferred for various reasons to administrative assignments for which he is unfitted but which he is *expected* to fulfill by virtue of the fact that he is an officer."[12] This principle is strikingly emphasized by the policies of rotation of personnel and of military occupational specialties (MOS). Tours of duty are usually of two to three years' duration, and when completed military men can expect to move again to a new and possibly quite different job. Such intense rotation is hardly conducive to the acquisition of expertise in a particular job. As a consequence, toward the end of their careers most military men will have acquired an incredible number of military occupational specialties—all of which are duly listed in their files.[13] More frequently than not, a man is expected to pick up the essentials of job performance by experience in the job itself, rather than by being equipped through previous training or aptitude for it.

However, the desirability of acquiring technical knowledge is now officially extolled; and since World War II large numbers of enlisted men and officers have been sent to military schools and civilian universities for further education. It should be noted, though, that subsequent utilization of this training is sometimes neglected, and the degrees or diplomas used for merit badges in the consideration of

70

individual promotions and for military public relations work in pointing out the high caliber of their personnel. Although a B.A. degree is becoming a prerequisite for officer rank, promotional possibilities for the individual do not seem to be unduly affected by specialized trappings. Almost to the contrary. To many military men the branches of service which are the most desirable in terms of prestige and promotion potential are those which have been traditionally considered the most "pure" or "military" in connotation[14]—for instance, the infantry in the Army. In general, these branches are the least specialized in terms of civilian technical knowledge and the most traditional in terms of military image and mission.

An ambivalent attitude toward technical branches is often encountered in ambitious young officers. While such training and experience equips one for a retirement career in the civilian world, during the military career itself remaining in a technical branch or job can be narrowly confining. Once in, it is often difficult to receive a transfer out; because of the comparative smallness of these branches, fewer higher positions are authorized and promotion ceilings exist. Even in the largest branches, technicians will find it necessary to seek general experience with the troops in order to receive promotions above a certain level. Thus from the military perspective the main chance still lies with being considered a leader of men and a generalist rather than a technician. This is, of course, congruent with the old heroic image of the military man, possessing the traditional virtues of bravery, discipline, patriotism, and so forth, and with the prime military mission of organized professional violence in service to the nation. There is the new competitive image

71

of the organization man; but the organization man is not necessarily seen as an expert either. In short, the problem is that organizational effectiveness in terms of expertise frequently does not articulate with the opportunity structure.

There are few large-scale organizations, if any, in which the hierarchy of positions is more rigidly defined as in the military. As Frederick Elkin observed:

> The new soldier learns that, theoretically for the sake of efficiency, there is a rule by impersonal hierarchy in which problems are resolved and decisions made according to rank. He learns that rank is all-pervading in the Army and that even for men of equal grade there are criteria for deciding which is the superior and which the subordinate.[15]

Adhering to the principle that every lower-ranking man is under the supervision and control of every higher one and that communication must follow the chain of command,[16] on the surface it would appear that this hierarchy could serve as a *ne plus ultra* example. In some ways it might, but again there are important differences between construct and reality.

From a graphic point of view, the hierarchy no longer exists in the shape of a pyramid, but has gradually changed to one which more closely resembles an odd diamond shape, or two diamond shapes, really, with the bulges occurring in the areas of officer 0–3's and enlisted men E–3's. This change has been spurred by the increase in new roles and specialties that have grown up in recent years.

It should also be noted in passing that one of the prime characteristics of this structure is the major disjunction in the distribution of authority and privileges that exists between officers and enlisted men. The Doolittle Board, ideas of efficiency versus nonefficiency, ideas of the democratic

72

army, and reorganizations notwithstanding, all of the military socialization patterns, norms, and codes continue to uphold this tradition. And the connective social tissues existing between the two divided segments is one of command-obedience and, as Vidich and Stein have described it, of "ritualistically specified caste relationships."[17] The shift from the techniques of domination to those of manipulation and persuasion as the means of command for which Janowitz compellingly argues might well be taking place; but, conversely, Brotz and Wilson have observed that "what finally remains of an order at the lowest echelons is often nothing more than a direct command, without apparent reason."[18]

Another interesting aspect of rank within the hierarchy is one which Coates and Pellegrin have pointed out. According to them, there are really two hierarchies, one of rank and one of function. These usually merge, but not always: "The rank of a military man becomes a pseudo personal quality which inheres in him regardless of changes in other aspects of his military career. His job may lessen in importance, but his rank remains the same and in time may increase."[19] Thus the bureaucratic role of the military man is directly and tellingly diffused into all areas of his life. Weber stated that "ideal" bureaucrats "are personally free and subject to authority only with respect to their impersonal official obligations."[20] Discipline and control of the military bureaucratic officer are not circumscribed by work time and place, but are omnipresent aspects of the career life. All of a man's roles external to the job are captured and colored by the encompassing net of rank. When Janowitz states that the fusion of the official and private spheres is "a basic feature of professional military life,"[21] or when Coates

73

and Pellegrin stress that "the military person has few spheres of action in which his behavior is not 'organizational' in its import and direction,"[22] they underline the comprehensiveness of military life.

Thus one can expect, and will find, that military rules and norms regulate almost every aspect of the military man's life. Coates and Pellegrin sum this up very well:

> While each regulation is specific, the body of regulations is diffuse, so that a wide range of actions of each member of the military organization is allowed. Thus there are not only regulations which govern how an officer will function in his job; but there are also regulations specifying how he will dress on numerous occasions, those persons with whom he will associate in certain social situations, the means by which he will advance his career, and so on. In this way, the application of regulations is not restricted to his military job but even controls his way of life.[23]

Those who have been prosecuted for their off-duty behavior have become painfully aware of the extent of bureaucratic reach and control.[24]

In the ideal bureaucracy, formalistic impersonality prevails. In the empirical situation there are always exceptions, but in general such questions as the following are relevant: Are the relationships between hierarchical levels impersonal? Do officials carry out their duties *"sine ira et studio?"*[25] Are general rules applied impersonally to all? On the whole, it appears that impersonality is prevalent in the administration of the establishment; but there are exceptions, and these exceptions are important. In order to examine this aspect of a bureaucracy, it is necessary to ignore the occasionally contradictory orders that exist in such a huge body of regulations, as well as the questionable legality of some of the regulations in the light of American Constitutional Law.

Arnold Rose contends that the following is the case: "Rules and orders are very badly enforced in the American Army. That is largely because discipline is regarded as something for the enlisted men and not for the officers, while it is officers who must see that the rules and orders are carried out."[26] Edward F. Sherman, a teaching fellow at Harvard Law School, declares in a recent article in *The New Republic* that the application of regulations is carried out in neither a fair nor impersonal manner, that some regulations in the Military Code are invoked "only when the commander wants to get someone," that they are used frequently to repress the rights of the individual rather than to effect military efficiency, that many rules and traditions are utilized expressly to forbid and discourage social association between officers and enlisted men and to provide special privileges for officers.[27]

With the large number of military regulations covering almost every area of military life, it is not surprising, perhaps, that some of the regulations are ignored—either because they are difficult to enforce or do not appear to be directly relevant to a particular situation or are so general and vague that their precise area of application is almost impossible to legally define. However, because they *exist* and *can be invoked* makes for a situation in which personal feelings and arbitrary judgments can thrive. Because there is an area where the decision for the application or non-application of sanctions is at the discretion of a commander or depends upon the political climate of the time and place, such regulations can be used coercively and as power levers,

The Nature of the Military Ethnic Community: An Overview

contributing to a condition of threat and unpredictability—
conducive to conformity but hardly conducive to efficiency.[28]

Article 133 of the 1950 Uniform Code of Military
Justice, prohibiting acts "constituting conduct unbecoming an
officer and gentleman" is an example of the vague and
diffuse regulation that can constitute legitimacy for indiv-
idualizing acts of repression.[29] Just what kinds of conduct
are unbecoming an officer and gentleman? These are not
specified, and so the regulation can be interpreted however
and whenever authorities see fit—can be ignored or wielded.

In Ankara, several military legal officers commented
that there were regulations against all sorts of behavior which
were violated with regularity. For instance, there is an Air
Force regulation prohibiting gambling and gambling de-
vices on government-owned or leased property.[30] Yet in
the Noncommissioned Officers' Club and in the Officers'
Club, both of which are housed in government-leased buildings and operated under the auspices of the military, slot
machines are an ubiquitous feature, their whirring clang
seldom still during off-duty hours. There are several military-
sponsored lotteries each year in Ankara, and tickets are
sold for these in government offices during duty time, and
the drawings are carried out on government property—all
of which is clearly illegal in terms of this regulation. One
military lawyer related that a fellow officer had asked him
for legal permission to set up slot machines and run a
lottery for a future event. He had had to tell him, "Don't
ask me, just go ahead and do it. If you ask me, I'll have to
tell you about the Air Force regulation against it." It is apparent, however, that if the occasion arises where the person
or the group or the cause is not popular, the regulation might

76

be enforced. Examples of arbitrary application or nonapplication of regulations are sufficiently numerous as to make questions on impersonality justified.

The discrete division between the ranks of officer and enlisted man is frequently cited as encouraging unfairness in the application of general regulations.[31] It is the responsibility of officers to see that the rules are followed; yet in some situations identification with fellow officers or with interests in maintaining officer privileges influences the decisions.[32] For that matter, given a situation in which two highly distinct rank-status groups exist, greatly differing from one another in regard to authority and privileges, and yet for which a body of general rules exists, it could be conjectured that the fair and impersonal application of these rules will frequently be subverted.

Suffice it to say, with Janowitz: "While the dominant trend is toward more modern types of authority structure and functional discipline, traditionalism, ceremonialism and sheer ritualism persist and even re-emerge."[33] The peculiarities of military life—its unique mission and ideology, its relative isolation from the societal mainstream, its highly corporative qualities, its solipsism—tend to maintain and reinforce the traditional aspects of the organization. The impact of modern technology, quickening rates of change, and the international problems that have come with a drastically contracted world are, it is true, corroding the rigid boundaries of this narrow corner of parochialism; but the accepted rationale of efficiency and new administrative practices is utilized by the military as a two-edged sword—to effect real changes, on the one hand, and to defend custom and pervading traditionalism as being *truly efficacious,* on the other.

The Nature of the Military Ethnic Community: An Overview

THE MILITARY ORGANIZATION
IN ANKARA

When a segment of this organization was transported to Ankara, it became a community of its own. And over a period of time certain properties and tendencies, bureaucratic and otherwise, have become more or less pronounced. Because the community is situated in a foreign milieu, and as such is an ethnic subcommunity as well as a military subcommunity, some of the traditions of the military have re-emerged in an intensified fashion as a response to external cultural threat. Patriotism, solidarity, unity, *esprit de corps* —and the closure implied in these group attitudes—sharpen the lines of identity between community members and outsiders.

Nationalism

The systematic inculcation of a heightened sense of nationalism is usually common to all armies. On the wings of patriotism, however, are also borne the hidden implications of this doctrine—that is, the disparagement of foreigners and that which is foreign to the nation. The indoctrination of this ideology is carried out on a rather simplistic basis—due, perforce, to its content and to the wide range in education and intelligence represented by both proselyters and receivers. Thus, in an overseas setting, particularly during the "cold war" period when a Manichean vision of bad communists versus good democrats is held by

78

some of the elite military men, this point of view is reduced to its lowest denominator—*we* versus *they*—and, in-
terestingly enough, becomes a further ideological rationale
for extreme conformity within the community. Excessive
concern for security and secrecy is partly the result of this
indoctrinated ideology; and the feeling that the external
threat is generalized and virulent is quite prevalent in Ankara. A statement made by an Air Force lieutenant colonel
sums up the tightening effect of such indoctrination on the
community: "Why, there are spies everywhere here in Ankara. I don't go to the race track anymore. There are too
many foreigners there."

Idealization of the United States

The effectiveness of this ideology in parochial circumstances, added to time and distance away from the United
States, contributes to an idealization of "home"—of the
"good old U.S.A." In almost all circumstances America,
American products, and Americans are seen as superior; and,
conversely, sometimes by default, Turkey, Turkish products,
and Turks are seen in the community schemata as inferior.

In this process of amplification, there is an inevitable
simplification and distortion. Other than viewing American
laws and cultural ways as the ultimate in reasonableness, the
primary emphasis is on the material advantages of American
life—America, the "land of the Big PX." Inherent in this
attitude, of course, is the idea that only a very clever people
(i.e., "we") could have developed such an advanced technology. However, it serves well as a self-conscious congratu-
lation, lending itself to an ethnic sense of superiority. At-

79

tendant to this is an hyperbolic sporting of what becomes defined as Americanness:[34] clothes, mannerisms, food habits, points of view. This Americanness does not reflect its pluralistic sources, is narrowly conceived and interpreted. Perhaps the group that most extravagantly, and insecurely, exaggerates its Americanness is the dependent teen-age group. Their consumption of American magazines, movies, and records is voracious; and on the basis of these a kind of archtype of the American teen-ager is collectively evolved and studiously copied. Their self-conscious posture is more than a little poignant, touched as it seems to be by their fear that upon their return to the United States they will somehow be found wanting.

The Military Mission

In the military organization the mission is always of paramount importance. In Ankara there are two missions, sometimes of questionable compatibility. Primarily, of course, there is the mission that is specifically military within the context of American national interests; secondarily, there is the mission of encouraging "good relations" with the indigenous peoples, which is seen as providing those conditions conducive to the successful accomplishment of the first. The approach of those in command toward the military people in Ankara is instrumental; community members are seen as a means of attaining the organizational goals, and they are explicitly impressed with their individual unimportance and expendability in the face of this.

The command conception of the instrumentality of the community members has tended to be narrow, with little

80

cognizance of how important the relationships of the *community* with the structure and goals of the organizations are. Techniques of domination are used more frequently in the community-wide sense than are techniques of manipulation. The attitudes of domination are reflected, for example, in the dearth of information about the community, about new regulations, and about the community relations with the Turkish community that are passed down from the upper reaches of authority. As a consequence, community-wide rumors and fears and almost fantastic interpretations of local Turkish-American relations are endemic in the community, and are seldom neutralized by facts.

This situation became sufficiently exacerbated in 1965 to cause concern among many of the consulting professionals—the school psychologist, the military psychiatrist, the hospital staff, counselors, and chaplains. It was their belief that the lack of communication, the fragmentation of community services, and the indifference shown toward people's needs on the community level resulted in general apathy and an extremely high rate of mental health problems. Going to the top group of generals and to the ambassador with their plans for a mental health program (which included a community council, suggested lines of communication, and the encouragement of member participation), they stressed that the mission *and the man* were inextricably bound up together. The elite response to this was interesting insofar as it was on two levels, the second canceling out the effects of the first. They acquiesced to the organization of a community council and agreed that a demographically organized "grass roots" approach involving the whole community might be helpful. Then they proceeded to implement this by fiat and discipline, by orders through the chain of command, without any real broadening of communication or without provision for increased participation. The solution to the problems engendered by domination and tight strictures of military control was assumed to be more of the same, with the main emphasis still firmly placed on *what* the mission was, rather than on the understanding that the paths to accomplishment are many and various and cannot be divorced from people.

Interchangeability of Personnel

As discussed earlier, the military organization is predicated on the dictum that personnel are not only replaceable, but can be rapidly and generally interchanged. This point of view, with its negation of personal variability, is mechanically applied; and masses of people are moved into and out of jobs in Ankara by the numbers. Thus people are frequently assigned to fill jobs regardless of whether they are equipped for them by training, aptitude, or interest. This approach, while doubtless useful in terms of speedily refilling job slots, often has grave consequences for the individual and for the community. Indifference to the client-public, an emphasis on rules to the neglect of content, and a mechanical going-through-the-motions sometimes result. Let one example suffice as an illustration. A young lieutenant, trained and experienced as an Air Force maintenance engineer, unhappily found upon his arrival that he was being assigned to duty as the Dependent Schools Officer. Needless to say, this job had nothing in common with his particular area of competence. His response was a rather apathetic acceptance that he had to put in his time and get the thirty-month tour over with. The social and psychological costs to him and his family, to the schools, and to the community seemed high. School administrators bitterly complained that no longer were necessary repairs made, that they seemed to have little control over maintenance people who had been hired through the military, and that they could no longer "communicate" with the establishment.

The Rotation Policy

Congruent with the interchangeability policy is the policy of intense rotation of personnel. In Ankara, from January 1, 1957 to March 2, 1967, the modal tour of duty for personnel accompanied by their families was thirty months. The "all others" tour of duty, which included single men and married men unaccompanied by their families, was usually of eighteen months. One might say, then, that on the whole a "generation" in this community was roughly of eighteen to thirty months duration. After March 2, 1967, the tour of duty for accompanied personnel in the Air Force was shortened to twenty-four months.[35]

Tours of duty are staggered, so that while the organization is not disrupted by periodic mass influxes and exoduses, people always seem to be coming and going, giving to the community a rather transient air. Because primary-group attachments to friends and neighbors are necessarily attenuated,[36] dependence upon the military institution is all the more complete.

Time Perspective

A community-wide frame of mind has developed that can be roughly labeled as the short-term perspective. Il-

The Nature of the Military Ethnic Community: An Overview

TABLE 1

TOTAL LENGTH OF TOUR BY RANK GROUPS (JANUARY 1967)

RANK[a]	1 Year		18 Months		2 Years		30 Months		3 Years		4 Years		Total	
	No.	%	No.	%	No.	%	No.	%	No.	%	No.	%	No.	%
E.M.	2	2	33	41	5	6	37	46	4	5	0	0	81	100
W.O.–3	0	0	7	17	2	5	31	76	1	2	0	0	41	100
04–above	0	0	0	0	5	11	32	73	6	14	1	2	44	100
All ranks	2	1.2	40	24.1	12	7.2	100	60.3	11	6.6	1	0.6	166	100

[a] E.M. = enlisted men; W.O. — 03 = warrant officers, second lieutenants, first lieutenants, and captains; 04 and above = majors and above.

lustrative of this perspective is the frequently verbalized question: "Why get interested? I'm leaving soon." The first year of the tour many Americans say they are "too busy getting settled" to get involved in the overseas milieu; the second year, as one Army wife put it: "It's too late now to get around Turkey much and to learn Turkish. I wish we had, but we've only got one year left." A high school boy wistfully said: "It doesn't pay to make good friends here. Everyone I know says that. Two years and it's all gone."

One manifestation of the short-term perspective is that of counting the days left of the tour in Turkey. Naturally, there are many who, when nearing the end of their tour, commence counting the days. But there are some who commence the counting almost from the moment of arrival. One dependent wife, who had been in Ankara but three weeks and had visited only the base exchange and the commissary, wearily cried: "When's the next boat home? I don't see how I can stand to wait. I cross off the days on the calendar, but there are so many left." A military man testily remarked: "I've been here eighteen months and twenty-eight days, and I'm numb now. I only hope I can wait out the eleven months and two days." For these people the tour is interminably long, a dreary sitting-it-out—complaining, bored, and dissatisfied. Perhaps for them, more than for the others, the easily calculable termination point of the tour is indeed a necessity and, as Sidney Adams and his colleagues have observed, "an important factor in maintaining morale."[37]

At the other extreme, there are those who have volunteered to come to Turkey, some for the second and even the third time. There are also those who have asked that their

The Nature of the Military Ethnic Community: An Overview

tour of duty in Turkey be extended. Those who requested transfer to Turkey made up 10 percent of a sample drawn from the American military population.[38] Voluntariness in itself involves some openness of attitude toward living in Turkey. It also involves, because of its comparative rareness, a degree of resistance to the more accepted attitude that it is preferable to leave Turkey as promptly as possible, never to return.

On the whole, the time perspective of military people in Ankara is oriented toward the future, toward the return to the United States. They see their stay as temporary, and the community is viewed as another way station in their nomadic military lives. It is possible that their involvement and participation in the American military community and in the Turkish majority community is neither as deep nor as extensive as it would be if they saw themselves as permanent or even semipermanent members.

Status Considerations

Due in part to the rotation rate, the interchangeability of personnel, and the distance from the United States, status considerations become channelized into those of rank and military position. In other words, the primary deference orientation is toward the militarily defined system of honor. Other distinctions are comparatively unimportant in the military world of Ankara. Status and class verifiers that are operative in the American civilian world, and to a lesser degree in the United States-based military world—such as those of residence, income, possessions, family membership, group associations, or even of personal excellence—have been largely robbed of meaning in Ankara. They are not crucial because they are seldom known and have little bearing on the immediate situation. The symbols of rank are highly and immediately visible and are peculiarly adapted to the rigidly structured, nomadic lives of the community dwellers. With but a glance, total strangers can immediately identify one another and know what kind of deference or authority behavior will be required and expected.

Political Participation in the Community

Nonpartisanship in the political affairs of the nation is a tenet of the American military establishment. In line with this, the military community in Ankara avoids any publicly expressed opinion or behavior that could be construed as having a political character. There are no American political groups or organizations to which one might belong in Ankara. Even in private social gatherings political discussions are infrequent; and controversial political issues, considered salient on the American scene, are conversationally avoided. The climate of political indifference is furthered by the dearth of critical literature available on the base exchange newstands. Glossy with the usual "slick" magazines, they present the critical reader with a political Barmecide feast.[39] Although a number of paperback books are also offered, works of political nonfiction are a rarity.[40]

There is little real representation in the local sense on military posts in the United States. In Ankara, since there are no American civilian communities just off post, local disenfranchisement is rather complete. All decisions on policy are handed down from on high with the explicit expectation

The Nature of the Military Ethnic Community: An Overview

that they will be complied with. There are no accepted channels through which criticisms or suggestions can be made or questions posed. Thus the power to control community decisions and community life does not lie, even minimally, in the hands of those affected. Discipline, obedience, and adjustment are seen as the proper responses of community members—and not just by those in command. One marginal person, a psychologist, observed that the attitude most "typical" of military people in Ankara was that of apathy: "They are told what to do, where to go, what to get. And they just sit there waiting for an order." It should be noted, however, that life in a community insulated from the economic, racial, and political tensions of the American world and from the controversies inherent in democratic processes does present an appearance of order and stability.

MARKS OF ETHNIC STATUS

There are many ways of identifying fellow community members. The obvious indicators vary from clothes, mannerisms, cars and distinctive license plate numbers to places where one expects Americans to congregate. The language, spoken with American inflections, is, of course, one of the most important identifiers; or, as Edward Sapir wisely said: " 'He talks like us' is equivalent to saying 'He is one of us.' "[41]

In the overseas setting Americans become much more

self-conscious of what constitutes American character,[42] developing a heightened awareness of differences from living side by side with another national group. Ethnic appearances and traits vis-à vis Turkish appearances and traits are not only a matter of group revelation and interpretation, but become further cultivated and even exaggerated by some group members. Some distinctions become key in the generalized community appraisal of fellow ethnics and of Turks.[43] There is little attempt in Ankara for either dependents or military personnel during off-duty time to "pass" as Turks or to "go native." The generally negative evaluations of Turks and Turkish culture and the highly positive evaluations of Americans and American culture, as well as the strictures imposed by military community life, effectively militate against this.

There are further, finer distinctions than just those based on nationality operative within the military community. Although the first ethnic consideration is founded on cultural bonds, the second and almost equally as important consideration is occupational. A strong "occupational ethnocentrism"[44] is evinced by military people in Ankara, resulting in a gathering-in of military community members and a shutting out of nonmilitary groups.

Representative Role and "Image"-Making

The official assumption in Ankara is that individual American behavior can serve as a basis for Turkish judgment and stereotyping of the American collectivity, that each American will be seen by Turks as containing the very essence of national character. Consequently, there is great

89

emphasis placed on how the "representative role" of the overseas American *should* be played in order to project a favorable "image" and to evoke a Turkish response of goodwill and cooperation toward Americans and American projects.

The assumption that the behavior of one person can serve as a basis for a national stereotype (if even that is necessary) is probably correct; and sociological observations that stereotypes of national groups take precedence over class, status, and individual distinctions have been made frequently.[45] However, the official conclusion that such "images" can be manipulated and are of such importance as to make national political actions and reality pale in comparison is much more dubious. Moreover, it is interesting to speculate on whether ethnic differences and isolation are not further deepened by the American official management of the representative role. It is possible that this official emphasis tends to increase national self-consciousness, to rigidify ethnic lines, and to make relaxed cross-cultural exchange more difficult.

From the moment of his arrival, the military person is told *not* to relax, that he is an ambassador of his country, that "every word, every gesture, every public appearance you make creates in the minds of the Turks a certain impression of the United States. Each personal contact you make affects the prestige of your country."[46] Throughout the tour of duty this admonition is both formally and informally reiterated. For example, in almost every monthly talk to his troops, one colonel would state: "You are in a glass house over here; at all times you are on exhibit." The effect on the receivers is various—from none at all in many to nervous ap-

90

prehension in some, to conscientious striving in others, to an expanded self-importance in a few.

With the military establishment in Turkey, the representative role is seen as having *specific* characteristics, rather than being one of a generalized attitude. The characteristics considered desirable are almost exclusively centered on order and neatness. A rigorous attempt is made to standardize the mode of dress and haircut, the condition of cars, and personal appearance in general. In other words, the characteristics emphasized are those upon which the military establishment places value, not those usually considered representative of a democratic society. Quotations from several military *Daily Bulletins* will perhaps illustrate this point:

> The dirty and general poor appearance of American military vehicles in the area are a discredit to the American image in Turkey and must be corrected immediately. . . . Effective immediately military vehicles will not be serviced at the Det 30 service station that are in a dirty condition.[47]

> ALL PERSONNEL: It has been observed that the privately owned vehicles operated by some of our people are noticeably unsightly. In most instances, our vehicles are easily identified as belonging to members of the U.S. forces, and the poor appearance of some of them is quickly noted by host nation personnel who take great pride in their automobiles. Owners should give the same attention to the care of their automobiles as they do to their quarters and person.[48]

> DRESS & PERSONAL APPEARANCES: The following is an extract of a USAFE letter, received at Det 30 dated 20 Oct 66: "All United States citizens overseas, regardless of their status, have a constant responsibility of insuring that

91

---

their dress, personal appearance and conduct reflects an image of our American Society in which we can take pride. Commanders at all echelons are requested to take appropriate action to bring to each military, civilian member and their dependents within this command a full responsibility to present the best image of our American Society."[49]

Personal Appearance—Men: (1) The face will be kept clean-shaven, but a short neatly trimmed mustache may be worn. A beard may be worn only when temporarily approved by medical officers for medical reasons. Such approval will be limited initially to three months, but may be extended if considered necessary by the medical authorities. (2) Hair must be neat and closely trimmed. It may be clipped at the edges of the sides and back, but must present an evenly graduated appearance.[50]

For dependents, women and children, and for military personnel during off-duty time, "appropriate attire" is also prescribed. Since the military sponsor is held responsible for the behavior of his dependents, institutional control over their dress and appearance is much more complete than it would be in the United States. In many of the school bulletins lists of forbidden attire are included. Outside the doors of several of the facilities—for example, the post exchange and the commissary—notices are posted which enumerate the kind of clothes which people are forbidden to wear if they wish to enter.

All of the middle- and higher-level officers interviewed who were in administrative charge of the community believed that neatness, order, and standardized dress were absolutely essential in winning Turkish goodwill. An occasional officer, caught up in the machinery of image-making,

92

expressed irritation that American civilians in the United States were not sufficiently impressed with the importance of projecting a "good image," that they were careless in how they appeared to foreigners. For how much more effective *the image* would be if it emanated from shore to shore of the American continent. One officer told me that the last time he had been in the United States he had seen "some kids in shorts and barefooted, if you can imagine, at Kennedy Airport." He was "shocked," he said. "Foreigners come in there. What do you think those kids do to our image?"

Along with the emphasis on a neat appearance goes the dictum of "no trouble." The fear that a drunken soldier, an inappropriate remark, or a fight between an American and a Turk will upset the delicate balance of Turkish-American relations is a very palpable one in higher headquarters. Illustrative of this are the following statements made at "Commander's Call" meetings with the Detachment 30 troops:

> I know that many people here are having a difficult time with their Turkish neighbors and their children. But the Americans *must* get along. If you can't get along, you should move to a new neighborhood.

> When you park on the streets downtown and a Turk comes up and asks for parking money—pay him! If he is authorized, he'll usually have tickets. But even if he has no tickets or authorization, pay him anyway. Don't cause any trouble!

The response of many of those hearing the statements above was one of frustrated irritation—an anger directed not at the commanders who made the requests, but at the

Turks in general for behaving in what was considered to be a clearly irrational fashion toward Americans.

The Nonimage: An Exercise in Legerdemain

After the demonstrations and riots in the summer of 1966, it was decided that the presentation of a good image alone was not an adequate measure. Somehow the obviously American military people would have to be whisked out of sight or made as unobtrusive as possible[51] so that their numbers, wealth, and attitudes did not further irritate the Turks. Several programs, dedicated to the ideal of invisibility, were put into effect. Examples of these follow.

Attempts were made to camouflage the school buses transporting American dependent children to and from the schools at Balgat Air Station. Previously the buses, after the children had been picked up, were driven in convoy down the main street of town, past the Turkish Parliament building, and on out a major highway toward Balgat. Thirty-seven Air Force blue buses made a rather obvious splash of color as they held up traffic twice a day at one of the busiest intersections; and in the Turkish Parliament a representative, if he was so inclined (and some were), had but to gesture out the window at the correct time to make his point that the American presence was indeed overwhelming. Following the invisibility decision of American officials, the buses were painted gray, olive green, with a few left Air Force blue. They were rescheduled and rerouted so that it would seem that only a few trickled past the Parliament building. However, school bus pickup times were not changed for the children nor were school opening times. So the trickle was

94

still pretty continuous, and as for the change of color, as one American punster quipped: "Instead of looking like U.S. military school buses painted blue, now they look like U.S. military school buses painted gray, green, and blue." The secret of this maneuver was not particularly well kept as the *Daily News,* a Turkish English-language newspaper, shortly ran a front-page article emblazoned "U.S. Cutting Profile Painting Buses," which commenced with the line: "It may be hard to camouflage a bus in the middle of a large city but that is what the Americans are trying to do in Turkey."[52]

Uniforms and American cars were another issue that was dealt with. It was ordered by TUSLOG, suggested by the other branches, that uniforms not be worn downtown and that private cars not be driven downtown. Americans were told to use military cars driven by Turkish chauffeurs as much as possible—not only for official business but also for any social engagements that took them away from the new part of town. It was suggested that private automobiles "should, whenever possible, be inconspicuous and unostentatious. Any special markings which particularly associate privately owned vehicles with U.S. owners should likewise be curtailed."[53] Two months later this suggestion was changed to an order:

> All personnel who have privately owned vehicles are reminded to remove all state-side markings, state-side plates, decals and other stickers. All cars displaying these markings will be issued tickets by the Security Police.[54]

Decals, necessary for admittance to the Balgat Air Station, had to be kept in glove compartments, to be shown only at the station gate. One commanding general who had brought

The Nature of the Military Ethnic Community: An Overview

a "big, white Cadillac" overseas with him, garaged the car and commenced negotiating to sell it. It was reported with high amusement by a few of his underlings that he feared either he or his wife would be attacked while driving "the big ship" through the streets of Ankara.

The problem of keeping Americans off the streets and away from everyday contacts with Turks was handled in several ways. Already there were sufficient facilities to take care of almost all of the needs of the American community, but there were a few loose ends. A full recreational program at the Balgat Air Station for the summer of 1967 was planned for American school children of all ages, in order to keep them away from their home areas as much of the day as possible. The routine shopping for fresh produce, previously bought on the local market, was made unnecessary when such items began being stocked at the commissary. Although a lack of funds caused by Vietnam war spending curtailed immediate large-scale American housing projects, plans were drawn up and funds were approved for the construction of enlisted billets and a few family housing units four miles out of town at Balgat.[55]

Fear and the sense of threat engendered by the Turkish demonstrations, the official military pronouncements, and by a plethora of rumors tended to keep many Americans out of the Turkish stores and away from the areas heavily populated with Turks.

Only one objection to this approach was heard by the researcher. A State Department official thought, contrary to the military policy of invisibility, that Americans should become *more* visible in some respects—that is, they should be *visibly* seen as involved and interested in Turkish life. "What

96

really perturbs the Turks," he said, "is not so much our general visibility as our not being interested in going to their soccer games or cultural events and our looking down on Turkish merchandise as inferior."

These programs are highly ambitious when one considers the difficulties involved in hiding so large and unwieldly a number of military Americans—over five thousand of them. The obvious solution of reducing the American military population in Ankara, or, barring that, of cutting down on the American facilities and curtailing the transport of American cars to Turkey, has not been considered as realistic.

OTHER AMERICAN GROUPS IN ANKARA

The American military community is only one of several small American worlds in Ankara, albeit by far the largest. It is estimated that there are 1,400 other Americans living there.[56] Of these, the majority is attached to government organizations, such as the Embassy, the United States Information Service, the United States Aid Mission to Turkey, and the Peace Corps. There is also a small business community of approximately fifty families. And there are exchange students, professors, and physicians living along the edges of the official communities. American visitors to Ankara, about six hundred a year, usually come on business,

The Nature of the Military Ethnic Community: An Overview

rather than as tourists. There are also those American men and women who have married Turks and are living in the wider Turkish community, but occasionally—rarely, as a matter of fact—some are invited to an American social gathering to add spice and curiosity. There are no American missionary groups because of the Turkish law prohibiting religious proselyting.[57]

In the main, these other groups exist on the fringes of the American military community, without noticeable impact upon its way of life. Government personnel utilize military-run facilities, and often they are also members of several of the larger associations, such as the PTA. Yet these very points of contact are sometimes generative of friction and resentment. The differences between jobs, organizations, missions, pay scales and allowances, privileges, and social worlds serve as irritants between the American groups.

The Military Community and Government Groups

From the general perspective of organization, the military establishment and the civilian government agencies are more or less separate. Although the programs and goals of both are supposed to be coordinated and to supplement one another, the priorities and interpretations are often different. Government officials occasionally state that just having a large military presence in Turkey has made their jobs more difficult and goals harder to realize. Funds for the respective organizations are separate; and seldom is there a pooling of resources on the community level. For that matter, although government civilians are permitted to use the facilities,[58] they are often required to reimburse the military,

98

either organizationally or individually. For example, they must pay tuition for their children to attend the dependent schools; they must also pay a minimal amount for medical and dental care. The feeling of division cuts through all levels, and the military saying that "we take care of our own, first" is not an overstatement. Even in the Air Force Family Services, a program which has been organized branchwide to assist military families in time of need, the volunteer director told me in reply to my question about the possibilities of aid to government civilian families, "If their need was great enough, I guess we'd help even civilians. But they come at the bottom of the list. Of course, they never ask."

In Ankara, it is at the places of congregation where the differences between the groups are the most evident. Many military people highly resent government personnel ("civilians") using "their" facilities; and government personnel are not only made aware of this but some have become rather defensive about it. Military people feel that the facilities are part of their fringe benefits, the prices and availability of American goods partially making up for their comparatively low salaries and their mostly involuntary transfers here. They feel that the government workers are well paid and more than amply compensated with extra allowances to defray the costs of overseas living, so why should their fringe benefits be shared with those who do not need them and have not earned them?

The inequities between pay scales and allowances of the two groups are a never-ending source of irritation for military people. But perhaps the most agonizing point of difference is that they do not possess diplomatic passports and diplomatic immunity, as do those attached to the State

Department. In a country where the host legal processes are not well understood—are often, in fact, sufficiently incomprehensible as to be thought sinister in intent—the possession of diplomatic immunity takes on an aura of great value. "Why don't we get them, too, in a country like this?" is an often reiterated plaint. Since there is a strong feeling that their vocation is more redolent of a higher patriotism and service than that of government workers, at least as great a protection from the perversities of the Turks is considered justified. The statement made to me by a military legal officer is possibly true of some: "The military attitude toward American civilians is not a pleasant one."

The point of view of government employees is often equally rancorous toward military personnel. Again and again one hears that it is the military people who make good diplomatic relations with the Turks so difficult to achieve, for it is they who are always getting into trouble—and it is the State Department people who must take time out to extricate them. The sense of aristocratic superiority of government people as against the loutishness of the military mass is occasionally expressed. One highly placed Embassy official summed this up rather well: "Military people aren't discriminatingly selected or oriented toward living abroad. They are less well educated. Now, State Department personnel are a much more select group, and they are oriented toward living abroad. The military exist in a cocoon, living very restricted lives—and not at all interested in the country. But, come to think of it, even in the United States they lead restricted lives, completely disengaged from foreign affairs. Really, it's the same old round wherever they go: from the job to the TV to the bridge club. Their behavior

GARRISON COMMUNITY

never changes. They never even try to learn the language."[59] A USIS official was even more explicit: "Conformity, routine, clubbiness, and authoritarianism sums up the military. The families are even very authoritarian. A sergeant can beat his son with a strap and never be condemned, and this isn't true in the usual American family. If anything, the military community overseas is even more rigid than in the U.S. Always being in that uniform does it. And it affects the families to a tragic degree." Besides feeling that in education and incentive they are better equipped for overseas living, they also feel that their social worlds are infinitely wider and more cosmopolitan.[60]

The Military Community and Nongovernment Groups

It is the military-issued privilege card that more than anything distinguishes between the military people and the nongovernment affiliated civilians. The "have-nots," although frequently very well paid, cannot shop at the commissary or the base exchange, and entry to the American theater, the Special Services library, and the Officers' Club is made much more difficult for them. The only American products they can buy, unless they ask card holders to get them something, are those available at exorbitant prices in the Turkish black market. Thus again the use or nonuse of facilities becomes a major divisive point—as well, of course, as the occupational and monetary differences.

Many of the American civilians feel rather bitterly about this "discrimination," as it is called. "After all," as one exchange student said, "we are American citizens." Perhaps the situation exists most poignantly for the children

The Nature of the Military Ethnic Community: An Overview

who go to the Dependent Schools as tuition students: after school, when the dependent children congregate at the snack bar or go into the base exchange to look at the latest records or clothes, they might as well take the early bus home, for they cannot enter; and most of the recreational facilities are also closed to them. As one businessman's wife said: "If you're not military here, you're nothing."

INTEREFFECTS OF THE AMERICAN MILITARY COMMUNITY AND OTHER AMERICAN GROUPS

Whether it is by size or organization, the American military community in Ankara seems to exert a far greater influence on other American groups than is the opposite case. The presence of civilian groups does not seem to have a noticeably ameliorating effect on military rigidities. Rather, it is indeed *possible* to conjecture that the secrecy and security-mindedness of the military is imitated to a greater extent by government people than would otherwise occur if left to themselves.

Perhaps one of the most interesting intergroup effects is that of the penetration of military rank into civilian groups as the predominant system of honor. Among both government and nongovernment civilian groups the problem of status identification often becomes acute among the insecure in their transient situations. Since the extremely obvious military system lies at hand, a curious search for status

102

equivalence with rank goes on, and a phenomenon of status borrowing arises. For example, the wife of a civilian worker with a G.S. civilian rating of 13 proudly mentioned that her husband's "rank" was the same as that of a lieutenant colonel. Some embassy people have irritably commented that their children have come home from school asking what the father's rank was.

The desire for visible, hard-line status is sometimes carried on even more frenetically, perhaps, among nongovernment civilians, who possess neither rank nor the tools of equivalence, the government or foreign-service ratings. Among some, status anxiety is manifested in the round of: Whom do you know? Whose names can you drop? Whose parties can you manage invitations to? And so on. Since the "rank" is not visible, those who wish to identify themselves with the elite must borrow status. And such comments signifying superiority as "you know, that *little* captain's wife" or comments signifying equivalence as "I'm having lunch with Mrs. so-and-so" are meant to be more than idle chatter.

It is the case, of course, that the highest-ranking officials of all American military and government groups in Ankara form an elite that cuts across communities. But for the most part, members of the military community live in relative isolation from any real incursions by American civilians.

The Nature of the Military Ethnic Community: An Overview

1. See, for example, the following: Morris Janowitz, *The Professional Soldier* (New York: Free Press, 1960), pp. 175–215; Charles H. Coates and Roland J. Pellegrin (with contributions by Norman A. Hilmar), *Military Sociology* (University Park, Md.: Social Science Press, 1965), pp. 323–408; S. E. Finer, *The Man on Horseback* (New York: Frederick A. Praeger, 1962), pp. 6–13. In an interesting study by Ernest A. T. Barth ("A Typological Analysis of Ten Air Force Bases—Host Community Situations," [Ph.D. dissertation, University of North Carolina, 1955]), it is pointed out that even in the United States the military community represents a kind of foreign settlement to many civilian communities and, as such, is exploited by them. This might work both ways, of course.

2. Willard Waller some years ago used the heuristic term of "inmate culture" when he spoke of certain institutions. What this can mean for the "inmates" has nowhere been more sentiently drawn than by Erving Goffman. With great acuity, Goffman states: "Now it appears that total institutions do not substitute their own unique culture for something already formed. We do not deal with acculturation or assimilation but with something more restricted than these. In a sense, total institutions do not look for cultural victory. They effectively create and sustain a particular kind of tension between the home world and the institutional world and use this persistent tension as strategic leverage in the management of men" ("The Characteristics of Total Institutions," in *Complex Organizations. A Sociological Reader,* ed. Amitai Etzioni [New York: Holt, Rinehart and Winston, 1964], p. 317). Other than by implication, Goffman has not specifically considered the importance of the situational context to the total institution, and the influences possibly exerted thus on the amelioration or extension of totality.

3. The term "garrison community" is being used here in this

very special sense, derived from Harold D. Lasswell's hypothesis of the garrison state and from Arthur Vagt's distinction between "military" and "militarism."

4. Representative of this school of thought is, of course, first and foremost Morris Janowitz. See, for example, the following books and articles for his exposition of this thesis: *The Professional Soldier* (New York: Free Press, 1960); *Sociology and the Military Establishment* (New York: Russell Sage Foundation, 1959); "The Military Establishment: Organization and Disorganization," in *Contemporary Social Problems,* ed. Robert K. Merton and Robert A. Nisbet (New York: Harcourt, Brace & World, 1961), pp. 515–552; "Hierarchy and Authority in the Military Establishment," in *Complex Organizations. A Sociological Reader,* ed. Amitai Etzioni; *The Military in the Political Development of New Nations* (Chicago: University of Chicago Press, 1964), particularly pp. 114–118. For a number of research studies undertaken in the context of Janowitz' thesis, see Morris Janowitz, ed., *The New Military* (New York: John Wiley & Sons, 1964). Another definitive statement in this regard is that of Samuel P. Huntington, *The Soldier and the State* (Cambridge, Mass.: Harvard University Press, Belknap Press, 1964).

5. Janowitz, "Hierarchy and Authority in the Military Establishment," *Complex Organizations,* p. 198.

6. Representatives of this point of view are, for example, as follows: S. A. Stouffer et al., *The American Soldier: Combat and its Aftermath,* Vols. 1 and 2 (New York: John Wiley & Sons, 1965); Felton D. Freeman, "The Army as a Social Structure," *Social Forces* 27 (October, 1948):78–83; Arnold M. Rose, "The Social Structure of the Army," *American Journal of Sociology* 51 (March, 1946):361–364; Howard Brotz and Everett Wilson, "Characteristics of Military Society," *American Journal of Sociology* 51 (March, 1946):371–375; G. Dearborn Spindler, "The Military—A Systematic Analysis," *Social Forces* 27 (October, 1948):83–88; Charles E. Bidwell, "The Young Profes-

The Nature of the Military Ethnic Community: An Overview

sional in the Army: A Study of Occupational Identity," *American Sociological Review* 26 (June, 1961):360–372.

7. Freeman, "The Army as a Social Structure," p. 82.

8. I believe that Janowitz occasionally makes this error. See, for example, "Hierarchy and Authority in the Military Establishment," *Complex Organizations*, p. 199.

9. Max Weber, *The Theory of Social and Economic Organization,* trans. A. M. Henderson and Talcott Parsons (New York: Oxford University Press, 1947), pp. 329–341. *From Max Weber: Essays in Sociology,* trans. and ed. H. H. Gerth and C. Wright Mills (New York: Oxford University Press, 1958), pp. 196–244.

10. Maury D. Feld has developed an interesting pair of constructs for the examination of the military organization, called the primitive and competitive models—which are, obviously, somewhat similar, if more focalized on the military organization, to Weber's ideal types of bureaucratic and traditional organization. See "The Military Self-Image in a Technological Environment," in *The New Military,* ed. Morris Janowitz.

11. Weber, *The Theory of Social and Economic Organization,* p. 343.

12. Brotz and Wilson, "Characteristics of Military Society," p. 373.

13. Hanson W. Baldwin (*New York Times,* Western Edition, October 21, 1963) reported that in an informal survey made on Governors Island of a 20 percent random sample of officers in each grade assigned to Headquarters, First United States Army, the average officer had seventeen years of commissioned service, *had acquired eight military occupation specialties,* made twelve PCS (permanent changes of station), had twenty-six major assignments (not including minor additional duties), and made at least sixteen moves (combat moves excluded) that required uprooting his family. In conclusion Baldwin stated:

"There are far too many transfers and shifts—so many that a great many service officers feel that they never stay long enough at any one job to master it properly."

14. For an excellent discussion of military career patterns and self-images, see Feld, "Military Self-Image in a Technological Environment."

15. Frederick Elkin, "The Soldier's Language," *American Journal of Sociology* 51 (March, 1946):419.

16. But of course informal organization exists throughout the military; and the chain of command, while lip service is paid to it, is sometimes by-passed—for reasons of efficiency, if none other.

17. Arthur J. Vidich and Maurice R. Stein, "The Dissolved Identity in Military Life," in *Identity and Anxiety,* ed. Maurice R. Stein, Arthur J. Vidich, and David Manning White (New York: Free Press, 1960), p. 503.

18. Brotz and Wilson, "Characteristics of Military Society," p. 372.

19. Coates and Pellegrin, *Military Sociology,* p. 110.

20. Weber, *The Theory of Social and Economic Organization,* p. 333.

21. Janowitz, *The Professional Soldier,* p. 199.

22. Coates and Pellegrin, *Military Sociology,* p. 113.

23. Ibid., p. 108.

24. A recent example of this is the courtmartial conviction of Army Lieutenant Henry H. Howe, Jr. for peaceful antiwar picketing during off-duty hours, dressed in civilian clothes. At first the charge was vagrancy, but this was dropped as clearly illegal. Later, military authorities charged Howe under three sections of the Uniform Code of Military Justice, one of these

being the charge that Howe was acting in a manner "constituting conduct unbecoming an officer and a gentleman."

25. This is the term that Weber used, explaining that he meant "without hatred or passion and hence without affection or enthusiasm" (*The Theory of Social and Economic Organization*, p. 340).

26. Rose, "Social Structure of the Army," p. 363.

27. Edward F. Sherman, "Military Injustice," *The New Republic* (March 9, 1968), pp. 20–23.

28. Sherman (ibid., p. 21) mentions that the courts-martial of Vietnam dissenters, Captain Howard Levy, Privates Andrew Stapp, Richard Perrin and others serve as a "continual reminder of the absoluteness of the demand for conformity within the military and the limited nature of soldiers' individual rights."

29. Examples of other Articles that are so vaguely worded as to be either useless or to grant license are the following: Article 134 forbids "disorders and neglects to the prejudice of good order and discipline"; Article 117 forbids "provoking or reproachful words or gestures towards any other persons subject to the Code"; and Article 88 forbids "contemptuous words against the President, Vice President, Congress, Secretary of Defense, Secretary of a Department or a legislature of any State."

30. Air Force Regulation 30–30, 28 June 1966, Section 10, p. 4, "Gambling, Betting, and Lotteries": "Air Force personnel shall not participate while on Government-owned or leased property, or while on duty for the Government, in any gambling activity, including the operation of a gambling device, in conducting a lottery or pool, in a game for money or property, or in selling or purchasing a numbers slip or ticket."

31. Although the disjunction between the two rank groups is defended by the military primarily on the basis of its necessity for combat command and obedience (as well as on the bases of professionalism, motivation, and tradition—i.e., "standing the test

108

of time"), this requirement has never been conclusively demonstrated. As an example of somewhat the opposite, the Israeli Army does not have the vast distinction between the two groups, yet its fighting capabilities have not been found wanting. Though historical examples of military organizations not having the rigid distinction do not abound, there are a few examples—e.g., Cromwell's army.

32. See the conclusions of the Doolittle Board, 1946.

33. Janowitz, "The Military Establishment: Organization and Disorganization," p. 525.

34. There are those few overseas Americans, of course, who "go native." However, in the American military community they are exceedingly rare. The conditions of life imposed by the military—the discipline, the lack of privacy—make this posture most difficult.

35. There were no official reasons given for this change, but rumors were rife, the explanations fitting into the general community interpretation schemata. However, Turkey is considered to be "an isolated area" type tour; and while the usual accompanied tour in Europe and Japan is for three years, the tour of duty in Turkey has always been less. Official recognition of the "hardship" elements of the tour is further accorded by the enlarged program of rest and recuperation flights (R&R) scheduled out of the country. Furthermore, dependents in this area are allowed to travel on a space-available basis with their sponsors on these flights.

36. The importance of primary group attachments for military morale has been indicated in the studies by Samuel Stouffer and his colleagues (*The American Soldier* 2:130–149) and in E. A. Shils and M. Janowitz, "Cohesion and Disintegration of the *Wehrmacht* in World War II," *Public Opinion Quarterly,* 12 (1948):280–315.

37. Quoted by David Tarr, "The Military Abroad," *The Annals* 368 (November, 1966):38.

38. This percentage of 10 percent, or 17 persons, is taken from a sample of 166 persons. Of this group of volunteers, 35.2 percent had been to Turkey before. It was interesting to observe the returnees and their changing attitudes toward Turkey in the face of the quite different attitudes of the majority. During their first tour, usually in the early 1950's, liking Turkey and wishing to return was a more prevalent attitude. Today the majority attitude has changed; and the returnee's enthusiasm in returning tends to dim over time and his attitude to become more congruent with that of the community. However, this will be more fully discussed in a later examination of community "deviants."

39. In many years of living on or near military posts, both in the United States and overseas, only once have I seen a periodical for sale on a post exchange newstand that could be considered of a critical type, though hardly liberal in point of view: the *National Review* at the post exchange at Carlyle Barracks, Pennsylvania (July, 1967).

40. The Special Services Library and the USIS Library in Ankara, though limited, do have some critical literature in the social sciences.

41. Edward Sapir, *Culture, Language and Personality* (Berkeley: University of California Press, 1961), p. 17.

42. For an excellent symposium on national character, see *The Annals,* Vol. 370 (March, 1967), particularly the discussions by Don Martindale on "The Sociology of National Character" (pp. 30–35) and by David Riesman on "Some Questions about the Study of American Character in the Twentieth Century" (pp. 36–47).

43. Community stereotypes, interpretations, and schemata will be discussed much more fully in a later section.

44. It was Arthur K. Davis ("Bureaucratic Patterns in the Navy Officer Corps," *Social Forces* 27 [December, 1948]:151) who first used this term, I believe, in regard to Navy officer groups.

110

45. Richard D. Lambert's article "Some Minor Pathologies in the American Presence in India" (*The Annals,* Vol. 368, November, 1966) is particularly enlightening in this regard.

46. *Information on Turkey for Air Force Personnel and Their Families,* 14 September 1964. Air Force Pamphlet AFP 34-8-22, p. 5.

47. *Daily Bulletin* (TUSLOG, Det. 30), No. 63 (April 4, 1967).

48. Ibid., No. 19 (January 30, 1967).

49. Ibid., No. 198 (November 2, 1966).

50. Ibid., No. 202 (November 8, 1966). The application of this particular order is usually up to the discretion of the military branch. However, here again the emphasis on this order is probably derived from the idea of proper representation.

51. A certain amount of unobtrusiveness was always practiced. For example, there are no street signs indicating the way to American facilities, nor have there been. One either knows or is taught where they are.

52. *Ankara Daily News,* February 5, 1967, p. 1.

53. *Daily Bulletin* (TUSLOG, Det. 30), No. 29 (13 Feb. 1967).

54. Ibid., No. 68 (11 April 1967).

55. Airmen living in the billets were called into a mandatory meeting and told that the new billets at Balgat had been approved and should be complete sometime in 1967 or 1968. Again this was not a well-kept secret, for it was reported in the *Ankara Daily News* (November 23, 1966) that "as money becomes available the visibility of the American presence will be lowered by moving U.S. personnel out of the cities to self-contained facilities nearby. Already large-scale plans for moving thousands of Americans out of Ankara to a facility at Balgat have been approved."

56. This estimate is based on the figure given in the *Joint Post Report, Ankara, Turkey,* compiled by the Embassy, USIS, and AID, 1965.

57. There is one American missionary in Ankara, of the South Baptist Convention. Since he is forbidden by Turkish law to hold meetings in a Turkish place, the American Embassy has permitted him the use of one of their rooms once a week.

58. Peace Corps personnel, with the exception of the administrators and professionals, are not allowed to use the commissary, the post exchange, or the clubs. Since only a few of the volunteers are stationed in Ankara, and these few live in the poorer Turkish sections, they are seldom known by military people.

59. He was fairly correct in this; however, it was amusing to be later asked to act as interpreter for him at the riding stables and to discover he spoke no Turkish at all.

60. Whether this is in fact the case or not, I do not know. However, having known a few government officials—Embassy, USIS, and AID—it appeared to me that most of their contacts with the Turks were, on the whole, of an official nature, and that these groups, in their own fashion, were as ingrown as is the military.

112

4

DEMOGRAPHIC, ECOLOGICAL, AND SOCIAL STRUCTURAL PROPERTIES OF THE AMERICAN MILITARY COLONY IN ANKARA

AN INFORMAL CENSUS

Any estimate of the number of American military people in Ankara by a civilian must be approximate, since population data are classified as a military secret. The Turkish government was said to have requested that the population figures be suppressed for the reason that, if divulged, the Turkish people might be highly perturbed by the size of the American military forces in their country.[1] The most reliable and semiofficial estimate given to me of the military population stationed in Ankara, including both personnel and their dependents as of December 31, 1966, was 5,126 persons.[2] Naturally, this varied periodically as there was a constant coming and going of personnel. Moreover, the community might have appeared larger at times, since American military groups and teams were often stationed there on temporary duty status or were coming in from other areas of Turkey on leave status.

The modal age[3] of adult military persons in the survey sample was in the range of seventeen to twenty-five years of age. This figure, however, was somewhat crude. It was more refined when the military people were separated into three rank groups: enlisted men (E.M.); warrant officers, second lieutenants, first lieutenants, and captains (W.O.–03); and majors and above (04 and above). Then the modal age of each rank group was as follows: 53 percent of the enlisted men were in the seventeen through twenty-five years of age category; 61 percent of the warrant officers, second and first lieutenants, and captains were in the twenty-six through thirty-two years of age category; 61 percent of the majors and of the ranks above were forty years of age or older (Table 2). There were very few people in the military community who were over sixty years of age, and these were usually dependent parents.

About 69.9 percent of the adult military people sampled in Ankara were married. Of the remainder, 6 percent were married but did not have their families in Turkey with them, 22.3 percent were single, and 1.8 percent were divorced, widowed, or separated (Table 3).

Those who were married and had their families with

TABLE 2

COMPARISON OF AGE BY RANK GROUPS

RANK	17–25 Years		26–32 Years		33–39 Years		40 Years & Over		Total	
	No.	%	No.	%	No.	%	No.	%	No.	%
E.M.	43	53	12	15	20	25	6	7	81	100
W.O.–03	4	10	25	61	10	24	2	5	41	100
04–above	0	0	3	7	14	32	27	61	44	100
All ranks	47	28.3	40	24.1	44	26.5	35	21.1	166	100

TABLE 3

COMPARISON OF MARITAL STATUS BY RANK GROUPS

RANK	Single		Married w. Family		Married w/o Family		Other		Total	
	No.	%	No.	%	No.	%	No.	%	No.	%
E.M.	30	37	40	49.4	10	12.4	1	1.2	81	100
W.O.–03	6	14.6	34	83	0	0	1	2.4	41	100
04–above	1	2.3	42	95.4	0	0	1	2.3	44	100
All ranks	37	22.3	116	69.9	10	6	3	1.8	166	100

Demographic, Ecological, and Social Structural Properties

them in Ankara had on the average 2.5 children living at home. The actual range, of course, was broad, from none to seven children. Of the children in the community, around 40.3 percent were of preschool age, 59.7 percent of school age.

Only one person in the sample had had fewer than nine years of formal education (.6 percent). About 47 percent had had either some university training or held university degrees; and 12.7 percent had gone to graduate school. Again, when the three rank groups were distinguished as above, it is seen that more education, as well as greater age, tended to correspond to higher rank (Table 4).

All of the occupations that exist in the military community are under the aegis of the military and are of course organizationally oriented. The proportionate numbers in each rank group could only be conjectured. It seemed, on the basis of observation and sampling, that the largest of the three rank groups was by far that of the enlisted personnel. Unlike the overall military rank configuration in the United States, the smallest rank group in Ankara was that of the warrant officers, second and first lieutenants, and captains. Most heavily represented in officer groups were majors and lieutenant colonels. A rough graphic representation would portray a vase shape, curving out from the small top elite to a relatively swollen upper half, curving in to accommodate the smaller lower-officer group, then gradually swelling out to a heavy base of enlisted personnel. This was possibly the case for officers because, in cross-cultural jobs, requirements were for more rank, prestige, and experience than company officer groups possessed.

116

TABLE 4

COMPARISON OF EDUCATIONAL ATTAINMENT BY RANK GROUPS

RANK	1–4 Years		5–8 Years		9–12 Years		13–16 Years		Graduate		Total	
	No.	%	No.	%	No.	%	No.	%	No.	%	No.	%
E.M.	0	0	1	1	52	64	28	35	0	0	81	100
W.O.–03	0	0	0	0	7	17	26	63.5	8	19.5	41	100
04–above	0	0	0	0	7	16	24	54.5	13	29.5	44	100
All ranks	0	0	1	.6	66	39.7	78	47.0	21	12.7	166	100

TABLE 5

COMPARISON OF TIME SPENT IN SERVICE BY RANK GROUPS

RANK	1–364 Days		1–5 Years		5–10 Years		10–15 Years		15–20 Years		Over 20		Total	
	No.	%	No.	%	No.	%	No.	%	No.	%	No.	%	No.	%
E.M.	7	8.7	28	34.6	14	17.2	12	14.8	17	21	3	3.7	81	100
W.O.–03	1	2.4	13	31.8	11	26.8	11	26.8	5	12.2	0	.0	41	100
04–above	0	.0	0	.0	1	2.2	12	27.3	9	20.5	22	50.0	44	100
All ranks	8	4.8	41	24.7	26	15.7	35	21.1	31	18.7	25	15	166	100

Demographic, Ecological, and Social Structural Properties

The modal length of time spent in military service was in the category of one to five years. This was the case for the largest percentage of enlisted men (34.4 percent) and for the largest percentage of the W.O.–03 group (31.8 percent). However, 50 percent of the 04 and above group had had over twenty years in the military service (Table 5).

In regard to occupational commitment, 65.7 percent of the military people sampled wished to make the military occupation a lifetime career—or, put differently, they either planned to spend, or had spent, at least twenty years in the military service. The highest percentage (97.7 percent) of those so committed were to be found in the highest rank group, 04 and above. In the W.O.–03 group, 58.5 percent felt committed. And 51.9 percent of the enlisted group planned to make the military life a career (Table 6).

TABLE 6 ────────────────────────────

COMPARISON OF CAREER COMMITMENTS BY RANK GROUPS

RANK	Committed		Not Committed		Undecided		Total	
	No.	%	No.	%	No.	%	No.	%
E.M.	42	51.9	27	33.3	12	14.8	81	100
W.O.–03	24	58.5	8	19.5	9	22.0	41	100
04–above	43	97.7	0	0.0	1	2.3	44	100
All ranks	109	65.7	35	21.1	22	13.2	166	100

About 60 percent of the military people were born in small towns and rural areas, while 38.2 percent were born in urban areas, and 1.8 percent were born in countries other than the United States.

118

For 44 percent of the military group, this was the first overseas military assignment; whereas 56 percent had been overseas one or more times before on other assignments (Table 7).

TABLE 7

COMPARISON OF OVERSEAS TOUR EXPERIENCE BY RANK GROUPS

RANK	First Overseas Tour		Previous Overseas Tours		Total	
	No.	%	No.	%	No.	%
E.M.	38	46.9	43	53.1	81	100
W.O.–03	30	73.2	11	26.8	41	100
04–above	5	11.4	39	88.6	44	100
All ranks	73	44	93	56	166	100

In January 1966 it was found that 22.2 percent of the group sampled had been in Turkey from one day up to six months, 47.7 percent had been in Turkey over six months up to eighteen months, and 30.1 percent had been in Turkey over eighteen months.

It is notable, when one compares the three rank groups distinguished herein, that certain attributes appear to be more or less characteristic of each. By inspection of the sample percentages, the enlisted group, which was also the largest group, included more young men, and included more single men. Its members were comparatively less well educated; and fewer of them felt committed to making the military occupation a lifetime career. The highest ranking group (04 and above) was composed of members who, comparatively, were the oldest, had the most education, and

119

who more frequently were committed to the military as a career. More of their number were married, with their families in Ankara. The middle ranking group, W.O.–03, in regard to these attributes lay somewhat in the middle, with one exception. On the whole, they had the least overseas tour experience of any of the three rank groups. The highest ranking group (04 and above) had more frequently had experience overseas. Enlisted men were comparatively positioned in the middle.

THE SPATIAL PATTERNS OF COMMUNITY LIFE

The territory of the American military community of Ankara could not be neatly delineated. There were points of congregation—work places, shopping centers, recreational facilities—but they were seldom contiguous. These, and the residential areas most populated by Americans, graphically presented an appearance of scatter in the southern part of the city. The traffic flow of Americans tended to be concentrated on the two to three main streets where these places were located; and many Americans seemed to know only these particular streets and to see them, primarily, as connections between American places. So even though American places were usually separated, the rounds of activities centering and carrying over from point to point symbolically lent spatial continuity. Put differently, the encapsulation of the

120

American military community was a state of mind, not one of spatial concentration.

The community had grown in a scattered fashion because there had been no American post or base with the usual concentration of housing, administrative buildings, and facilities.[4] Rather, the acquisition of buildings for American administrative and facility use and of apartments or houses for personal use had been carried out piecemeal on the competitive basis of availability and cost.

Settlement Patterns

The new part of Ankara stretches along a four-mile boulevard, running from the old section in the north to the President's Mansion on a high hill at the extreme southern end. The farther south one goes from the new city center the more raw and unfinished the landscape—hillsides gouged out, new construction going up. Almost everywhere, however, from November to May the city was more or less blanketed in smog. This was due not only to the geographical and climatic peculiarities, but also to the extensive use of a low-grade lignite for fuel. The elevation of an apartment—whether by floor or by hillside—became a critical criterion in the choice of a living place. The practical grounds of escaping the worst of the smog were fully as operative in the search for dwellings as prestige, the view, and so on. To make an obvious but relevant parable out of this: the poor folks lived in the smoggy bottom areas, and the rich folks lived on the smogless heights.

Basically, there were three considerations involved when Americans chose living places: there was the desire to live

121

within close proximity to fellow Americans and to American work places and facilities, to live in as prestigious an area as possible—near to one's rank equals or superiors; there was the consideration of living conditions—amount of smog, newness and attractiveness of the apartment or house, density of habitation and amount of open space in the area, and so on.[5] In regard to the first consideration, a very distinct enclaving tendency among Americans was noticeable. Clusters of Americans settled around almost every American facility; and seldom did an American family or bachelor live off somewhere by its ethnic self, surrounded only by Turks. Some Americans felt isolated when separated from their fellows by only one or two apartment buildings. One of the military chaplains mentioned he had been told by a congregation member that visiting friends just half a block away was like traveling through enemy territory.

The latter two considerations were tied in together, for the farther and higher one went from the city center, the better the living conditions, the thinner the smog, the more prestigious the area, *and* the more expensive the apartment or house. It was the cost, of course, that most forcefully operated as an internally segregative factor. As a consequence, one found an ecological separation of military ranks in Ankara: the higher the elevation, the higher the rank. It was true that such separation was often raggedly defined and that there were transitional areas, usually halfway up the hills. Here, middle-income people were moving into the new apartment houses, but some of the old, large, gracious houses insecurely remained in the face of apartment building, still being retained for high-ranking personnel.

Nonetheless, most areas could be roughly classified in terms of prestige; and one found that a certain range of ranks was represented with greater frequency in certain areas than in others. Probably the most prestigious and expensive area was Cankaya, the hill where the Officers' Club was located, as well as the President's Mansion. It had been nicknamed "Whiskey Hill" by the Turks, who said that there were so many Americans up there that all they needed to make it a frontier town was a sheriff. As one went down from the hills (from Cankaya and Gazi Osman Pasha), the density of habitation increased, the dearth of open spaces and patches of grass became apparent, the smog was more concentrated during the winter months, the rents were cheaper, and enlisted personnel were more in evidence. Right in the middle of the new city were several sets of billets, where most of the single enlisted men lived, sharing apartment-type accommodations with up to twelve persons in each apartment, depending upon rank and assignment.

Facilities and Services

The military facilities and services available to the community were indeed adequate for providing the conditions for social and economic self-sufficiency; and American life in Ankara was mostly circumscribed by them. Almost all needs were bureaucratically cared for.

For educating the young, there was a nursery and kindergarten school. There was an elementary school and a junior and senior high school. There was a cooperative school for mentally retarded children. And there was an

123

education center for adults where high school courses, correspondence courses, and university courses could be taken. The community also had one library.

Although there were no churches as such, space was allotted for chaplains' offices, for group meeting rooms, and for religious services; and chaplains—Protestant, Catholic, and Jewish—were assigned to Turkey to care for the religious needs of the military flock.

Medical care was rather extensively provided by a hospital, an outpatient clinic, a pharmacy, ambulance and medical evacuation units, and even a "Bio-Environmental Health Engineer."

Although one was permitted to ship an American automobile to Turkey, other means of transportation were available also: school buses, shopping buses, and military vehicles.

There were various military control agencies in Ankara: an Air Police unit with forty policemen,[6] a security and law-enforcement unit, and several intelligence units.

Almost all necessary items and quite a few luxuries could be bought at the commissary, the base exchanges,[7] and the liquor store. Even a thrift shop was operated by volunteers for charitable purposes, and one could sell no-longer-wanted items and buy secondhand merchandise. Purified drinking water could be picked up in jugs at six places in the city.

Services of all types were available. A post office, legal services, social services (such as the American Red Cross and the Air Force Family Services), a laundry and dry cleaners, a tailor shop, an electrical repair shop, a shoe-repair shop, a beauty shop, a nursery, and a mortuary provided

124

for almost any exigency. Information was officially provided by the military daily bulletins and by the organ newspapers; and the *Stars and Stripes* newspaper was flown in daily from Germany.

A variety of recreational possibilities existed for the American community member. There were several clubs—the Officers' Club, the Noncommissioned Officers' Club, the Special Services Club, the Youth Club (AYA), and the Rod and Gun Club. There was a movie theater with 750 seats, a bowling alley, two gymnasiums (one of which was also used as a roller-skating rink in the winter), a hobby shop, a swimming pool, riding stables, tennis courts, basketball courts, a miniature golf course, and little league and softball diamonds. Downtown there was the Ankara Community Center, where tours of the city were arranged, where a game room, a lounge, and club rooms were available. A new youth center was being built at the Balgat Air Station. For eating American food away from home or mess hall, there were the restaurants at the NCO Club and at the Officers' Club, as well as five snack bars located at various buildings in the city. For those who wished to venture from the city for entertainment, a wide variety of sporting equipment might be borrowed from Personnel Services Supply.

Needless to say, the administration and supervision of all of this was somewhat formidable, since it was completely handled by one organization, and simply to have kept it all going required a rather impressive number of personnel. The official rationale for furnishing the community so extensively and completely with these material accouterments could perhaps be summed up as follows: Exploiting the local resources would place an intolerable burden upon the

125

area for a group of this size; and the local economy could not absorb the number without dislocation, shortages, and inflation, leading to a keen competition, possibly conflict, over scarce items between American personnel and local inhabitants. Secondly, such facilities were necessary for the morale of American military people; they lessened the adjustments that had to be made by the transient population to the foreign milieu, for things were "just like home." Thirdly, they were an important source of institutional control over community members, keeping them off the streets, out of trouble, busy, and "buying American." Fourthly, the physical and mental health of the military community was taken into account. Supplies and services could be inspected and controlled. And finally, tradition played a role. For years, ever since the era of sutler exploitation, along with the troops and the flag has gone the counter, busily dispensing toothpaste and chewing gum. Today, the military establishment *expects* to furnish the facilities, and personnel *expect* to have them.

Yet every event has unforeseen consequences—and so with this. Such facilities, I believe, tended to make a social type—the overseas provincial; for self-sufficiency does not encourage contacts with or appreciation for the outside world. Even in the base exchange superficial acquaintance with Turkish goods was not possible, since none was stocked. Somehow this seemed to reinforce the feeling that the local products were inferior and that only American products were well made and sanitary.[8] Moreover, most Americans felt that they could not do without American products, that they could not adjust even minimally to a different way of life; and as their wants became elevated to the status of

126

needs, their way of life became equated with material goods.

In answering a survey question on whether the respondent thought that American military facilities were "an absolute necessity for overseas American military life," 93.4 percent of the sample (or 155 persons) said "yes," 3 percent were "undecided," and 3.6 percent said "no." When asked why they believed as they did, their answers most frequently stressed that the cost of maintaining an American standard of living on the Turkish economy would be prohibitive, that the Turks would be sure to cheat Americans, that Turkish products were inferior, that the morale and the physical and mental health of the Americans would be gravely endangered. But perhaps the comments of some of the respondents better illustrate these attitudes.

From the enlisted rank group:

> Most important, very few Turk businessmen speak English and if they do, they won't. Things we are used to buying are unavailable on the Turk market. All Turks will cheat on money transactions.

> Americans, especially dependents, are not accustomed to the inferior products overseas.

> I joined the Military, not the Peace Corps.

> It is hard enough with these facilities and would be impossible without them.

> These items are considered necessary at home. I was sent over here so I should be able to get these items of necessity.

> The morale problem is bad enough as it is. Take them away and the place would go to pot.

> Because it is a strange and wicked country with a usurping attitude and mentality—they are out for every penny

127

they can squeeze out of us legally and illegally, plus some more!

I would not eat anything off of the economy.

These facilities bring a small touch of home to the foreign atmosphere you are surrounded with.

From the W.O.–03 group:

I feel we are American citizens and should have as much of the American way of life with us overseas as possible. We are not here because we like it but because it is our duty to the country. Therefore, our country should support us with these activities.

The natives would take advantage of us.

I think the impression we Americans give the Turks is important to our mission. We are less likely to make an unfavorable impression if we are a happy lot and friendly.

We shauld not be required to lower our standard of living by being deprived of American products, particularly in a country like Turkey where everything is generally inferior, if not completely worthless.

From the 04 and above group:

Were it not for American facilities our existence in Turkey would be intolerable.

The point is to raise these people to our standards; not to sink to theirs. Further—we have the wealth, organization and inclination to enjoy ourselves as members of a capitalistic nation should—so why not?

Turkish food is not fit to eat, and their clothing is so high and inadequate you can't buy it.

Those who responded to the question by saying that the facilities were not absolutely necessary made such comments as the following:

128

An enlisted man:

We're spoiled! Dependents, especially in Ankara, should be prohibited.

An Air Force Captain:

Because we know people, European and American, who exist on the economy more than military people do and they manage quite nicely—also it's an opportunity to speak with Turks if you shop in their stores.

From the 04 and above group:

Not a necessity but nice to have—would tend to create better relations if we did without.

It seems to arouse antagonism both among the military and Turkish communities.

Having lived on the Italian economy we realize it can be done without detriment.

The three most important facilities to these Americans were, in order of written preference, the hospital, the commissary, and the post exchange. When these preferences were classified by rank groups, enlisted personnel thought that the hospital, commissary, and post exchange were the most important. The officer groups (warrant officers and above) believed that the hospital, commissary, and schools were the most needed facilities.

Temporal Sequences

Military life routines were much the same in Ankara as they are in the United States. For all but those on special duty, the hours of work were from eight o'clock in the morning until five o'clock in the evening. Saturday mornings for troops and their commanders were usually inspection

129

days; but for the rest of the military people it was a day off, as were Sundays. The rhythm of life in the homes was primarily dependent upon the husband's work schedule and upon the children's school times. Generally, there were no seasonal variations in this schedule; and in offices summers and winters were distinguishable only by changes in uniforms.

Leave time was a matter of personal choice and of permission from one's superior. All American holidays were celebrated. Turkish holidays could be noted only by the closing of facilities staffed mostly by Turkish workers or when a number of one's Turkish coworkers were absent.

SOCIAL STRUCTURAL PROPERTIES OF THE COMMUNITY

Rank

The internal structure of the community was based on the rank hierarchy. This hierarchy was divided into two major categories, officers and enlisted men; and the effects of the bifurcation were evident in every aspect of individual and group life. Position was derivative of rank: that is, rank was a prerequisite for filling a position, rather than that which devolved on the man by virtue of his holding the position;[9] and the importance of a position was indicated by the rank qualification. In Ankara, generally speaking, the hierarchies of class, status, and power were fused in the one

130

hierarchy of rank. Discrepancies between these dimensions for rank groups did not exist to any notable degree. Within a rank group, of course, there was some differentiation between individuals on the bases of power and status because there were differences between the within-rank positions they held.[10] Some positions were more strategic in terms of power and prestige, several factors being determinative in this respect: for example, the number of people over which the position-holder had authority; the proximity of the position-holder to the seat of power (e.g., the general or the commanding officer), or, barring that, the relative independence he had from direct supervision; the accouterments of prestige that went with the position, such as the car and chauffeur assigned for personal use, the size, location, and furnishings of the office, and so on.

Among men whose rank was the same and whose positions were roughly equivalent, there were further finite distinctions that were peculiarly relevant in some circumstances. One of these was the date of rank. Even when men of the same rank did not work together, date of rank automatically determined degrees of superiority, thereby indicating who in a specific rank group would have first choice as to government housing or government furniture, who would be the "ranking man" (that is, in charge) in a government apartment house, and so on. In one American government apartment house in Ankara, one of the first things that four colonels and one Navy captain (all 06's) found worthy of discovery about one another was who ranked whom. He who had been of 06 rank the longest was considered to have the most authority in the living quarters; and the colonel who had received his rank most recently was patronizingly re-

131

ferred to as "Junior" by his ranking compatriots. There were a few positions in the community, as in any military setting, where temporary usurpation of power was possible. The job of aide-de-camp to a general was one of these, for it was the aide (or aides) who usually acted as a primary communication link between the general and subordinates. Oddments of background could enhance individual prestige, although they were not necessarily convertible as means to rank mobility: for instance, a military academy education, high-ranking relatives, effective job performance, and so on.

The elite. The key stratum or the decision makers of the community were those who were at the command posts of the various units. At the time of this study, the elite nucleus consisted of six Army and Air Force generals and one Navy admiral. They were primarily responsible for the accomplishment of the military missions, as the administrators of the community, as the ethnic representatives to high-strata Turks and foreign dignitaries, as the military occupational representatives to other American groups in Ankara and to visiting American political and military leaders. Within this group local and political responsibility and communication were centralized. They filled the master positions—at the center of the military web. Their influence radiated out, enhanced by the education of secondary positions, for these men were also chosen almost automatically to be the chairmen of the boards, the presidents of the clubs, and to fill as many of the honorific positions as they would consent to.

It was difficult to discover much about these men, so surrounded were they by aides and assistants, so cloistered in a fog of deference,[11] so insulated by power and prestige

132

from the impropriety of questions. A consciousness of rank-kind pervaded their number; and when one member proved to be rather incompetent in his job, their allegiance (or so it appeared from the observer's point of view) was to kind, rather than to profession. Four of the seven men had been schooled at one or another of the military academies; all had spent their working lifetimes in the military establishment. Naturally, these men had differences in manner and personality, but as a group a certain uniformity in military and elite perspectives was manifested toward the outsider. If some of the political and social attitudes of this elite were sometimes simplistically dichotomous, it was possibly due in no small measure to the very real limits that lifetimes in the military and latter years in the closed, small world of high rank had imposed upon them.

Second-echelon elites or cadres were composed mainly of colonels, those in command of smaller units or those directly responsible to the general for seeing that his orders were carried out. These men and their wives seemed to be the most conscious of rank prerogatives and to evince the most status anxiety. Commitment to the military life, internalization of its norms, acceptance of its ideology have become critical at this point, for it is at this stage of the career that an ambitious man can founder. Selection for the next promotion—to that of brigadier general—is not based on seniority or staying power. The received definition of military merit, sufficient for acceptance into the circle of elect, is difficult to ascertain when applied to oneself; and anticipatory socialization on this level requires an even more rigid adherence to military norms. Thus it appeared to me that if there were a rank-center for traditionalism, that if there were a group who could be considered the custodians of the official culture, it would be found here.

Ministrants of the establishment. An interesting group, important for the organization and noteworthy in its effects, were the specialists in human relations (psychiatrists, chaplains, and so on) and such professionals as lawyers and administrators. Not all those involved in these activities were ministrants, but some were. Self-appointed, they identified themselves with the establishment, responding to the local definitions rather than to those of external profession or calling. These were the middle-range organization men of the military: the men in the blue and olive-drab serge suits. Usually of the captain, major, or colonel ranks, in two areas in particular were their efforts notable in Ankara: in the area of adjustment to military life and in the area of "good relations" with the Turkish community.

Those who felt they had to reconcile the putative needs of the community with the ideology, the order, and the convenience of the establishment often did so with the rhetoric of "adjustment." One specialist in human relations said that he felt forced to "identify with the military bureaucracy" in order to help people, in order to save the maladjusted for duty. Mental health for him was adjustment to the military situation, regardless of the merits or defects of that particular situation—in effect, a denial of the relevance of individual values as against the larger purposes of the organization. Another man, a lawyer, told of what he considered the patently unjust trial of several American servicemen in a Turkish court. They were now serving sentences in a Turkish prison for crimes he did not believe, on the basis

134

of the evidence, that they had committed. Was there no way to effectively object or to request retrial? Yes, after each court case there were NATO-SOFA (NATO-Status of Forces Agreements) sheets to be made out by the American lawyer; and, on these, statements could be made to this effect. Had he done so? No, for he knew of one "idealistic young military lawyer who got a black mark on his efficiency report for saying a trial was unfair, and, too, you get the reputation of being a rebel." And, anyway, he preferred to "wait for the few really important cases." One chaplain mentioned that when congregation members came to him, seeking his help to return to the United States because they could not bear the situation, he told them, "No, you're not going to get out of this that easy. You've just got to hack it."

In the area of "good relations" with the Turkish people, military men who acted as representatives of the establishment to lower-ranking personnel were obligated to reflect the importance of this secondary mission. An adequate presentation was *expected* to take into account two levels of thought: the extraneous goal of good relations, on the one hand; and, on the other, the infinitely more important organizational belief in the virtue of corporative solidarity, patriotism, and community definitions. The mark of the good organization man lay in his capacity to appear to conform to expectations on both levels. Discrepancies between these two expectations were verbally resolved in the presentations of middle-ranking men by such statements to the troops as "We all know that Turks are emotional like children, but we American military people understand this and can get along with them." The inability to effectively bridge the

135

gap of social reality and appearance is illustrated by this example: At an annual Boy Scout dinner in Ankara, which included both American and Turkish guests, the officer in charge of the proceedings gave a long speech lauding the brotherhood of man and of the Boy Scouts. Toward the end of the speech he mentioned that one of the enlisted leaders had had an automobile accident in which he had badly injured a Turkish pedestrian: "You might have had an accident, but at least you are one of us who can say, 'I got my Turk!'" A presentation in which congruence of official expectations would be achieved was one in which lip service was paid to the extraneous goals of the organization and yet there was also the covert reaffirmation of organizational and community beliefs.[12]

Systematized privilege. The privileges that are inevitably associated with rank are institutionally and systematically invoked. The privilege gap that exists between officer and enlisted man is particularly evident, reinforced by reduced interaction and highly defined nuances of deference and social distance. The distribution of system rewards is very unequal, whether in terms of power, prestige, or who-gets-what-when in the military world—and ultimately, of course, in terms of self-conceptions. In a milieu in which authoritarianism is the rule it is not surprising, furthermore, that some people seek to maximize social distance from subordinates and to minimize social distance from superordinates; the possibilities for extending authority and distinctions in small but invidious ways is built into the system. Although lower ranks are in principle protected by military regulations and norms from arbitrary demands of upper ranks, in prac-

136

tice they are more or less accessible. Sometimes this accessibility can be noted in trivial instances: a group of officers' wives in Ankara occasionally "borrowed" the summer furniture off the patio of the noncommissioned officers' family quarters, and certainly without expecting to lend their own furniture in return; in the personal favors requested of lower-ranking men, both parties aware that this is a one-way relationship; in the terms of interaddress and respect between upper and lower-ranking groups. But trivial, or not so trivial, it was resented. As one goes up the scale, inaccessibility grows, and rank provides a protective shield against encroachments on individual dignity.

Consciousness of rank penetrated every facet of personal relationships and of military life. Wives and children were fully as sensitive to rank differences and involved in them as was the military husband. They, too, were classified as subordinates or superordinates on the basis of the military member's rank: Mrs. X, the wife of Sergeant X; Mary M., the daughter of Colonel M. Utilization of the husband's or father's rank as a tool of latent power occurred among some wives and, to a lesser degree, even among children. One young child was told by an older "upper ranking" child, "You'd better keep your cat quiet, or one day soon I'll see to it that you and the cat aren't going to be here." One "ranking" dependent in an apartment house believed that the small children's play area should not be for children, but for grass; and because of her son's rank, she managed to enforce this, making the children play in the parking lot or on the street: "Things must look nice. We have to keep up appearances. Children suffer, I know, but that's the way it is with service children." A general and his family stayed

137

temporarily in one apartment house while their apartment was being painted. Only the general's wife and a lieutenant colonel's wife had to do their washing and drying in the basement, since the other permanent residents were of colonel's rank and were assigned washers and dryers in their apartments proper. The general's wife told the lieutenant colonel's wife that she thought washing times should be divided—a reasonable request. However, she went on to specify: "You may have Saturday night, since we usually go out then. I'll take the rest of the week, since I like to spread out."

Ways of looking at superordinate and subordinate ranks had become stereotyped; and it was felt by many that the social space, style of life, and possessions should be commensurate with these definitions. Conformity within this framework of superior-to, inferior-to, equal-to relationships was rewarded, creativity and critical spirit were not. Thus in an overseas military community, where there was little in the daily life and activities that did not have an aura of "government issue," many of the avenues of individual escape were effectively cut off, the sources for nonmilitary identities narrowed, and rank, in many ways, became the measure of the man.

Education

The newcomer; socialization rituals of the welcome. The military person going overseas takes with him, of course, his particular cultural and individual baggage of traits, attitudes, and perspectives. But even before he left the United States the alchemy of community socialization commenced

138

in the forms of brochures sent to him from his new unit in Ankara, letters from his overseas military sponsor, and any conversations he might have had with friends or acquaintances who were previously stationed in Turkey or who had "heard what it was like there." When he arrived he was usually met at the airport by his military sponsor, and the community socialization process, previously intermittent and of diluted strength, became direct and relatively unmediated, continuing throughout his entire tour.

Prearrival orientations of American military personnel. Seen in a historical perspective, Americans for some time manifested pejorative attitudes toward Turks and Turkey, although they had had little real contact with either.[13] Stereotypes of the Turkish character, current for some years in the past, were summed up in the pat phrases of "the Turkish barbarian" or "the Terrible Turk," stressing such characteristics as cruelty, religious fanaticism, and a ferociously warlike spirit. Not until recently, particularly during the Korean War, was this representation ameliorated by such terms as "brave and loyal." Nevertheless, it was apparent that the hoary stereotypes still took their attitudinal toll of the incoming military personnel, leading to rather fearful and unfavorable expectations. Several American military people said that when they received their orders to Turkey, they were filled with the ambivalent emotions of curiosity and forboding.

Prearrival orientations took several forms, their amounts and comprehensiveness varying with rank and unit of assignment. Each branch of service—Air Force, Navy, and Army —sent its own orientation brochures; and, on the whole,

Demographic, Ecological, and Social Structural Properties

these were quite factual guides, with sections on Turkish customs, traditions, and history, but for the most part devoted to matters of personal concern, such as port call and travel authorization, shipping of private automobiles, legal arrangements, housing and living conditions, and so on. Another means of orientation was the sponsor system, sometimes called "the Buddy Program." Someone of equivalent rank from the unit to which the newcomer was assigned was appointed to correspond by letter with him on matters pertaining to his new position, the living situation in Turkey, and the like—to give, in short, a personal touch of warmth and welcome to the incoming person. These letters were supposed to be informative, encouraging, and attitudinally noncommittal; however, some letters were occasionally none of these, such as the following: "Welcome to Ankara (ugh), Turkey (ugh)!" As can be noted in Table 8, in the survey group the highest-ranking officers more frequently received letters and pamphlets from their newly assigned station than did middle-ranking officers or enlisted personnel.

When the survey group was asked whether any Americans, in writing to them, commented favorably or unfavorably on the situation, some of the written replies were as follows:

From the enlisted rank group:

Comments were favorable, *but untrue.*

They painted a rosey picture as they were not allowed to write anything bad. Letters from my sponsor were censored.[14]

The sponsor's comments were better than what this place is.

140

When I got the assignment I had no doubt that I would like it. My sponsor's letter put the first doubt in my mind.

TABLE 8

RECEIVAL OF PREARRIVAL WRITTEN
ORIENTATION BY RANK GROUPS

RANK	Yes		No		Total	
	No.	%	No.	%	No.	%
E.M.	51	63	30	37	81	100
W.O.–03	35	85	6	15	41	100
04–above	41	93	3	7	44	100
All ranks	127	76.5	39	23.5	166	100

I was written and told of the unusual behavior of the people. It was difficult to understand these until I arrived there and saw for myself it was all quite true.

From the W.O.–03 group:

They wrote of essential needs. What to expect of work and life. Their comments were not either favorable or unfavorable. They didn't like to live in Turkey but put up with it.

They wrote complete information on housing, car, health, appliances. Comments were neither favorable nor unfavorable but objective and quite accurate. However, it is hard to relate the experience here—you must live it to believe it.

Person we replaced wrote a short letter, saying they were very glad to leave Turkey. Letter was very little help.

Comments were mixed, mostly about housing conditions. Most were in the nature of, "So you're coming to Turkey—sorry about that!"

141

His information was totally wrong, and had we known the truth the family would never have come, and we certainly would not have brought the car!!!

From the 04 and above group:

They wrote favorable comments, but when we arrived at the airport and conversation was used instead of correspondence the comments changed to very unfavorable.

They said the living was difficult in some respects, but different and could be fun. They warned that the Turks were a dour, not too friendly people.

They told us to be sure and bring our sense of humor!

Some who received orders for Turkey sought or were found by those who had previously been stationed there. One young enlisted man said: "Even in the United States the reputation of a tour in Turkey is terrible. When I got my PCS (permanent change of station orders), everybody in my office sympathized with me; and one fellow who had been here said it was really lousy." Some of the survey group (23.5 percent) received no prearrival orientation at all. One soldier told me that he had had none, so he hadn't known what to expect: "And, boy was it ever a big shock! With some kind of orientation I could have gotten used to the idea before I got here."

Those who were assigned to duty in JUSMMAT as advisors to the Turkish military were usually sent to Washington, D.C., for classes and a short Berlitz course in the Turkish language at the Military Assistance Institute.[15] There was also a brief orientation course given to their wives. One wife, in recalling the orientation, said:

That was a terrible orientation! For example, they told us

142

such silly stuff as, "Don't cross your legs in front of a Turk," and "Don't touch a Turk," meaning don't slap him on the back or such. Now this couldn't be less true. We've found they like to be slapped on the back. By the time they got through with me, I was terrified. And when I first got over here I was still so scared I would hardly walk out the front door.

Those slated to become military attachés or area specialists were given the most complete training.

It is interesting to note that among those of the survey, regardless of the quality of orientation and response, the majority expected to like Turks and to enjoy their tour in Turkey (Table 9).

TABLE 9 ─────────────────────────────

EXPECTATIONS OF LIKING TURKS AND
ENJOYING THE TOUR BY RANK GROUPS

RANK	Yes No.	Yes %	No No.	No %	No Opinion No.	No Opinion %	Total No.	Total %
E.M.	50	62	9	11	22	27	81	100
W.O.–03	32	78	2	5	7	17	41	100
04–above	39	89	0	0	5	11	44	100
All ranks	121	72.9	11	6.6	34	20.5	166	100

Postarrival orientations of American military personnel. Most American military people upon arriving at the airport were met by a sponsor, friend, or duly assigned person, who helped them through customs and drove back to Ankara with them in the unit-assigned car. It was at this point of

Demographic, Ecological, and Social Structural Properties

shaking hands with the sponsor that community socialization in the prevalent attitudinal schemata commenced with
intensity. After twenty-nine kilometers (eighteen miles) of
conversation, then possibly dinner, the newcomer was beginning to feel less alien. As can be noted below (Table 10),
enlisted men in the survey group less frequently felt that
they were warmly welcomed than did officers. It was the
sponsor's duty to continue to assist his assigned newcomer
until he was thoroughly settled, giving him advice about
housing, shopping, places to go, taking him here and there,
introducing him to fellow workers and friends. In this early
period the newcomer's involvement with his new acquaintance was often quite intense, and he was drawn into the
ready-made community and taught how to see his new
world. Of the survey group, 92.8 percent said that after
arriving in Turkey they had been told what they could
expect in the months to come. When asked if they thought
the comments were favorable or unfavorable about life in
Turkey, 65.8 percent said they thought that all or most of
the comments were unfavorable. A comparison of prearrival
and postarrival orientations was interesting in the study
made, insofar as the former, by means of correspondence,
were more favorable expressions than those expressed during face-to-face conversations (see Tables 11 and 12).

The following are some of the comments these people
wrote, describing their postarrival orientations:

From the enlisted rank group:

> Comments were unfavorable. I was told exactly what the
> conditions are and how most Turks feel toward Americans.

> Most everyone hated it and soon convinced me that I
> would also.

144

TABLE 10

OPINIONS OF THE WELCOME BY RANK GROUPS

RANK	Warmly Welcomed		Not so Warmly Welcomed		Ignored and Lonely		Undecided		Total	
	No.	%	No.	%	No.	%	No.	%	No.	%
E.M.	46	56.8	20	24.7	15	18.5	0	0	81	100
W.O.–03	26	63.5	9	22	1	2.5	5	12	41	100
04–above	36	82	4	9	3	7	1	2	44	100
All ranks	121	65.1	33	19.9	19	11.4	6	3.6	166	100

TABLE 11

OPINIONS OF THE CONTENT OF PREARRIVAL ORIENTATIONS BY RANK GROUPS

RANK	All or Mostly Favorable		All or Mostly Unfavorable		Neutral		No Comment		No Orientation		Total	
	No.	%	No.	%	No.	%	No.	%	No.	%	No.	%
E.M.	13	16	16	19.8	16	19.8	7	8.6	29	35.8	81	100
W.O.–03	12	29.3	15	36.6	8	19.5	2	4.9	4	9.7	41	100
04–above	15	34.1	9	20.4	15	34.1	2	4.5	3	6.9	44	100
All ranks	40	24.1	40	24.1	39	23.5	11	6.6	36	21.7	166	100

Demographic, Ecological, and Social Structural Properties

TABLE 12

OPINIONS OF THE CONTENT OF POSTARRIVAL ORIENTATIONS BY RANK GROUPS

RANK	All or Mostly Favorable		All or Mostly Unfavorable		Neutral		No Comment		No Orientation		Total	
	No.	%	No.	%	No.	%	No.	%	No.	%	No.	%
E.M.	8	9.9	51	63	4	4.9	10	12.3	8	9.9	81	100
W.O.–03	3	7.3	28	68.3	2	4.9	6	14.6	2	4.9	41	100
04–above	7	15.9	30	68.2	2	4.5	3	6.9	2	4.5	44	100
All ranks	18	10.8	109	65.8	8	4.8	19	11.4	12	7.2	166	100

The facts—good and bad—were told as they exist.

Unfavorable comments—which I find true.

I was told generally about the "filthy and stupid" Turks. I can't even remember hearing any favorable comments.

We were informed of the poor water pressure, lack of electricity at times, etc., and they were merely informative comments to aid us with these new inconveniences. They were neither favorable or unfavorable. We learned about Turkey and Turks the hard way.

Very unfavorable! After six months here I think this is a terrible place—the tour should be *shortened!*

They were a backward, ignorant people—many thieves— had to be watched constantly.

From the W.O.–03 group:

I had the impression that most people were not happy there.

Comments were very unfavorable and unfair. I was extremely angered by sponsor's attitude. Comments were made in the presence of a Turkish National right at the Airport. I was extremely embarrassed.

They told me about a few robberies and how one man nearly scared the new chaplain's wife to death. Also, they were ready to go home. Work was drudgery. They did a good job. A very good job.

Be careful driving—especially women. Watch children's toys—apt to be stolen. Comments not unfavorable.

We heard many complaints from Americans about Ankara itself, the Turkish people's attitude toward Americans. It was all very unfavorable but we were optimistic and thought the American people were unduly bitter. As time passes we find the early comments quite true.

147

Unfavorable, told of taxi drivers trying to clip you, bad markets, driving conditions and problems of getting along with people, and their ridiculous judicial system.

From the 04 and above group:

They told us just the way things were—the truth—favorable or unfavorable.

We were warned about sanitation, drinking water, and driving conditions. Mostly all unfavorable. They spoke favorably about the weather and other Americans.

Generally unfavorable, i.e., "terrible drivers so be careful or don't drive at all!" "rude people," "dirty country," "watch out for beggars," and "everyone has his hand out."

All info I received was on the bad side. As to people being uncooperative and not giving the Americans an even chance, I felt it was completely overdone.

Formal orientations, called "Inbound Briefings,"[16] were given every month by Detachment 30. Attendance was mandatory for Air Force personnel; wives and other branch personnel were welcomed.[17] This monthly orientation program usually included talks by people from Family Services, Red Cross, and Personal Affairs regarding help that was available in the community. There were discussions on military missions and on the American facilities available in Ankara. An Air Police representative warned of driving hazards and the precautions that should be taken. Someone from the medical unit discussed health problems. All in all, the emphasis was almost entirely on the personal problems likely to be encountered during the tour; and its psychological impact was apparently quite great. One woman said: "The Det. 30 orientation was negative and terrifying. It

148

frightened me to death about eating Turkish food and about driving over here." Another stated: "I became so fear-ridden about Turkey, I wanted to go straight home." During one orientation meeting a sergeant, representing the medical unit, discussed for some time that illness might strike at any moment and, therefore, a great deal of care must be taken with water and food. Someone insouciantly questioned him: "Isn't it better to just go ahead and relax and enjoy Turkey, rather than constantly worrying about the food and water?" Dramatically, the sergeant replied: "You go ahead and drink the water, eat unwashed vegetables and fruit, eat out at Turkish restaurants. You just go ahead, but then look in the mirror everyday and watch your eyes getting yellower and yellower and yellower."[18]

There was very little said in the official orientations about Turkey and Turkish customs that would encourage people to venture out from the American community. The dearth of information about Turkish culture was noted by several sergeants one day, when they mentioned that they had known quite a few Americans who had been invited to go to Turkish homes but hadn't gone because "they didn't know how to behave and they were afraid of doing something wrong or making trouble or, worse, causing an incident."

The threatening quality of the official orientations was frequently justified by officers on the basis of "forewarned, forearmed." One officer flatly said:

> Yes, the orientations are fearful, and they are designed to be that way. Newcomers must be aware of the dangers involved in being over here. This fear is healthy! Without fear people would go out and drive on the streets thinking

149

it was just like the States. And when they get into an accident, they've had it!

Adult education. In all of the military units in Ankara the importance of more education was stressed on the practical grounds that it was needed for further promotions. Accordingly, the Education Center offered university night classes, correspondence work, and high school diploma work. The grades that the Air Force expected the students to achieve in the courses offered were summarized in an announcement placed prominently on the Center bulletin board:

> In setting goals on which we can base our standards of performance within TUSLOG Detachment 30 the following definitions of terms are established:
>
> UNSATISFACTORY   equals an obviously intolerable condition.
>
> SATISFACTORY   equals a condition that can be tolerated only for that minimum essential period of time it takes to raise that rating to excellent.
>
> EXCELLENT   equals the minimum acceptable standard for normal accomplishment of tasks.
>
> OUTSTANDING   EQUALS THE DESIRED GOAL WHICH ALL PERSONNEL AND UNITS ARE EXPECTED TO ACHIEVE AND MAINTAIN.

The university classes were fairly well attended, having their highest enrollment of the study period in September, 1966, of 193 students.

Classes in the Turkish language were offered at the Center.[19] In 1967 the beginning course ran for a period of four weeks with a total of thirty hours of instruction. In

150

the years preceding, the course had included forty-five hours of instruction, but the number of hours had been decreased because, as the advisor said:

> There is a fantastic dropout rate in the Turkish classes, approximately fifty percent. We usually start with around fifteen people, and if we're lucky we'll end up with eight. Oddly enough, there is very little interest in Turkish classes or in Middle Eastern history, and we have a hard time having them go. Students use the excuse that they'll never use Turkish again after they leave here.

Seldom was a second course in Turkish offered, since the requisite number of ten students, sufficient to justify giving a course, rarely signed up. In the study group 54.9 percent were not interested in learning more Turkish, while 38.5 percent were interested in doing so (Table 13).

TABLE 13

INTEREST EVINCED IN LEARNING MORE TURKISH BY RANK GROUPS

RANK	No		Yes		No Comment		Total	
	No.	*%*	*No.*	*%*	*No.*	*%*	*No.*	*%*
E.M.	42	52	31	38	8	10	81	100
W.O.–03	28	68	13	32	0	0	41	100
04–above	21	48	20	45	3	7	44	100
All ranks	91	54.9	64	38.5	11	6.6	166	100

Participation in the education program in Ankara was considered by the authorities to be low in comparison with participation at European centers. In discussing this the education advisor sadly commented: "I don't understand it,

Demographic, Ecological, and Social Structural Properties

TABLE 14

SELF-JUDGED TURKISH LANGUAGE CAPABILITY BY RANK GROUPS

RANK	Not a Word		A Few Words		"Kitchen" Turkish		Good Turkish		Fluent Turkish		Total	
	No.	%	No.	%	No.	%	No.	%	No.	%	No.	%
E.M.	7	9	30	37	39	48	4	5	1	1	81	100
W.O.–03	0	0	10	24	29	71	2	5	0	0	41	100
04–above	1	2	15	34	22	50	4	9	2	5	44	100
All ranks	8	4.8	55	33.1	90	54.2	10	6	3	1.8	166	100

but in Germany the participation is much higher, even though there are many things to do and to see there. Guess if people are happy they do more."

The education of children. The Air Force provided schools and teachers for children from the first through the twelfth grades. The schools were administered by the principals, the District Superintendent, and the Base Commander, who was advised by a nine-member Board of Education. Since the Base Commander was responsible for logistical support to the schools, this meant that any military people detached for duty to the schools or any employees, other than teachers, took their orders from commanding officers and not from school administrators. A Dependent Schools Officer, appointed by the Base Commander to work as the liaison officer between the school principals and the military agencies, was in charge of the maintenance of the physical facilities and of the operation of the school bus system. The kindergarten, nursery school,[20] and School for Exceptional Children were cooperatively managed by the parents. There were other school possibilities in Ankara, but few military parents appeared to be interested: one American military child attended the British Embassy School; two military children attended the French Embassy School; and none attended either the German Embassy School or any of the Turkish schools.

The enrollment at the elementary school at Balgat on November 23, 1966, was 1,098 children, 890 of whom were military dependents. Every year, according to the principal, the enrollment had increased, with "an annual growth factor between 5 and 15 percent." Planning was difficult,

Demographic, Ecological, and Social Structural Properties

since any time a change in military mission might mean a drastic increase or decrease. The junior and senior high schools had 852 students, 601 of these being military dependents. Since the senior high school was the only American one in Turkey and was the most centrally located for quite a few other countries having none, children of thirteen to nineteen years old were sent here and two dormitories had had to be built to accommodate them. These housed 170 of the high school students, 105 of them being military dependents.

The military-directed schools accepted children from the various embassies, also; but they were prohibited by Turkish law from accepting Turkish children. Even permitting foreign embassy children to attend, however, was becoming a problem as the American enrollment continued to increase. One school administrator described the situation as follows:

> It's difficult to justify taking non-American children when our schools are so crowded, and a continuance of this policy might mean that the school sessions will have to be run on half-time. But if the base C.O. says, "Do it!" we must do it.

With the exception of the 170 dormitory students, the school population was transported from Ankara to Balgat by a fleet of school buses each day. The system of bus monitors was administered by the military liaison officer. Every parent had to take his or her turn monitoring the school buses. The participation in the parent monitor system was excellent, possibly because a one-day absence was reported to the assigned parent's military commander, and two

154

absences were punished by expelling the monitor's child from school.

The enrollment at the kindergarten was forty children in 1967; at the Nursery School it was eighteen. The School for Exceptional Children had only five children; however, it was believed by teachers and parents that there were several more than this number in the community. Air Force policy at that time was that a military man could not take a mentally retarded child overseas with him. So the Air Force serviceman was faced with leaving his family in the United States, or requesting that he not be sent overseas—thereby decreasing his chances for promotion, or taking his family and hiding the child.

There was no segregation in these schools—either of officers and enlisted personnel or of whites and Negroes. And only one problem regarding racial integration came up during the two years of study. When room assignments were made at the boys' dormitory in 1966, one white boy objected strongly to having a Negro roommate, but to no avail. Within an hour his father, a colonel and a commanding officer, called the director and demanded that his son's roommate be changed immediately. The director, knowing the military regulations regarding integration, told the colonel that he would need the objections in writing before they could be considered: "Naturally, I didn't get them, since the colonel knew if he put anything like that in writing he could be hung." Other dormitory students, he continued, heard about the incident and informally ostracized the prejudiced boy: "The social pressure was quite effective, and we have no problem now."

Demographic, Ecological, and Social Structural Properties

Several administrators said that they believed the students in the American schools were a scholastically superior group, that there were few poor students, few average students, and many very good students. The reason given for this phenomenon was: "The children come from superior parents, either heavy on brass or high government officials. Only about 5 percent of the children come from homes where the father's rank is below that of staff sergeant." Only one school official disagreed with this assumption, saying: "This is pure snobbism. As far as I know, none of them has ever been accepted by any of the Ivy League Colleges. And even more to the point, their averages on the National Merit Examinations have never been compared with those of any other group."

The custodial function of the schools was in some ways perhaps more extended than in many schools in the United States. Dress and general appearance were more standardized; and, of course, there was more control in the community, and this penetrated into the schools, as well. The school administrators interviewed felt that the relationship between the military establishment, military parents and the schools was better than the relationship between parents and schools in the United States, or as one put it: "The parents know how important education is. Education is needed for their promotions, so they stress it for their children, too." Military authority was sometimes utilized by school administrators. One principal described it rather well:

> There is more control in these schools. The military expects obedience. If you are told to do something, you do it. If a child becomes obnoxious, I just call up the father's commanding officer, and he brings pressure to bear on the

GARRISON COMMUNITY

father. The father, pressed by his C.O., really talks to the child. After all, the father is responsible for all his dependents and their actions. The Base Commander is God. If Dad wants his promotion, he must control his kids.

According to stories circulating among some of the students and parents, children in the dormitories were highly controlled. One military wife said: "The school dorms are a disgrace, more like prisons than dormitories. There have been four suicide attempts there, just since September [1966]." Dormitory officials believed that because of the local situation children had to be highly controlled. Girls were never allowed to be alone in taxis: "Ninety-nine out of one hundred would probably be O.K., but it's that one case we fear." They were not permitted to go to the old section of town alone: "There are too many crevices and alleys that the girls could be pulled into. The Turks have often pinched girls, even when they're escorted by a chaperone."

Besides the usual curriculum in the schools, there was also a host nation program, designed to acquaint the students with the customs and history of Turkey. The program was started in 1963. In 1967 it offered to students from the third grade through high school two sessions a week with a Turkish teacher. The Turkish language, however, was not taught in any of the American schools. The reasons given by administrators for its not being offered were the following: that it took too much time; that the children weren't interested; that if they really wanted to learn Turkish, they would "pick it up" from Turkish friends; that they wouldn't remember it after they'd left Turkey, or as one principal said, "Where would they ever use it again? It's not like French or German." An English language teacher in the high school,

Demographic, Ecological, and Social Structural Properties

feeling that it was "a pity," nonetheless, that his students were learning little or no Turkish while living in the middle of Turkey, commenced giving them ten or fifteen Turkish words each week to memorize. Within two weeks, at a PTA meeting, military parents came to him expressing a great deal of consternation over this "waste of time." Even those who were not adamant about his "sticking to his subject matter" told him they saw little reason for their children to learn Turkish, since "we're going home soon, anyway."

Although the Turkish teachers for the host nation program thought that most of the children were very interested and curious about Turkey, all of the American teachers, counselors, and administrators interviewed believed that they were not interested and that some felt actively hostile toward Turks. In this, as the oft-reiterated phrase went, the children "reflected their parents' feelings and lack of interest." One counselor, in discussing the difficulties she believed American military children faced in Ankara, said:

> It takes children far longer to adjust here, probably because the problems are greater. Children hate Turkey, and they say they can hardly wait to go home. They don't want to come to school, and when they do they seem so unsure of themselves—timid, in fact. Many of the children cry a great deal and very easily. They pick up that fear from their parents, and the parents get it from those damned orientations. The parents become so fearful that they don't let their children ride alone in taxis or eat any Turkish food. Pretty soon the children are afraid of everything.

In talking with school personnel it was apparent that the school children "reflected" not only the attitudes of their parents, but of their teachers, as well. The teacher rotation rate was rather high: at the end of the 1965–66

158

school year, the elementary school lost 88.1 percent of its teaching staff; and the high schools lost 70 percent of theirs.[21] Among the various irritations expressed by the teachers, one of the most prevalent was that they had to spend so much of their time maintaining or repairing the physical plant because the logistical support was so poor.[22] Others asserted that Turkey was a "miserable, frustrating place." One woman, who had talked at great length about the children's unhappiness and hostility toward the Turks, attributing the cause to parental attitudes, said: "I can sure understand why teachers leave this god-awful hole after one year!"

In summary, most of the administrators either approved or were reconciled to the military influence on the schools. In some cases, it proved a convenience to them, resulting in comparatively submissive students and parents. Where the authority of the military institution ended and that of the school began, or vice versa, did not seem distinguishable to the students interviewed, for misbehavior in one area brought repercussions from both. "Keeping the children American" presented no problems in these schools or in the community, since their exposure to the country in which they lived was so minimal as to have little positive effect. Apparently this was seldom recognized as a loss by the children, parents, or school personnel. The only loss that was felt by the children—and this profoundly—was that of being away from the United States.

Economic Life of the Community

The American military community in Ankara was unusual economically insofar as there was neither unemploy-

Demographic, Ecological, and Social Structural Properties

ment nor the uncertainties of seasonal work for the heads of families. At least one member of every family was employed by the military establishment. The salaries and allowances, supplemented by a station per diem allowance[23] as compensation for higher overseas rentals, were adequate for most in providing a more or less lower middle-class standard of life, although enlisted people with large families sometimes found it difficult to get along. A few people, mainly enlisted men, who wished to further supplement their income, engaged in part-time, after-duty jobs as clerks at the base exchange, night managers of one or other of the clubs, or as salesmen of cars, insurance, or mutual funds. These extra jobs were few and highly prized. For wives who were qualified, there were occasionally teaching or substitute teaching positions open at the American schools. Secretarial positions were fairly plentiful, and there were also a few jobs available as nursery attendants and as base exchange clerks. Most of the higher-paying American civilian positions in Ankara had been filled by people hired in the United States, rather than locally.

No one interviewed or questioned seemed to know of any American working on the Turkish economy. This was understandable as Turkish work permits were almost impossible for Americans to procure; and the wages offered were so low in comparison with what they were accustomed to that almost no one seemed to be interested.

Teen-agers found it difficult to earn money in the American community. The sort of work they might have ordinarily done, such as washing cars, cutting grass, or waiting on tables, was done much less expensively by adult Turkish help. However, in the summer a military program

GARRISON COMMUNITY

had been set up, providing jobs for teen-agers between the ages of sixteen and eighteen.

Besides the legitimate ways of making a living in the American military community, nonlegitimate means also existed. They were legally hazardous, but sufficiently lucrative to tempt a few. These included illegal currency conversion, the black-marketing of American exchange products, and the smuggling in of goods from the United States through the American Post Office for resale on the Turkish market at inflated prices. Flurries of these nonlegitimate activities intermittently became sufficiently serious as to warrant full-scale investigations by the Office of Special Investigation (OSI).[24]

The NATO Status of Forces Agreements between the United States and Turkey permitted Americans to be employed by American facilities without needing to have Turkish work permits. However, according to the American labor attaché, this had become a point of contention for many Turks, who believed not only did the Americans not really need the money, but this was Turkey—their country—and Turks were entitled to these jobs, particularly in the face of a high rate of unemployment. Because of this fairly prevalent attitude on the part of the Turks and because of the resentment caused by a wage differential between the salaries of Turks and Americans working at American facilities,[25] a number of problems had arisen. For example, in the base exchange system in 1967 only 7½ percent of their 200-man labor force were Americans; yet difficulties between the two groups were manifest. The Turks greatly resented being paid less than their American counterparts; and because American workers were cautioned never to dis-

Demographic, Ecological, and Social Structural Properties

cuss their salaries with Turkish workers, "The Turks," according to one American dependent worker, "are always asking me what I make." As an informal segregative pattern of work relations grew up between the two groups— the Turks eating together, talking together, and helping one another, and the American group doing likewise—numerous other difficulties in work relations and hiring policies arose. The Turkish employees came to feel that they were being discriminated against in hiring and promotion policies; and with these reports going into the Turkish labor unions, restiveness and dissatisfaction began to be hardened into resistance. Disagreements between American administrators and hiring firms and Turkish labor unions increased, and strikes, which would have been extremely disruptive to the American military community, were threatened by the unions.[26]

Religion

There are no Christian churches in Ankara, nor can they be built legally. Although the Turkish Constitution guarantees freedom of religion, Turkish law forbids proselytizing or attempted conversion of any Turkish citizen. Thus, as interpreted, the building of a church, the dissemination of religious literature, the engaging in any type of religious activity other than that sanctioned by government agencies, are offenses, punishable by imprisonment. This meant that the religious activities of the American military community had to be held in military buildings or on Embassy property: Catholic masses were conducted in the JUSMMAT auditorium; Protestant services were held either at the Balgat School or at the Base Theater; Jewish services were held in a meeting room at the billets.

Six military chaplains had been assigned to Ankara: three Protestant ministers, two Catholic priests, and one Jewish rabbi. It was assumed by the chaplains that two-thirds of the churchgoers were Protestants and most of the remaining one-third were Catholics. According to the Jewish chaplain, his congregation consisted of thirty-two members. The study group reflected somewhat different proportions (Tables 15 and 16). Other than the military religious services, Catholic services at the Italian Embassy, Episcopalian services at the British Embassy, and Jewish services at the Turkish Synagogue in Ankara were open to Americans. For those who preferred a more fundamental form of Protestantism, an American preacher of the Mission of the Southern Baptist Convention was permitted to use a room in the American Embassy to give services every Sunday night; and between sixty and sixty-five people regularly attended. A number of chapel lay organizations had been established, and one of the best-attended religious events was a five-day tour of the Holy Land, taken every month by fifty-eight people and escorted by one or more chaplains.

Participation in the chapel and in the Catholic organizations was believed by the Catholic chaplain to be far more active in Ankara than was usual in the United States, even though "the unity of a military post is missing." He did not believe that religious feelings were suddenly intensified in the overseas setting, but rather that religious meetings were "the only way people can get together." The need for increased religious participation did not seem to be operative among the Protestant congregation.

163

TABLE 15

RELIGIOUS AFFILIATION BY RANK GROUPS

RANK	Protestant		Catholic		Jewish		Other[a]		None		Total	
	No.	%	No.	%	No.	%	No.	%	No.	%	No.	%
E.M.	54	67	21	26	0	0	0	0	6	7	81	100
W.O.–03	29	71	6	15	1	2	3	7	2	5	41	100
04–above	36	82	8	18	0	0	0	0	0	0	44	100
All ranks	119	71.7	35	21.1	1	.06	3	1.8	8	4.8	166	100

[a] "Other" was interpreted by those respondents checking this blank to mean Eastern Orthodox Church.

TABLE 16

FREQUENCY OF CHURCH ATTENDANCE BY RANK GROUPS

RANK	Never		Rarely[a]		Occasionally[a]		Frequently[a]		Every Sunday		No Answer		Total	
	No.	%	No.	%	No.	%	No.	%	No.	%	No.	%	No.	%
E.M.	29	36	16	20	6	7.5	9	11	19	23	2	2.5	81	100
W.O.–03	7	17	9	22	5	12	4	10	16	39	0	.0	41	100
04–above	9	20.5	8	18	4	9	9	20.5	13	29.5	1	2.5	44	100
All ranks	45	27.1	33	19.9	15	9.0	22	13.3	48	28.9	3	1.8	166	100

[a] These terms were quantitatively specified in the questionnaire to mean the following:
Rarely = 1–4 times per year.
Occasionally = 5–11 times per year.
Frequently = once a month or oftener.

Demographic, Ecological, and Social Structural Properties

The Turkish prohibition against proselyizing also forbid church-sponsored charity and good works by Christian congregations for non-Christians. The restriction of organizational charity to the military community itself seemed to have an important effect on the attitudes of the Protestant and Catholic chaplains toward the Turkish people. A Catholic chaplain described the situation as follows:

> Charitable gift-giving and organizations for charitable purposes are very much a part of American chapels. This lack of charitable relationship greatly affects American relationships with the Turkish people. There seems to be few other ways Americans and Turks can get together.[27]

A Protestant chaplain spoke with bitterness about the prohibition, summing it up in this fashion:

> Charity is against the Turkish law. We cannot sponsor or help an orphanage or a hospital. Why, I can't even give them an old shirt. The Turks don't admit that such problems, like orphanages with inadequate funds, exist; they don't admit a need. A person cannot even ask a Turk to come to a church meeting or a youth group with him, as this is considered an attempt at conversion. Their idea of religious freedom means freedom from harassment by other religions. They hardly admit that Christianity is a religion.

It was apparent from these and other remarks by chaplains that the military chapel, at least in *this* overseas context, was to a degree dependent for its vitality upon the organized giver-receiver relationship with the external milieu. The problems and complaints voiced by the Christian chaplains appeared to have little relevance to the Jewish chapel situation in Ankara. The Jewish rabbi had been in Ankara for two years and, unlike the other chaplains inter-

166

viewed, was not a military career man. He said that the small Jewish congregation had strong personal contacts with the Turkish Jews in Ankara. Primarily the bonds were those of religion and the experience of discrimination; whereas the cultural ties, to be sure, were quite attenuated. American Jews, as individuals, did not really move within the Turkish-Jewish community, yet there was a felt sense of sharing between the two groups. Americans occasionally went to the Turkish synagogue in order to be in a synagogue again, rather than attending services in an ordinary room. Organized charitable giving was not a tenet of the Jewish chapel in Ankara, so its blockage gave rise to no organizational crises. Rather, giving was based on the immediate needs expressed by Turkish Jews—intermittent, casual, and un-organized—that were responded to by individual American Jews: the rabbi kept a cash box with a few lira in his office in case someone would drop by with an urgent request for help; he had given some kosher wine for Passover service to a Turkish rabbi (kosher wine was unobtainable on the Turkish market); a member of the congregation had recently helped a Turkish woman with her children's educa-tion. It was the kind of giving that was unpremeditated, unplanned, unorganized—and unnecessary to the vitality of the organization.

In discussing the adjustment of the American Jews as a group to living in Ankara, he said:

> The Jewish community has always been isolated to a greater or lesser degree. Historically, we have always been the few among the many. So adjustment to isolation and the emotional difficulties of being undesired in a strange environment is not a new one for us. The strength and

167

warmth of the Jewish family have helped. We have our own religious newspaper here; and my wife and I always hold open house, so people have somewhere to go when they want to talk. Yes, we have always been a small minority group, so the effect here on us is not as devastating as it is for a Protestant or a Catholic.

In comparing the three religious groups and the comments of their chaplains, questions can be tentatively posed regarding their adaptation to alien surroundings. It is possible that when accepted and powerful groups, such as those of the Protestants and Catholics, are removed from their home environments to alien situations where the expected status is not accorded and where the group definitions of itself and its actions are, in fact, rejected or put into question, response to the incongruence of external and internal definitions might be that of bitterness, hostility, and withdrawal. On the other hand, when a religious group such as that of the Jews has been molded by the historical experiences and memories of isolation, comparatively low status, and rejection, expectations of acceptance in a new environment are considerably modified. So in Turkey the Jewish expectation and Turkish response were somewhat more commensurate, precipitating neither crisis nor withdrawal on the part of the Jewish congregation.

To sum up, the religious organizations in the military community did not, on the whole, seem to play a significant role in the life of the community. Rather, the chapels were frequently seen by community members as adjuncts of the military life. Conducive to this attitude was that the military conditions of life seemed to have as much effect on chaplains as they did on anyone else: they wore uniforms; they had rank; their weekday working hours were quite similar; and their surroundings were quite as profane as anyone else's—being the same workaday military buildings. Charitable giving, under the aegis of the organization, seemed to be necessary for the viability of the religious institution in Ankara, helping to distinguish its functions from those of other commodity-dispensing military units. It would seem that the *need* for charity did, indeed, begin at home.

Leisure-Time Activities

The range of activities possible for the American military person was wide and various in Ankara: from informal socializing with friends and neighbors at the snack bar or at home to formal parties given at one of the clubs, from organization meetings to swimming and impromptu touch football games. Much of the entertainment possible in a town in the United States was available in Ankara, with the diversity of recreation that a foreign city and land offered, as well. Several Turkish and Turkish-American clubs were open for American military membership: such sport clubs as the Kavaklidere Tennis Club,[28] professional organizations like the Turkish-American Lawyers Association, charitable groups like the Cocuk Sevenlar Dernegi, special interest groups like the Turkish-American Coin Club. Perhaps the best-known cross-cultural organization was the Turkish-American Association and its subsidiary, the Turkish-American Women's Cultural Society. Both offered classes, tours, charities, and social events. The latter group was extremely popular with Turkish women and with American government officials' wives. In 1967 the Society had a total

169

membership of 605 people. Of that membership, 70.9 percent were Turkish women and 29.1 percent were American women. American military wives, almost all of whom were officers' wives,[29] made up approximately 8.9 percent of the total membership and 30.1 percent of the American membership. However, those American military people who joined Turkish clubs, who frequently went to Turkish restaurants, sporting events, and the theater, and to other Turkish entertainments were in the minority. To the majority, frightened by the orientations and community rumors, they offered little appeal. For that matter, most Turkish recreational possibilities were not seen by them as *real* possibilities.

Patterns of association in the community tended to be largely military and to remain within rank groups: for example, captains and their wives and higher ranks tended to spend time with other captains and their wives and higher ranks. Rank group, military unit, and proximity seemed to greatly determine the web of friendships. One officer, in talking about the social life of his unit, said: "When we give private parties, asking outsiders is frowned on." In a very consequential way the two most important clubs in the community, the Officers' Club and the NCO Club, reinforced the basic pattern of rank exclusion, since, of course, membership in either club was accessible only to the appropriate ranks. This pattern continued in wives' clubs and informally in certain types of activities and organizations, as well. Some clubs such as the Ankara Riding Club or the Duplicate Bridge League had never had enlisted personnel as members, although ostensibly it was possible for them to join. Even some of the volunteer organizations tended to become monopolized by either officers and their wives or

170

by enlisted personnel and their wives. Some recreation centers such as the bowling alley were more frequently patronized by one group than another. For many units the most social mingling between officers and their families and enlisted men and their families occurred during the Christmas holiday season when there were such occasions as the "Kiddies' Party" for all children of the unit. Another means of inter-rank group participation existed in unit sports: both officers and enlisted men would play together on unit football or basketball teams. Patterns of rank-group segregation were not formally operative for children and teen-agers in the schools, clubs, or recreation areas. However, residential area, preference, and parental patterns of rank exclusion and guidance tended to influence the young.

Membership in most of the community clubs in itself conferred no status; for that matter, it was obligatory for officers and enlisted men to become members of their respective clubs. However, attendance and participation in some clubs, such as the unit officers' wives clubs or in clubs in which the commanding officer's wife was particularly interested, were considered by many wives (and some husbands) as essential steps toward the husband's next promotion.[30] The internal organization of most of the clubs and organizations was instructive insofar as almost invariably the highest-ranking members were either the top club officers or, barring that, they provided the irresistible *deus ex machina* in the wings. Even in the community-wide associations, such as the PTA and the Boy Scouts,[31] this was the case.

Social participation, both within the community and external to the community, was found in the study group to be greater among officers than it was among enlisted men: the higher the rank, the greater the amount of participation. However, this will be discussed more fully in the next chapter.

Family Life in the Military Community

Military wives and children are classified as dependents. The ramifications of this classification are more profound in the overseas setting than they are on military posts in the United States:

> DEPENDENT ACTIONS: American personnel of all ranks, grades, components and agencies are reminded that they are responsible for the activities of their accompanying dependents, minor and adult, and will be held accountable for their activities.[32]

Nonetheless, the role of the military wife was much the same in Ankara as it was elsewhere, although the situational context made its enactment somewhat more difficult. Some of these activities which had been handled routinely before presented themselves as obstacles in Ankara. Few American military wives, for example, could speak Turkish well enough to adequately communicate with most Turks; and so talking to people with whom they had to deal every day—servants, shopkeepers, landlords, taxi drivers, neighbors—became an exhausting experience, fraught with misunderstandings and frustration.

Since Turkish help was inexpensive, most American military people had a servant, and the amount of household work and child care was greatly reduced for the wife. But there was little to substitute as a time filler for many women,

172

whose personal resources for making satisfying use of the ample leisure time were meager. There were no television stations; telephones were rarities; few women had relatives or long-time friends in Ankara, and they had to depend on casual acquaintances for friendship and support; and the volunteer and club work[33] that some women did were not usually seen to be of sufficient importance or interest to elicit great involvement. Boredom, loneliness, lethargy, the sense of being isolated were frequent responses; and over the morning cups of coffee with friends and neighbors, complaining about the facilities, the Turks, the servants, the life often became an inevitable feature of the conversational motif. Some women went daily to the commissary and the base exchange, just to look around and see if any new merchandise had arrived. The arrival of shipments of celery or avocados (or whatever) merited announcement in the daily bulletins, and carloads of women would drive out to Balgat, as much for the excitement and the sociability, of course, as for the articles.

American wives who said they were "happy" in Ankara were rare, but there were a few. Some of those spoke rather good Turkish, some spoke little Turkish; some had had overseas experience before, some had not; some traveled a great deal, some did not. The only characteristics they shared, apparently, were an interest in the life around them and a certain flexibility of response.

Many of the children and teen-agers in the American military community manifested a lack of interest in the country in which they were living. They appeared to be involved in and circumscribed by the American military community. The closing in of their world commenced im-

Demographic, Ecological, and Social Structural Properties

mediately. One military family, having just moved into an apartment, sent their two children out to play. A few minutes later the children rushed back into the apartment, saying they had been introduced to "The Turks." They excitedly told their parents that the American children in the neighborhood fought a coalition of "the German kids and the Turks. And when the Turk kids come near our building, the American kids say, 'Get out of here!' " Sometimes the only Turks that these children knew were those who worked for the Americans—the janitors, the secretaries, the maids.

Facilities for children near the home were more often than not lacking, particularly safe and satisfactory play space. The lives of both children and teen-agers seemed to be rather rigidly supervised, with parents, neighbors, military and school authorities imposing rules of conduct. There were almost no places to get away from authority—no weedy corners in the backyard or drugstore hangouts. The military exerted an effort to keep teen-agers, in particular, busy by organizing free-time activities, the object being to keep them out of trouble. And, according to the Air Police, juvenile delinquency rates were very low. As one officer explained: "Our kids are somewhat sheltered. We keep them busy, organized, and supervised to prevent their getting into trouble. Because when a teen-ager is in trouble overseas his parents are in trouble, too."

The language barrier tended to keep American youngsters together,[34] and sometimes they felt "hemmed in" with "nothing to do here." More than anything, probably, they missed the corner drugstore and other teen-age hangouts, although they did have the snack bar. Supervision was so close that the teen-ager found few secluded spots for dating.

174

There were several discothèques downtown, but many of the teen-agers were not permitted to go to these. Since there was no television, it was likely they talked more, read more, engaged in more sports and games, and spent more time with their families. One youth director described some of his impressions of teen-agers in Ankara:

> Youngsters hate being away from the U.S. They think the teen-agers there have a wonderful, wonderful time. One of the biggest drawbacks here is that there is no competition with other schools. There is only intramural football, plus one basketball trip a year to Greece. Some of the boys are really sad that they are missing these years of high school football; and a few of them think they've missed fame and glory, saying, "I could have played two years of high school ball. I might even have been All-State." There are some, I know of six or more youngsters right off, who say that they hate Turkey and they hate Turks. They feel that if they were in the U.S. they would be glowing successes, and the fact that they aren't they blame on Turkey. One boy told me he had his own car in the U.S. and had dated the two best looking girls in school. Come to find out, he hadn't had a car at all, and I don't know about the girls. It's the parents that are the big problem. If they're unhappy and the home is falling apart, what can you expect from the children?

Men were affected, of course, by many of the same problems as their wives and children. A few husbands told me that they felt they should not have brought their families to Turkey, and that they would send them home if they could afford to. One man asserted: "It's impossible to live here. It is very dangerous. I feel that my family's physical safety and health are threatened."

For the single man living in the barracks, the con-

175

sequences of group living were, in many respects, much more profound. Discipline and lack of privacy are always intrinsic to the barracks situation; but during off-duty time, it is possible at most posts to get away for a few hours—to see a girl, to drink, to talk. Excitement, sex, relaxation—these are what the town just off post has often symbolized to soldiers. This was not the case in Turkey. There were few inexpensive places to go and drink, and some of these were considered dangerous.[35] There were few Turkish girls who were willing to go out with American soldiers, and most American girls were not permitted to date them. In talking with a group of young enlisted men at the billets, they told me that they knew of only one airman who dated a Turkish girl, and she had to be brought home by eight o'clock at night. Another group of enlisted men said they knew of a fellow over at JUSMMAT who was "doing very well with a Turkish girl. She only goes with Americans, but I guess she's always asking for things, money and stuff." On the whole, because of the strictness of customs regarding women and the differences in religion, dating Turkish girls (if one could find one to date) was so difficult, it was "not worth the trouble."

With all the cross-cultural differences involved, it was not surprising that marriages of Americans and Turks were fairly infrequent. According to the Consular Section of the American Embassy, they had processed only fifteen American-Turkish marriages from April 1966 to May 1967. The head of the section said: "Most of those marriages were military. When you consider the number of unmarried American soldiers over here, fifteen marriages in thirteen months is extremely low. It is much, much higher at other posts."

176

There were some single military women in the community, but proportionately their numbers were few. Almost entirely, they were officers of lower or middle ranks and were working as nurses or in administrative jobs. Their social life was ordinarily an extension of work relationships, most of their friends coming from the work group; and their usual mode of living was sharing an apartment and household expenses with one or two of their female fellow workers. Many of these women had come to Turkey with the hope of doing some traveling during weekends and leave time; however, they were warned by commanding officers that it was dangerous for women to travel alone or in pairs, and it was strongly suggested that driving out of the city be done only in groups.[36] Considering that their friends usually worked at the same place they did, for several to get leaves at the same time was a near impossibility. Most of the women interviewed said that although their jobs were quite satisfying, they felt confined in Ankara and would be glad to leave when their tours were over.

Style of life. The living places available for rent were predominantly apartments. Individual houses could be rented, but they were older, more expensive, and the tenant had to procure his own heating fuel and wrestle with the multitudinous problems of maintenance. For the unwary American, who took many living conveniences for granted, innumerable pitfalls existed in choosing a place, and reminder lists were often handed out to him from Detachment 30 when he went apartment-hunting: Were the drains covered so that the rats did not come up through the open sewer line? Were there closets and cupboards? Were the windows

177

screened? Was there a hot-water heater? Was there a water storage tank on the roof and a water pump in the basement so that when the city mains were shut off, water was still available? Were the gaps between window and door frames so large that the soot and coal dust omnipresent from November to May and the ordinary wind-blown dust from May to November would seep in? It was usually suggested that rental leases be checked by the American legal section before signatures were affixed, for if not correctly worded and attested to, innumerable controversies over costs, maintenance, heating, and so on might develop between the landlord and tenant. Some arrangements that have been simplified to the point of effortlessness in the United States were lengthy and complicated in Turkey. For example, if one rented a house in Ankara it was necessary to estimate a sufficient amount of coal for the entire winter season early in the fall, since the coal supply commenced to run low around December. As it was, one did not simply order and pay for it —negotiations at that point had hardly commenced. There was the haggling over the cost of the coal *(caveat emptor!)*, there were separate arrangements to be made for its delivery to the house, then new arrangements, possibly with different laborers, had to be made to have it hauled from the truck or wagon to the coal shed, then even more arrangements had to be made to have it broken into smaller pieces, suitable for a furnace or a stove. All of this obviously took time, and involved much discussion and bargaining. The entire series of arrangements could have been looked at as a grand occasion for the competitive game of bargaining, or, as was more often the case, as a long nightmare of small frustrations. Electricity was more expensive in Turkey than

178

in the United States, and less dependable. In the two years of study, dinners cooked on camp stoves and eaten by candlelight, from necessity rather than for atmosphere, were far from rare. Moreover, circuits were usually inadequate to take the electrical load of more than one large-current American appliance at a time. And every month or so there were the difficulties involved in paying the utility bills; neither paying nor not paying was simple for an American.

Although few people had telephones, the ring of the doorbell was a constant noise factor in everyday living; and the interruptions by vendors of vegetables, fruit, pottery, water, wood, buyers of old clothes and household articles, beggars and solicitors continued intermittently from dawn until dusk. Difficulties with servants often seemed to be innate with such relationships, particularly for newcomers, primarily due, of course, to cultural and class misunderstandings. Many of the servants were recently from highly traditional villages, and the attitudes derivative of this way of life—expectations of a paternal relationship with employers, order and way of work, standards of sanitation and cleanliness, time perspective (why hurry?), ideas of seemliness and propriety of dress and behavior—were contradistinctive to those of the American employer. Stealing was sometimes a major problem with servants, and Americans often felt a sense of helplessness in knowing how to deal with it. Living on the physically intimate, yet emotionally distant, terms with a maid or houseboy every day, with whom one had little adequate communication, was for many an enervating experience.

In certain respects, the military style of life was only an intensified version of what it had been in the United

179

States. There was still the abiding absorption in manners, and the higher the rank the more intricate the minuet. Calling cards, receiving lines, formal invitations, precise terms of address to superiors, "command performances," discussions on the proper silver or china to use—these features persistently lingered on in the military social limbo. Entertaining often exuded a quaint and creaky formality, likely to be generally found only in this last stronghold of yesterday's America. Relevant to this style, for example, was the curious importance that the term "lady" sometimes took on in certain rank groups. This appellation, bestowed only upon officers' wives by military tradition, was used by them sometimes as a term connoting highest praise, or in its absence implying derogation. Ladylike properties seemed impossible of definition and elusive of description even to those for whom it held significance—but unquestionably they belonged to oneself and to wives of higher-ranking officers.

The interiors of most of the homes bore a similarity of appearance to one another. Military families were permitted to bring their household goods with them, so the furniture was definitely American. In all of the homes visited (probably around 150) I saw but one piano; record players were infrequent, books could usually be counted on the fingers, and even magazines were few. Brass and copper items bought in Turkey were standard items; and articles from the Orient, Latin America, and Europe bespoke of other overseas tours of duty. However, many of the household effects that are usual in a settled home in the United States had had to be jettisoned along the way or had never been acquired because of the exigencies of the nomadic military life.

180

Health and sanitation. Undoubtedly one of the greatest sources of anxiety in Ankara for the American military family was that of health and sanitation, and at times fears became obsessive. Illustrative of this was one woman's commentary: "Turkey is just a big rock pile with germs sprouting out of every rock." However, fears were not entirely unfounded, and moderate and consistent health precautions were necessary: water had to be treated; fresh produce had to be soaked in a chlorine solution; meat shops or restaurants merited careful selection. Dysentery and respiratory problems aggravated by smog were constant problems for the Americans. The rate of hepatitis was rather high among the American military population at times.[37] Rabies was a constant threat, as there were many semiwild city cats roaming about the streets.[38]

Mental health. A prevalent rumor in American military circles was that an extremely high number of people who suffered from some mental health problem. This was usually attributed to just being in Turkey. Several people related that the early period of adjustment for wives was so difficult that it resulted in what they called "the first-month-in-bed syndrome": women became so depressed by the barren surroundings and the alien life that they refused to get out of bed to cope with the harassments of another day. Extreme fearfulness on the part of some military wives did occur: some women refused to drive; a few women were known to meet their children at the school bus stop, escort them home, and never permit them to play outside; one woman would lock all of her windows and doors the

Demographic, Ecological, and Social Structural Properties

moment her husband left, barricading herself and her pre-school children inside the house and never answering the door until he came home.[39]

Comparative figures of mental illness in Ankara vis-à-vis the United States were classified military information, inaccessible to those who did not have "the need to know." However, there were indications from professional and embassy personnel that possibly there was some truth to the rumors. A psychiatrist said: "I think this is one of the worst situations I have ever seen." A psychologist thought that the military community situation in Ankara "triggered off preneurotics and prepsychotics—in particular, young wives and mothers feel threatened, and husbands feel their virility challenged here by the big, mustachioed Turkish male. In general, however, these people in Ankara are from the disintegrating communities in the United States, and they come here for the *coup de grâce.*" Embassy officials said that they knew there was a higher number of military people suffering from psychiatric problems in Ankara than there would be in the United States; but the actual figures were impossible to arrive at, since many American military men would not go to the military hospital for treatment. In order to keep such visits off their records, as they might prove detrimental to their careers, they went to Turkish psychiatrists. Several Turkish psychiatrists estimated to an embassy official that at least 50 percent of their patients were Americans. This same official came to the conclusion that mental illness was likely endemic to the military career and the men it attracted, since it seemed to occur with much greater frequency among them than it did among Foreign Service employees. And he posed the question: "I can't help

GARRISON COMMUNITY

but wonder why mental illness in these people comes out quicker here than it does in the United States."

NOTES

1. The figures mentioned in Turkish newspapers and in conversations often seemed to overestimate the American military population; however, the figures gleaned from American sources seem to be underestimates. Therefore, for whom the secret classification is considered necessary becomes a moot point.

2. With this population broken down to units, the estimates were as follows:

Air Force: Headquarters, Detachments 30 and 37	2,400 people
Other Air Force Units	1,100
Army Units	500
JUSMMAT (includes Army, Navy, and Air Force Groups)	1,000
NATO (4 Navy people, 16 Air Force people)	20
CENTO	96
Total	5,126 people

3. These figures were based on the results of a sample of 166 people, randomly selected from the American military community in Ankara. For further explication of the design and methods used, see the appendix on methods.

4. Many Americans sorrowfully commented on this lack of an American post, feeling that their lives in Ankara would have been infinitely better if they could have all lived together.

5. Some Americans are not faced with these problems. A few houses have been rented by the United States government for some of the generals; there are several sets of billets for single enlisted personnel; American CENTO people live together in three rented apartment houses; and those high school students whose families are not stationed in Ankara live in dormitories at Balgat.

6. In December, 1966, the officer in charge of the Air Police unit requested a 50 percent increase in police force.

7. There were seven exchange stores in Ankara: one large one at Balgat, two middle-sized stores at Maltape and at JUSMMAT Headquarters, and four small stores in other parts of the city.

8. An Iranian general, when discussing American military facilities in a private conversation, remarked: "It's too bad the U.S. spends so much money to make enemies."

9. The classic American example of the exception to this rule is the career of General John J. Pershing, who was an Army captain at the time he was plucked from the ranks.

10. The salaries of a rank group fall within a specific range; the individual's salary within this range is dependent upon his years of military service.

11. It is interesting to note the myths that are cultivated regarding these men, not only by those who see them very little but also by those who work closely with them. The myth-making extends even to the families of the elite. One general's secretary told me in perfect seriousness that "her general's wife" had never been to such a mundane affair as a shower for a bride-to-be, although she knew as well as I that both the general and his wife had come from lower middle-class homes in the Western United States.

12. Either Erving Goffman's concept of roles and presentations or Leon Festinger's concept of cognitive dissonance might provide analytical tools for studying this comunity phenomenon.

184

13.   In the 1930's three separate studies were conducted to explore ethnic prejudice and stereotypes. Daniel Katz and Kenneth W. Braley asked one hundred Princeton students to order their preferences regarding these groups of people: Negroes were preferred least, Turks next to least. Although the students had had no contact with any Turks, they associated, in the given order, the following traits with them: (1) cruel; (2) very religious; (3) treacherous; (4) sensual; (5) ignorant; (6) dirty, etc. In an earlier study Bogardus asked 110 businessmen and schoolteachers on the Pacific Coast about the degrees of intimacy to which they were willing to admit certain ethnic groups. Of the twenty-three ethnic groups listed, Turks were preferred least. In the Middle West, Thurstone constructed a scale on the basis of the likes and dislikes of 239 students. From 21 ethnic groups, the rank order of the Turk was number 20.

14.   It is not known whether there was censorship of sponsor correspondence or not. However, according to "U.S. Element Treaty Org. Instruction," No. 14–66, 13 October 1966, the following was requested of the sponsor: "A copy of each item of correspondence, written or received, should be provided to the Administrative Office for file."

15.   According to Ralph F. Paige and Frank J. Zagorski ("Preparation for the Cross-Cultural Relationships of American Military Personnel" [Thesis, Graduate School of Public and International Affairs, University of Pittsburgh, 1960], p. 46), the Military Assistance Institute in Washington provides MAAG officers "with 130 hours of intensive formal instruction in U.S. studies, communism and the cold war, military assistance and area and country studies."

16.   "Outbound Briefings" were also given to departing personnel. The content of these had to do with clearing customs, sale of household articles to Turks, immunizations, and the packing and shipping of automobiles and household goods to the United States.

185

17. Twice yearly an Inter-Agency Orientation Program (AID, USIS, and the Embassy) was presented; and any military personnel who wished to come were permitted to do so. During the October 31–November 4, 1966 program, new military people were particularly encouraged to attend; and it was later estimated that 25 percent of the audience was composed of military personnel.

18. The sergeant was obviously referring to the jaundice effects that sometimes accompany hepatitis.

19. This course was sponsored by Detachment 30. The University of Maryland also offered an occasional class in Turkish. JUSMMAT had sponsored classes in Turkish until 1966, at which time they were discontinued.

20. Since the Air Force was not required to provide kindergarten or nursery schools, the cost had to be borne by the parents. The tuition, which ran around $208 for a nine-month session, seemed particularly expensive to enlisted people.

21. If figures for teacher retention rates in dependent schools in Germany are used for comparison, these figures are not quite so startling. I have been told that the usual loss there is around 50 percent.

22. Teachers and administrators repeatedly told me that they spent a great deal of their time involved in janitorial activities. For example: Because of the crowded conditions at the Balgat schools in the fall of 1966, the third and fourth grades had to be moved to a building downtown. Over the Christmas holidays the entire heating system of this school building was stolen—furnace, pipes, everything. When school reopened, the teacher and students had to wear caps, gloves, and coats, and they studied around a portable electric heater. After getting a new heating system, the temperatures then soared to 95 degrees. Next came a fire in the electrical circuit system. One day when I was sitting in the principal's office, a frantic call came from this school, requesting waste paper baskets. The roof was leak-

186

ing, water was coming down in streams, and without baskets innundation was threatening.

23. Station allowances were given only to those living in Turkish apartments or houses. To give an approximate idea of what they ran, sergeants received $1.30 per day, colonels $2 per day. Military pay scales are so easily accessible that they have not been reprinted herein.

24. From Christmas, 1966, through January, 1967, the O.S.I., I was told, went on a "crash program" to uncover some of these American overseas enterpreneurs. According to the rumors current at that time, eighty-five Americans were arrested and charged with the offense of black-marketing.

25. For example, an American company, Tumpane, which acted as a liaison between the United States government and Turkish labor, paid one American secretary $530 a month and a Turkish secretary $132 a month (both worked in the same office). The differential was defended on the grounds that the Turkish government preferred that Turkish salaries were more in line with those earned downtown, and that the living costs for the Turks were far less than those for the Americans.

26. In the autumn of 1967, after this study was completed, the Turkish employees of the company which services American personnel in Turkey (Tumpane) went on a thirty-day strike. Seven hundred of the strikers, according to the newspaper accounts, roamed through the military bases scattering garbage. The union demands had to do with the improvement of working conditions and employment security and with increased wages.

27. In regard to charitable relationships between Americans and Turks, there were in fact many possibilities open to American *individuals*. Several American women in the community went to one of the orphanages every week to play with the children, bringing them games and gifts. One club, the Cocuk Sevenler Dernegi, had been organized for the express purpose of aiding and donating to an orphanage. However, neither of

187

these examples—individual and organized—was under the auspices of organized Christian religion. A well-educated Turkish woman told me in regard to this: "Of course the church groups can give charity, but the gifts must be given by the American people—person to person—and not by the church or the church group as such."

28.   American membership made up an estimated 7 to 9 percent of the Kavaklidere Tennis Club membership and approximately 47 percent of the Ankara Golf Club membership. However, what percentage of this was American military membership is not known.

29.   I have been told that there were no enlisted men or their wives in either the Turkish-American Association or in the Turkish-American Women's Cultural Society. However, the statement must remain tentative, since verification was not possible.

30.   Just how popular and accepted the image of the military organization wife has become is reflected in the following quotation from a newspaper (which would accept little that was not received opinion): "Generally speaking (no pun intended), conformity is the key word for wives who want to help their husbands' military career. . . . The wife can make a major contribution to her husband's promotion effort by being 'a contributing, acceptable, noncontroversial member of the community at a base' as one Air Force wife put it" ("American Week-end," *Army Times* Supplement, 21 September 1966, p. 6).

31.   For example, in the Boy Scouts the roster of officials read like a military hierarchy in miniature, starting at the apex with a general, of course.

32.   This notice was frequently reprinted in the military daily bulletins of both JUSMMAT and Detachment 30.

33.   According to one volunteer program director, participation was very low, and she queried: "Why are people over here always so busy doing nothing?"

188

34. Very few of the teen-agers that I talked to had any Turkish boy or girl friends, and cross-cultural dating was really rare.

35. One of these places was the Kit-Kat Bar, where American soldiers had been known to be cheated and beaten; and, according to two American lawyers, two American soldiers had been "framed" on the charge of kidnapping prostitutes because they refused to pay inflated checks.

36. This warning was followed closely after a lieutenant was murdered, returning from Istanbul to Ankara with a Turkish male companion in a hired taxi. Robbers had stopped the car and shot driver and passengers.

37. Embassy personnel received gamma globulin shots twice annually to protect them from hepatitis. Whether or not this treatment was effective was not clearly known, but it was believed by medical authorities that it helped greatly. Military personnel did not receive these shots, unless they were suspected of coming down with hepatitis, and they greatly resented the discrimination.

38. For example, the number of animal bites of American personnel from October through December, 1966, was 102 cases. Since some of the animals could not be found, 27 of these people had to go through the rather lengthy and painful anti-rabies treatment.

39. The fear that some American women manifested toward "the Turks" was at times incredible. I took one older woman shopping in the old section one bright afternoon, and as we began leaving the department store area and started walking into the narrow streets, filled with tiny hole-in-the-wall shops and men sitting or standing about staring at passers-by, she became so agitated and fearful, clutching her purse tightly to her breast, that she begged I walk her back to get a taxi to return home. What she had heard or what she believed it was that frightened her to this extent was not clearly expressed at the time.

5

CLOSURE
AND
INNOVATION
IN A
MILITARY
COLONY

AREAS OF INTERGROUP TENSION

At the points where the Turkish and the American military communities were apt to intersect, tension often
developed. Since interpersonal communication and understanding had not effectively evolved as the principal means
of settling differences between the two communities, contacts were sometimes fraught with hostility and conflict.
The following is a discussion of some of these problems.

The Legal Perplexities

Under the terms of the NATO Status of Forces Agreement American military personnel and their dependents in Ankara were subject to Turkish laws. In case of violation during off-duty time Americans could be apprehended by the Turkish police, tried in a Turkish court by Turkish authorities, and, if found guilty, sent to a Turkish prison.[1] However, and this was a point of contention for the Turks, if a Turkish law was violated by an American serviceman while he was on duty, he was then considered under the legal jurisdiction of the American military authorities. The NATO Status of Forces Agreement further specified that members of the American military forces must be afforded adequate legal safeguards based upon American standards of fair trial and treatment. Many American military people did not believe that this provision was adhered to in Ankara.

Turkish law,[2] on the whole, was not well understood by Americans in Ankara. Some felt that it was irrational and unfairly applied to them, while others, according to a State Department official, didn't seem to realize that they were "in a foreign country and under its laws." The Turkish set of Insult (or Courtesy or Dignity) Laws, in particular, seemed almost incomprehensible to them. Basically, there were three sections to this law: insult of the Turkish nation was prohibited, with penalties for violation of one to six years imprisonment; insults of the symbols of the Turkish nation (for example, the Turkish flag, money, statues or pictures of Ataturk, and so on) were punishable by imprisonment up to three years; insult of a Turkish national (extended to include foreigners, as well) was prohibited

191

and punishable by imprisonment for fifteen days up to six months. An air policeman, in commenting about several recent trials involving "Americans insulting Turkish nationals," said: "This law seems to be made against Americans. Ordinarily, however, when an American is hauled into court for this type of offense, he gets away with only apologizing to the Turk. Occasionally, he has to go to jail for a short term."

Driving and traffic laws were particularly frightening to Americans, since the idea of "comparative negligence" was thought to be unjust and inequitable for Americans.[3] It was generally believed, even by American officials, that Americans involved in any traffic accidents were almost always found guilty, regardless of their actions. One State Department official told me: "Americans are usually adjudged guilty because of their greater ability to pay than the dolmus [shared taxi] or taxi driver." A military legal officer[4] said: "If you get in an auto accident, you run a double risk. If you're just there, you're automatically 50 percent at fault. If the accident is minor and no one is hurt, it is likely an American will be found 100 percent to blame, even if he's not. And if someone is hurt, then it's very likely that you will be physically molested by gathering crowds of Turks."

Currency regulations were also seen as an area where American servicemen were unfairly discriminated against. The legal rate of exchange was nine Turkish lira to the American dollar; however, tourists were afforded a more generous rate. Moreover, black-marketeers dealing in currency would exchange an American dollar for anyplace from

192

eleven to eighteen Turkish lira. Complaints about this were numerous, and as one American official stated: "The soldier feels he cannot afford to take the brunt of American foreign policy. Everyone, anyone, gets more for the dollar than he can. It's devastating to his morale."

Customs laws were angrily described by Americans as "ridiculous." They were permitted to bring all of their household goods and a private automobile into the country duty-free, but upon leaving they had to account for each item. If they had thrown an item away during the tour in Ankara and had not had it officially removed from their customs list, they were liable for duty on it. If they sold an item, either the seller or the buyer had to pay customs on it. Since Americans usually possessed numerous items and over a period of time things get lost, stolen, misplaced, this was a source of great irritation for them.

In addition to the bewilderment, fear, and anger that Americans expressed in regard to the Turkish laws and legal practices, they also felt that they received little or no adequate protection or help in these matters from American officials. The Air Police unit was restricted in its jurisdiction to American leased property, although they were often called in by Americans or as witnessing authorities by the Turkish police in cases involving Americans. The top military administrators and lawyers of the Staff Judge Advocate Section were believed not to care particularly: "They remain above it all." The American State Department, which was thought to have the only really effective power to intercede on the behalf of American military people, was seen as indifferent to the military person's plight if he became caught in the

Closure and Innovation in a Military Colony

inscrutable meshes of the Turkish legal machine. Several comments from lower-echelon military lawyers and military officials illustrate this last point of view:

> Those Americans who do not have diplomatic immunity are fearful, knowing that for scant reason they can be sent to Turkish prisons. They do not feel that the State Department cares about their safety over here. American State Department officials are more interested in diplomatic relations than in individuals.

> Americans are quite defenseless here. The U.S. government gives them no safeguards whatsoever. So they're at the mercy of the Turkish government and courts, and they get no legal protection. The trend in the last eighteen months has been toward an increasing number of lawsuits and cases brought against Americans.

> The State Department ignores the legal problems of the American military people over here, even when a man's life is at stake. Oh, they might intercede if an American general had problems, but they certainly wouldn't help a poor airman or dependent. I can't remember, nor can anyone else in my section, when they've ever helped anyone.

Because these attitudes were not confined to a small circle of officers, but were generally felt throughout the community, military people sometimes saw themselves as defenseless. Enlisted men, in particular, felt betrayed by those whose "duty" it was to protect them. Typical of some of their remarks are the following:

> I don't like it at all! Our Air Force don't care how we live so long as we get the job done. Big wheels got it made, and it's one long picnic for them. For us it's thirty months of punishment, penance, harassment, and ill will.

> I feel that the American GI should have more privileges,

that we should be able to stand up to these people when you are taken advantage of, which happens quite frequently.

I have hated every minute of my time here and will never return. I have felt like a person in prison as our Status of Forces Agreement has put the GI at the mercy of the Turks. Seventy-nine days to go and can't wait. It's not easy to take being spat on when you walk in the streets.

I do not like the attitude of the U.S. cowering to the Turks. We are the greatest nation in the world and to bow to Turk people only makes the situation worse. If we would demand our rights and equal treatment, we would get it.

A *few* Americans sell us all out. If an American is right, defend him or we all lose face.

Americans should not be in Turkey. It's bad for both Turks and Americans relations. Any and all cases involving illegal acts should be handled by American courts not Turks. If any American should be caught doing something illegal the American government should see to it he is taken out of this country before they would allow him to be handed over to Turkish authorities.

It should be mentioned in passing that many Turks felt that Americans flagrantly disregarded their laws and did so with impunity, even though they were guests in their country.

Competition

In almost every field where the same things or advantages were sought, rivalry between Americans and Turks developed: housing, servants, products, service at shops, even playground space. It was immediately apparent to both Turks and Americans to whom a landlord catered: did the sign in the window say "For Rent" or did it say "Kiralik"? Servants

Closure and Innovation in a Military Colony

were said to prefer to work for Americans because they could ask for and receive much higher wages. The competitive situation was viewed by both groups, with the exception of those who profited from it, with some sadness and resentment. Turks resented the increased rents, the increased costs for servants, the increased prices for produce; and they blamed the American community members with their high standard of living and their big salaries for causing the inflation. Americans, on the other hand, felt they were cheated, that two price scales existed—a reasonable one for the Turks and a larcenous one for them.

With this assumption, along with several others in mind, the Americans sometimes demanded more services than those usually provided at Turkish shops. For example, at a beauty shop one American dependent indignantly stated that she had almost gotten pushed out of "her turn" to have her hair combed when she emerged from the hair dryer: "No damned Turk is going to get ahead of me. You know we pay twice as much as they do. They even wash their hair before they come so they won't have to pay for a shampoo. When I pay more, why shouldn't I go first?" Competition to be first served or best served cropped up frequently in Turkish stores and produce markets. Turf rights in various fields were contended: for example, American and Turkish children might battle, in one way or another, for playground areas or whatever they designated as such. Sometimes streets and highways became the field of contest, with dangerous maneuvering for rights-of-way, parking places, and car-passing precedence.

While for single American soldiers rivalry with the local males over the local girls is usually intrinsic to the

196

overseas military situation, in Ankara Turkish women were usually either too highly controlled by customs and families to be counters in a dispute or their "reputations" were sometimes thought to be so questionable that dating them was hardly considered a victory.

Conflict

Disparities in value systems. The differences that existed between the value systems of the Turks and of the American military members were sometimes seen as an unbridgeable gulf. Perhaps some of the underlying sources of misunderstandings and feelings like "I don't understand these people at all" lay in Turkey being a Moslem country and one which in some respects was still quite traditionally oriented. Turks sometimes expressed distaste for the different ethics that Americans had imported into their country, and particularly irritating to them were the American attitudes toward women and liquor. Conversely, the highly paternal family arrangement in Turkey and the predominance of the male role in all areas sometimes led to jolted self-conceptions in Americans.

A basic difference between the two groups occurred in their attitudes toward what was considered as public and private areas of living and responsibility. The private areas of American family life, for example, were often not seen as such by Turks. Turkish servants would open closed doors and walk into bathrooms and bedrooms. Turkish neighbors would unabashedly stare into American apartment windows with great curiosity and interest. Yet, in terms of public responsibility as seen by Americans, Turkish life was com-

197

paratively privatized and family-oriented. Where many Americans felt that both individuals and organizations should be somewhat responsible for the orphaned, the injured, the indigent, and so on, Turks were believed to be indifferent. The Turkish attitude toward animals particularly bothered many Americans, who had seen or heard about instances of cruel treatment: horses beaten, cats thrown into construction lime pits, kittens stepped on by workmen, dogs poisoned. To permit this in a society was thought by Americans to be morally reprehensible in both the public and private sectors. As an American psychiatrist said: "When Turks throw poisoned meat out in the street to kill dogs or when they beat horses—then such brutality exacerbates the situation for Americans."

Violation of the American work ethic was viewed with indignation by Americans. Seeing Turkish men spend hours in the tea houses while the women worked seemed particularly to anger them. Concepts of how work should be done also differed between the two groups. Technologically oriented, Americans believed in using machines instead of the masses of men with which the Turkish contractors usually worked. Naturally, this was seen within the context of efficiency, rather than within one of traditional work modes, high unemployment rates, and a comparative scarcity of machines.

Several officers and dependents summed up their views on these cultural differences in the following manner:

> Ninety-five percent of the differences between Turks and Americans are due to religion. We'll never get to know them, they're so unlike us. Only 5 percent of the Turks are Europeanized somewhat, but we still won't get along with them.

GARRISON COMMUNITY

Their country is like it is today because of a lack of Christianity and love.

The basic problem in Turkey is that we expect to deal with Europeans (and they think they are), but we deal and live with Orientals.

The average Turk constitutes about 85 percent of the Turkish population. He is the Turk from the village and is very illiterate, stupid, and lacks common sense. The other 15 percent have a thin veneer of civilization. Scratch the surface, and we are back to the other 85 percent.

Disparities in living standards. American military people, on the whole, expected to live in much the same fashion in Ankara as they had in the United States. This included a "decent" place to live, an automobile, and the availability of American foods and products. Some Turks expressed irritation at this, considering the American style of life an unnecessarily conspicuous display of wealth[5] in the midst of poverty; more than anything, however, they resented the base exchange, stocked with so many of the articles that were either not available or were extremely expensive in the Turkish market. The black markets, almost the only outlets for American base exchange goods, were deplored as indicators of the moral degradation the Americans had brought in their wake—yet their patronage was so extensive that no real attempt was made to close them. While angered with the influx of American goods, Turks often considered these products better made and more desirable than Turkish products. For example, Americans were able to sell torn and worn-out articles of clothing for the labels alone. These labels were then cut out and sewn into new Turkish-made clothing, which with American labels would sell for a much higher price. Cheap, mass-produced ceramic articles from the United States were thought more beautiful, I was told, than Turkish folk art. These attitudes had a certain *ressentiment* quality and sometimes led to situations that were extremely embarrassing for Americans. For instance, when Turkish friends or work counterparts asked them to buy something for them in the base exchange, even though it was against the Turkish law, it was difficult to say no. One American woman wrote:

> Our most pleasant experience was being hospitably received by Turks in their homes. Our most unpleasant was discovering that the same Turks had a shopping list to present.

To further complicate the problem, some Americans used only American products and served only American foods when they entertained Turks. One Turkish woman asked:

> Why don't Americans when they entertain have a few Turkish things in the house, too, rather than all American products—like a few Turkish cigarettes or nuts, that sort of thing? Turks become afraid to ask the Americans back to their homes because they think Americans like only their own products. Most Turks can't afford to buy American products from the black market, and they are afraid to serve Americans Turkish products, afraid that they will be offended.

On the other side, some Americans manifested little sympathy for or understanding of the poverty they saw around them and expressed distaste for "the way the Turks live," interpreting it as deliberate slothfulness. Believing they, in contrast, were seen as "rich Americans" and ruthlessly exploited as such, a certain "victim" psychology could be noted in their responses:

200

They don't want *us*—only our money. It is not a place for Americans.

I don't like being exploited as a "rich American." I can feel antagonism with stares of people when shopping in Turkish markets.

I don't care for Turkey. You are taken advantage of because you are an American, they steal you blind. You have to be constantly aware so as not to be called the Ugly American.

Living in Turkey has been the most undesirable place I have lived in twenty-seven years of Army life. We as Americans have to be constantly on guard. I have not felt welcome here. It is the only country in which I have served that a feeling of constant harassment has existed. These are petty—however, just to clear the country for return to the U.S. one must begin at least sixty days in advance just to get the paper work accomplished. Americans shy away from going on the economy to shop for fear they will be spit upon or a rude remark made. If the Turkish people and government want all the help they seem to want some attempt should be made to make life easier and more pleasant for Americans.

Ami Go Home!

The relations with Turks were good before Cyprus. Americans in uniform walked down the streets and got smiles. Now we get spat upon and so do our cars. I have been spat on, and my car has been spat on. (An American official).

Frankly, here I feel like a Negro must feel in Alabama.

There is a sense of not being wanted.

Overall, I am treated like a third-class citizen.

The accounts of unpleasant "incidents" with Turks

Closure and Innovation in a Military Colony

were legion in the American military community: spitting, stone-throwing, children slapped by Turkish workmen or janitors, cars scratched, car lights broken, air let out of tires. One sergeant told me that he "hated to feel so hated," and he recalled that several times when he had gone to one of the base exchanges that Turkish youngsters had stood outside, throwing rocks at Americans, shouting, "Lousy Americans!" In 1967 the *TUSLOG Daily Bulletin* warnings about Turkish children throwing stones at American cars entering and leaving the Balgat area were frequent. Riding horseback through villages around Ankara and Balgat was described as frightening: "Once your back is turned, you'd better start galloping because they throw rocks at the horse, and you might be thrown." American children occasionally took the brunt of this hostility. In the summer of 1966 American Air Police had had to ride American buses in one section of town, because Turkish juvenile gangs waited at the bus stops for the American children to get off so that they could beat them with bicycle chains.

In one instance, problems became so exacerbated between Turks and Americans—particularly between the children—at an apartment complex near the Balgat Air Station that a meeting had had to be called by the Base Commander. Approximately forty-five people, mostly enlisted men, attended; and when asked if there was anyone there who had had *no* problems with the Turks at the complex, only six hands were raised. Others spoke, as follows:

> Our children out there have to defend themselves, and the only way they can do it is for them to run. I have to make cowards out of my kids and tell them, "When they hit you, run into the house."

202

They pulled a knife on my kids. You can't win! You've got to tell the kids to run home.

They were trying to hit my children with a ball bat, then my wife ran out, and this one big Turkish kid got a big rock and was going to hit my wife with it.

For some Americans, the unpleasant "incidents" they had been involved in, or had witnessed, or had heard about were generalized as typical of the entire tour of duty:

I so far have tolerated Turkey. The housing is only part of the reason. Living with the Turks is the hardest. While eight months pregnant I've had grown men spit at me and throw rocks at me from buildings they were constructing. I had a taxi driver run over my feet so as not to have to pay me my change. Those are only two incidents. There have been several more. Including one Turkish baby sitter, sixteen years of age, whom I paid five lira an hour to watch one three-year-old girl. Friends informed me she was leaving her locked in the house alone as soon as my husband and I left. Now judge for yourself why most Americans literally can't stand Turks!

Only Hell and the USSR could be worse! Spit at and almost going to jail.

I don't like living in Turkey and returning to the U.S. is all I want to do! I personally have been spit on. My two teen-age daughters have been chased home by dirty old Turk men, had rocks thrown at them while waiting for the school bus. This should be an *unaccompanied* tour of fifteen months and *no* P.O.V. [privately owned vehicle].

Incidents were sometimes viewed with anger and fear, but the demonstrations and riots, more than anything else, aroused general anxiety among the community members. One official explained it thus:

203

Closure and Innovation in a Military Colony

In other countries where American military are stationed, it's felt with demonstrations and riots that the difficulties can and will be worked out between the two countries, and the individual American will be protected. Americans don't think it's true here. There's an unpredictable quality about our experiences with the Turks. People are afraid. They feel the country won't take care of their personal safety.

Perhaps the most frightening series of riots and demonstrations of the two years of study occurred in the summer and autumn of 1966. The first of these took place in Ankara on August 6, 1966. Two American airmen, when driving an official station wagon through the new part of town to pick up the mail for the American Post Office, accidentally struck a Turkish woman. They stopped the car and got out to see if she was all right (her injuries were minor). Then someone from the gathering crowd shouted, "Kill the Americans!" After that, the two airmen barely had time to rush back into the car, lock the doors, and throw up their arms and hands to protect their faces and heads. The crowd, variously estimated as consisting of between 500 and 1,000 people, found paving stones and began hitting and smashing at the car. Eventually, the Turkish police came, reinforced by two truckloads of soldiers, and rescued the two airmen. The station wagon was "completely destroyed."[6] During the time of this riot, people at the American movie theater, several blocks away, were told that the movie would not be continued and that they were to return to their homes immediately.

This was followed by various minor demonstrations, riots, and threats of labor strikes. For example, on November 12, 1966, an "anti-American demonstration" was held in

204

front of the USIS building. Two Turkish English-language newspapers stated that the demonstration was organized in general against "American imperialism" and specifically against the firing of Turkish personnel from AID. Signs carried by the demonstrators were typically captioned as follows: "Yankee Go Home!" "Turkey Is Not LBJ's Ranch," "Turkey Will Not Become Viet Nam," "People of Viet Nam, We Share Your Revenge," "Turkey is Not an American Colony," "You Can Not Buy Us With Dollars," "Yankees, Leave Independent Turkey," and so on.[7]

The day after this demonstration in Ankara, on November 13, 1966, a riot of rather large proportions broke out in Adana, a city in southern Turkey where an American air base was located. This was covered by the international press, as well as by the Turkish press:

> . . . [A]bout 5,000 Turks rioted here (Adana) last night, badly damaging several buildings, overturning foreign cars, and chasing Americans through the streets. Nearly 1,000 cars were damaged.[8]

> An anti-American crowd of 6,000 Turks Monday smashed U.S. buildings here and nearly lynched eight American airmen they considered to have behaved improperly towards Turkish women. Police set up barricades in the city center to stop the riots and arrested 35 of the demonstrators. . . . By early morning it appeared the trouble was over. . . . The trouble began in front of a local movie house when a number of Turks accused eight airmen stationed at the Incirlik base of behaving improperly towards the women. Within moments the crowd had built up to some 6,000 persons and the eight Americans were in danger of being lynched.[9]

In the wake of the demonstrations and riots came more

Closure and Innovation in a Military Colony

rumors, more fear, and an intensified drawing in of American military community lines, a tightening up of the feeling of "we on the battlements" against "they, the attackers." One night, shortly after the Adana riot, a firecracker went off with a bang outside of the military library. One American soldier in the reading room jumped up, a bit white, and cried: "My God! Are they shooting at us now?"

IMPLEMENTS OF CLOSURE

Within the American military community certain elements of the military organization and of the ethnic situation seemed to exert a more salient force toward closure than did others. The following is an attempt to locate some of these.

The Milieu of Secrecy

> Large-scale organizations create the milieu within which they flourish.[10]

Whether deliberate or not, the manufacturing of a social climate in which the virtues of military force and organization are seen as necessary is a basic tendency in the military establishment. After all, without enemies who needs protection? And without full-scale, insidious, organized enemies, who needs full-scale, insidious, organized protection? In Ankara this process was as operative as it is frequently in other places, and two components involved

206

seemed to actively promote the type of milieu which was closed to the external population and which repressed the internal population: one of these components was an ideology in which the world was defined in the Manichean terms of communists and communist-fighters; and another was the interest of organizational members to increase their forces, to extend their power, and to protect their segment of the organization from inquiry, public accounting, and disapproval. The former was utilized in the service of the latter, for in a world that was negatively evaluated as one of treachery and strife, where the forces for good and evil were not always unmixed, the reasons for a large, powerful military organization to exist and to bar its secrets, however defined, not only from those without but also to some of those within were defensible. Secrecy was extended sometimes to become an extremely effective defensive weapon for the military organization based in Ankara, even against higher American military and civilian authorities from the United States. For example, witness the following TUSLOG regulation, the main section of which has been printed in its entirety below:

> 1. Because of adverse publicity received by U.S. Military Forces in Turkey, the eyes of Congress, Department of Defense, and higher Headquarters are constantly on us. Thus, many subjects in this geographical area which might be routine in other areas have the potential of becoming controversial or delicate issues of international significance.
>
> 2. The presence of Army, Navy, and Air Force elements in Turkey, operating under diversified commands, requires cohesive coordination in all delicate and controversial matters. Accordingly, it is imperative that this headquarters maintain an informed, unified, and well coordinated posi-

tion on all delicate and controversial matters arising within or requiring action of this command. Toward the accomplishment of this end, the following policies are established to become effective immediately.

(a) No staff agency of headquarters or commander in the field will answer or take final action on correspondence pertaining to delicate or controversial matters without first coordinating with and securing the concurrence of the Command Section, this headquarters.

(b) The action agency or commander in the field will submit the proposed response to the Command Section sufficiently in advance of any suspense date to permit full and unhurried coordination with other interested agencies, as may be required.

(c) No member of this command should express any official comments on controversial subjects unless the command position thereon has been crystallized and release thereof is authorized.

(d) When meeting with inspection teams of higher headquarters and visiting VIPs, each member of this command is admonished to exercise extreme care and prudence in discussing controversial or delicate subjects.

3. The following are examples of delicate and controversial matters:

(a) Illegal currency transactions.
(b) Black market activities.
(c) Smuggling and customs.
(d) Cases pending before the Turkish criminal and civil courts.
(e) Incidents involving American personnel and Turkish nationals.
(f) The Turkish lira rate of exchange.
(g) APO system.
(h) Dependent school system.

This list is not intended to be all inclusive. In case of doubt, the matter should be treated as controversial and the policies herein stated are applicable.

4. Every member of this command is charged with the responsibility of carrying out the policies herein set forth. Each staff head or commander of units concerned will be held responsible for any violation thereof.

Contributing to the atmosphere of closure was the existence of numerous secret units[11] stationed in Ankara. Their main work, doubtless, was to keep a check on "subversive activities" in the Middle East; however, they were sometimes utilized, or on their own initiative felt it their duty, to investigate military members who were thought to deviate from the received conception of what the American military man or dependent should be like. It was possible for such agencies to create victims, for even an investigation sufficed to make one somewhat suspect. Perennial distrust seemed to be a characteristic of some of the agents. One told me how diabolically clever the opponents were: "Leftists play the biggest role here; and they counter every move we make. They twist and distort everything we do." Another said: "They might say there are no communists here, but there are plenty." Two sets of labels existed for some of these people, which they applied, I believe, with little care: "Leftists" or "Communists" and "Communist Dupes" or "Catspaws" or "Fellow Travelers."[12]

Awareness of "leftist" dangers was stressed to all personnel, and mandatory briefings on the "reporting and investigation of espionage, sabotage and subversive activities"[13] were given. On Air Force bulletin boards a notice was tacked up requesting that any suspicious persons or activities be reported immediately. Generalized suspicion and

209

fear of questions seemed to generate from these sources. A child guidance counselor, who wished to send out an informal questionnaire to the parents regarding their children's after-school activities and the extent of their participation in the Turkish community, was told she could not do so.[14] A principal reluctantly gave me a printed school brochure saying, "Well, I guess it's not classified." A chaplain, whom I wished to interview, would neither talk to me nor permit me to leave his office without first calling the Office of Special Investigation (OSI) and the military psychiatrist.[15] One base commander became so fearful that some of the actions requisite to his command ground to a virtual standstill. According to a secretary: "He locked up everything in his safe, and would never take anything out. No one knew what was going on, and nothing got done. And no one could do anything about it."

Suspicious aversion toward variation or nonconformity, often in the most trivial instances, could be noted throughout the community. Some verbalized this in terms of what it did to their own lives, or as one person said: "I feel so hedged in here, so restricted." This chafing at constraint was not unusual, and the repression of nonconformity possibly intensified inner-community tensions and hostility toward external groups. Perhaps this phenomenon has nowhere been summed up so wisely as by G. H. Mead: "Just in proportion as we organize by hostility do we suppress individuality."[16]

210

THE SIZE OF THE AMERICAN
MILITARY COMMUNITY IN ANKARA

I don't blame the Turks for feeling resentful. Imagine putting ten thousand Turks into San Francisco, giving each family a new car, and plunking them down in the city with the attitude that they don't want to be there. How would the Americans feel toward them? (An American military officer in Ankara)

The fact remains: The presence and actions of the large American military presence in Turkey is tinder and fuel for the anti-American fire. (*Outlook,* Turkish-English language magazine) [17]

Are we too numerous? No, not at present. The problem is not our numbers. What's the difference between a few hundred or a few thousands? (Ambassador Parker T. Hart) [18]

There are various reasons why there is indeed a difference between the effects of a few hundred and a few thousand American military people in a foreign city. The effects of size were not inconsequential upon the American military community. As numbers grew, American facilities sufficient for a life apart were added. Participation with the local people became unnecessary. Decreased contacts with Turks lent credence to gradually forming pejorative stereotypes; and walls, even those of words, not only keep people out, they also keep people in.

Was the increase of American forces in Ankara necessary? Frequently, I have heard American military people

211

say that the military units in Ankara were "grossly over-staffed." At TUSLOG I was told that various units could be cut in half, and no one would notice. At JUSMMAT some Americans said that since the Turkish military no longer wanted American advice, there were many Americans who had little, if anything, to do. Detachment 30, the largest unit in Ankara, was said to be overstaffed, that men had little to do and were bored and dissatisfied.

Although the cultural impact of increased numbers of Americans on Ankara itself has never been adequately studied, on the basis of Turkish newspaper articles and numerous conversations with Turks it is possible to suggest further effects. To many Turks that which might have been admirable or at least tolerable on the small scale seemed to be monstrous and threatening on the large. What seemed to be at first a handful of bewildered strangers became an influx of foreign troops, which were perceived by some as posing a menace to Turkish independence and polity. And as the increase became visible, the disparity of living stand-ards and values between Turks and Americans became more apparent—and resented. It also became obvious that Ameri-cans were beginning to live apart from Turks, isolated from the Turkish mainstream of life, seldom learning the lan-guage, infrequently participating. And this was eventually interpreted to mean that Americans as a group felt superior to the Turks and viewed that which was Turkish as valueless.

Communication and Rumor

The usual means of receiving information were limited for the Americans in Ankara: there were no television

212

stations; there were only a few daily English-language programs that could be received on the radio, and no Armed Forces Network; there were few telephones; there was no genuine military community press. Of course, American magazines and several newspapers could be bought at the base exchange newsstand. But even the military newspaper, the *Stars and Stripes*,[19] was printed in Europe, and its primary focus was the European Command. There were several Turkish English-language newspapers and news magazines, but these were slanted toward the diplomatic audience. And then there were the various American military organs,[20] which were the media of official thought and communication and were not, of course, independent.

Wives, possibly, felt more isolated than other groups since they often had to wait until their husbands and children came home to hear "the news." Men were somewhat better informed, since they went to work, they received the daily bulletins, and at the periodic Commander's Calls some information might be disseminated.

The most feared contingency was that it might be impossible to contact people in time of emergency: for example, if children were injured at school, it was difficult to inform the parents; or, in case of a community-wide emergency, the problems of general notification were grave. In the case of the latter, an Area Warden System had been organized; but even those involved were somewhat dubious about how effectively it would work, since the absence of only one or two wardens might mean that a whole area would go uninformed.

Information about what was going on in the community, about Turkish-American relations, about even rou-

213

tine events was often difficult to secure. And there were no legitimate ways to request information or to ask questions or to air grievances. Thus as an Embassy official said: "Everything in the military community seems to be via the grapevine." Gossip and rumors tended to fill the informational vacuum, and the primary channel was word-of-mouth. The rumors prevalent in the community were somewhat indicative of where the most pronounced gaps in information lay and, ultimately, were quite possibly symptomatic of underlying community sentiments, anxieties, and fears. Sometimes rumors were based on incidents, but greatly enhanced and exaggerated. Some were entirely imaginary. But good or bad, morbid or hopeful, mostly true or entirely false, they provided knowledge of a sort not forthcoming from elsewhere.

Examples of a few of the most prevalent rumors are enlightening.

The Mark of Zorro. This was a rumor which was illustrative of the feeling that a general Turkish conspiracy was being directed against Americans. According to the rumor, a letter "Z" was being placed on apartment buildings in which American military people lived, indicating to beggars, vendors, thieves, and murderers where Americans could be found for whatever purposes they had in mind. One woman questioned wrote: "Peddlers and beggars swarm to our homes, and if we won't give lira they mark a big Z over our doors or deface our homes in some way." That a Z was marked on several apartment house walls was a fact, but then it was fitted into a conceptual structure and related to other experiences and fears. Other events, coinciding in time with the Z, were worked into the story. The extensiveness and credibility of the rumor could be noted: even an officer in the Information Office told the story as fact to illustrate the point he was making regarding the organized harassment of Americans. One woman, a secretary, reported that after she and her husband left for work in the morning someone managed to get into her apartment almost every day and took all of the fuses out of the electric fuse box. Then just before she returned home, the unknown someone would replace them. Thus the spoiled food in her refrigerator was attributed to Turkish machinations—to the Turkish Zorro. Several people reported to a military law agency that the apartment janitors in Ankara were being organized against American residents, that they were being told not to do anything for Americans and to hit and hurt American children when no one was looking, and so on.

This rumor became sufficiently widespread and embellished to require an investigation by the Security Law Enforcement Agency. Apparently, a Z was placed on apartment buildings in certain areas to inform vendors and beggars and so on that the people within, regardless of nationality, could not speak Turkish and, therefore, not to waste their time. At one apartment house someone erased the Z and found, subsequently, that many more Turks than usual who could not speak English came to his door requesting to buy or sell things. It was curious that the results of the investigation were never made public. Thus the rumor was still circulating as fact some months later when I left Ankara.

Mayhem on the outskirts. This rumor had variations, but in general it ran that an American couple (sometimes accompanied by a Turkish friend) set off for Istanbul. They had

Closure and Innovation in a Military Colony

gotten but a few miles from Ankara when they accidentally struck a village child. (Sometimes the child in the story was killed, sometimes only injured.) A maddened mob of villagers came out and surrounded the car. From this point in the rumor, the rest of the story became, over time, successively more dramatic, gory, and horrifying. At first, either the American man or the Turk (depending on the source of information) was able to produce a gun, and they all escaped back to Ankara. Later, the protagonists in the story were all torn to pieces. I heard this rumor from at least ten very different sources; and it was always told fearfully in the hushed tones of the true horror story. In checking the rumor at four agencies,[21] I was told that it had "never happened," that it had no basis in fact whatsoever. This rumor was not publicly denied, directly or by inference, for it semed to be felt that to officially deny meant to accredit.

Other rumors. Another rumor which militated against traveling about the Turkish countryside was in the words of one person: "You can't travel in this country. Turks sit on the hillsides along the roads and roll rocks down on you until you're forced to stop. Then they'll rob you, and heaven knows what else." There was the rumor that it was very dangerous to walk in the streets of Ankara, particularly at night, and at any time in the old section of town. Yet, according to the law-enforcement agencies, during 1966 "not a single American was accosted or molested in the streets of Ankara." A rumor that American personnel in Turkey apprehended for black-marketing activities were immediately reassigned to Vietnam as a kind of punishment was dis-

216

pelled, perhaps incorrectly—I do not know, only by a Tukish English-language newspaper, which entitled its front-page article as follows: "Vietnam Assignment for Black-marketing Denied by Officials."[22] To my knowledge official corroboration of this never appeared in any of the military organ papers.

Often even the most routine information was not made public. Apparently, explanation of events or of orders was not deemed necessary by military authorities. For example, in the *TUSLOG Daily Bulletin*[23] it was stated that only certain set rates as specified should be paid for taxi fares from the Air Station at Balgat to Ankara. Seven days later this notice appeared: "TAXI FARES FROM ANKARA AIR STATION: Paragraph 3, Official, Daily Bulletin #188, 19 October 1966 is in error and is revoked (CAS/15)."[24] Why? Community members decided for themselves *why:* it was because "the Turks" wouldn't let Americans have fair rates. It was just one more way in which Turks were "clipping" Americans. Actually, however, there was a Turkish law which specified extremely reasonable basic taxi rates, but extra specified charges could be made for each added passenger, parcel, and service. This was never explained, and Americans expected to pay only the basic rate, regardless of the number of passengers, grocery sacks or parcels, and the help required from the taxi driver.

Information tended to be confined to either top levels or to law-enforcement and secret agencies. There was really no way to generally dispel rumors or fears except through official channels, and the official reaction often seemed to be to either classify the information[25] or to ignore it. Communication with the community most often came on the

217

level of a directive. Thus new rumors were accreted to old rumors and passed on from "generation to generation" as historical fact. With sinister inflections such remarks as the following were often heard: "There are a lot of incidents with Americans that go on that we never hear about. They're kept quiet." "Americans never know what is *really* going on." Most of the rumored incidents tended to give substance to the community-held image that the American military people were threatened by the Turks, that they were isolated, and that their only defense was to cling together.

Community Ideology and Stereotypes

The military community, it is believed, provided peculiarly optimum conditions for the growth and totalization of an interpretive framework within which certain experiences were ordered in a sufficiently comprehensive fashion as to seem reasonable. In a milieu where the dominance of the military institution diminished the effectiveness of challenge and resistance from other institutions, where individualism was an irrelevant value as against group life, where external contacts were restricted, the babble of dissent was muffled to a whisper. Community ideology and the stereotypes therefrom, continually reinforced by intense intragroup interaction, tended to become mutually confirmed and supported by community members—and, for them, confirming and supporting.[26]

In the analysis of the stereotypes most frequently used by the military community, certain composite patterns appear. Basic to this pattern was the assumption of the innate superiority of the American military member and group and

218

the innate inferiority of the Turkish majority member and group. In conjunction with these feelings of ethnocentrism a set of justifications had arisen: a rationale that Turks were inferior *because* of certain specified cultural, psychological, and physical traits.

The conviction of the excellence of American culture and the defectiveness of Turkish culture was one which sustained the community sense of ethnic and military honor in a milieu where comparison was not only possible but might at certain points prove to be pernicious and, ultimately, threatening to group solidarity. Furthermore, and importantly, such honor could be claimed by *any* military community member from any stratum. To lower-ranking personnel, in organization and community positions where status dignity was attenuated and status humiliation endemic, this form of honor was accessible; and if the need for feeling superior to some group existed, which it might have in an organization where positions were prescribed by hierarchical relationships, it could be satisfied to a degree here. Therefore community-patterned stereotypes could be further analyzed on the basis of codified structures of rank perception, for the internal selection and use of such stereotypes seemed to depend somewhat on the differential relational properties and needs of the community groups applying them.[27]

The vocabularies of prejudice. In comparing the descriptions of the "average Turk" written by study group respondents, it was found that the following were the most usual characterizations cited, in order of frequency: Enlisted men saw the "average Turk" as (1) arrogant and excessively proud, (2) anti-American and unfriendly, (3) stupid, dirty, and crude, (4) treacherous and dishonest, (5) overly national-istic and patriotic. As one enlisted man neatly summed it up: "He thinks he knows everything." The W.O. to 03 rank group saw the "average Turk" as (1) arrogant and overly proud, (2) treacherous, dishonest, and stupid, (3) dirty and backward, (4) crude and discourteous. The 04 and above rank group believed that the "average Turk" was (1) stupid and ignorant, (2) nationalistic and crude, (3) arrogant and excessively proud, (4) childlike, highly emo-tional, and anti-American, (5) shrewd and grasping, (6) overly religious.

Of the sixty-five comments by enlisted personnel, forty-seven were unfavorable, eight were mixed, ten were favorable. Thirty-seven members of the W.O. to 03 rank group re-sponded to the question, and of these comments sixteen were unfavorable, fifteen were a mixture of favorable and unfavorable remarks, six were completely favorable. The 04 and above rank group responded with forty-one com-ments, twenty-two of which were unfavorable, fourteen mixed, and five favorable. The percentages for all ranks in the study group were roughly as follows: 59.5 percent were unfavorable, 25.9 percent were mixtures of favorable and unfavorable remarks, and 14.6 percent were favorable.[28]

In response to the question, "How much have you personally liked the Turks?" the following data resulted (Table 17).

On the basis of participant-observation data, such com-ments as the following were heard from enlisted men and dependents:

I hate Turkey! They treat you like dirt, like Communists. Why they act as if they are better than we are!

220

TABLE 17

COMPARISON OF ATTITUDES TOWARD TURKS BY RANK GROUPS

	POSITION ON SCALE[a]											
	1 (Neg.)		2		3		4		5 (Pos.)		Total	
RANK	No.	%	No.	%	No.	%	No.	%	No.	%	No.	%
E.M.	13	16	26	32.1	22	27.2	15	18.5	5	6.2	81	100
W.O.–03	5	12.2	8	19.5	11	26.8	12	29.3	5	12.2	41	100
04–above	2	4.5	11	25	9	20.4	15	34.1	7	16	44	100
All ranks	20	12	45	27.1	42	25.3	42	25.3	17	10.3	166	100

[a] 1—Not at all; 2—Not so much; 3—Don't care either way; 4—Pretty much; 5—Very much.

Closure and Innovation in a Military Colony

I only have 139 days to go. I guess I can make it. I've had both my cars damaged. I have been cheated and lied about by these animals and no defense against them. I have been called names and spat upon for no other reason than being an American and being here. I have had to deal with the Turkish military and have never had so much frustration in my sixteen years of service. The Turkish nationals that work for the American Government as its contractors are a constant source of irritation to everybody by their attitudes—their anti-American attitudes.

Officer groups seemed to have greater verbal facility in justifying any prejudices, separatism, and lack of success in carrying out organizational missions that they had had:

There's no hope for Turkey to ever catch up with the Western world industrially or psychologically. Even the middle class has a peasant mentality.

There's no hope for Turks. No hope at all for these people. They are centuries behind, and they'll never catch up.

We can have an adult approach, but you have to have another adult on the other side to talk things over with. That's why it's hopeless.

It was interesting to note that the vocabulary of prejudice for some people was similar to that which was directed at minority groups in the United States; it had now been transferred to the Turks. One soldier wrote: "I have had no pleasant experiences in Turkey. To put it mildly, I don't care for Turks—they remind me of the niggers back home." Some said that they were "dirty," "stupid," and that they "smelled." Some categorized Turks as a "race," with the implication of genetic inferiority. Even when one woman felt a respect for some Turks, the stereotype remained: "I

222

have met some that are kind. Yet they all have the same blood." In the conversations of some Americans, derogatory expressions so inevitably preceded the word "Turk" as to become prefixes. For others, names dredged up from the past were used as shorthand characterizations, such as "The Terrible Turk" and "The Turk Barbarian." Sometimes a dichotomization of kinds of Turks was made on this basis: "The Terrible Turk," wild and free on the streets and in the shops, and "The Tamed Turk," who worked for Americans.

Counterstereotypes. In the study group, out of 144 comments 21, or 14.6 percent, where favorable. The most frequently used words to describe Turks by this group were, in order of frequency: (1) friendly and warm, (2) courteous and hard-working, (3) honest and fair.[29] Typical comments by rank groups are as follows:

From the enlisted rank group:

> They are friendly and very helpful. They'll go out of their way to assist you with any problem. If it hadn't been for Turks I would have been in sad shape upon arrival.

> They are very fine people. I worked with them in Korea.

From the W.O.–03 group:

> They are very friendly, warm, and outgoing people. They appear to be quite happy with their lives. They are very friendly with one another and usually friendly to Americans.

> They are very warm and friendly, very interested in you as another human being. They're extremely delighted when you compliment them on Turkey—a very proud people.

223

From the 04 and above group:

I would say they are friendly in social contact and willing to help you to know their ways when you yourself evince a sincere desire to know and like them.

They are short, dark, and very helpful outside of the city. Within the city, they are fairly overt in their dislike of Americans, but really with effort on your part they are likeable enough.

Some military members in the community, particularly those who spoke Turkish fluently and who had asked for reassignment to Turkey, were extraordinarily resistant to the prevalent stereotypes. One man, when told by American neighbors that they had just been spat on downtown, said he did not believe them, that he knew of no instances when Turks spit on people. Those who held counterstereotypes to be "true," received, of course, some support from the secondary military goal of good relations with Turks.

SUMMARY

The range of community members' attitudes toward Turks and toward social participation with them seemed to run the spectrum: from that expressed by one airman, who said with intense feeling that he would like to sit on a corner with a machine gun and "mow all the Turks down— men, women, and children," to the other polarity expressed by an officer, who said that Turks were infinitely nicer and more intelligent than Americans. The social climate of the military community gave little support to either expression, and the majority had taste for neither massacre nor paeans of praise.

For many of those who expressed ethnocentric sentiments, the reconciliation of these sentiments with the secondary organizational mission of good relations was achieved by the ideology of justification: that is, we can't get along with these people because they are thus and so. This was particularly the case in higher-rank levels. The logical construction of the community ideology was interesting to note: If Turks and Turkish culture were inferior, then why learn the language or the history? If Turks took advantage of Americans, were dishonest and treacherous, then the feeling that Americans were victimized was perfectly rational, and the following comment was appropriate to the situation: "When you pass a Turkish national on the street you don't know whether he is going to shake your hand or stab you in the back." If Turks were centuries behind Americans in technical, cultural, and psychological development, then lack of success in work and living together was justifiable.

Since the community situation was one in which anti-Turkish sentiments were fairly prevalent, and yet military controls and the contextual power situation were such that they could not be aggressively expressed, submerged hostility and the frantic desire to return to the United States and never again see Turkey were the only safe responses.

Extra-Community Innovation
on the Official Level

Under the rubric of people-to-people programs[30] the United States military establishment has worked to create favorable attitudes among host nation populations toward American military forces all over the world. The strategies used to achieve this goal have been primarily three: public relations offices have been set up to provide information about the United States and about the purposes of the American troops stationed in the country; aid and service to the host country have been furnished; interpersonal relationships between American military people and local people have been encouraged.

In recent years the community relations program in Ankara has been greatly restricted by political developments. During the Turkish Revolution of 1960 any overt actions on the part of American servicemen and dependents that could have been construed as favoring one side or the other were prohibited. The Cyprus crisis of 1963 and the subsequent intergroup tensions further restrained the development of a viable program. As a consequence, it had become one of expediency, a grasping at whatever opportunities arose.

Information programs were difficult to carry on, since the Turkish press and radio were not particularly cooperative. According to one information officer:

226

Publicity for our community gestures is not pro-American. Ankara is worse with its community relations program than any other place in Turkey. Maybe it's because it is the capital. Yet, I don't understand that either, because it also happens that there are more American personnel here than in any other place in Turkey.

Unable to set up a Turkish-American Community Council (a primary goal for public relations work overseas), the military groups directly responsible for good relations frantically cast about for some program that would either further their cause or appear to do so. They finally arrived at the idea of arranging air trips to Europe for various hand-picked, high-level Turkish groups, hoping that these people would feel sufficiently impressed and appreciative after the trip to go forth as friends of the United States. At the time of study only one trip had been taken, although a subsequent one was planned for a group of Turkish doctors. One officer glowingly described the trip as a kind of triumph:

> The idea is that the U.S. government at its own expense flies up a big group of Turks to see NATO areas and U.S. bases you see. So far we've done only one trip. We took up a group of Turkish Socialists, all with Ph.D.'s or near Ph.D.'s. Many of them had never been outside of Turkey. The effect was great! They were reading Marx and stuff like that when they flew up; but they weren't reading that stuff when they flew back.

The biggest and most organized civil-action program carried out by the United States forces[31] during the study period came about as a result of the series of earthquakes in Eastern Turkey in August, 1966. At least 2,300 Turks were killed and a similar number injured. American military groups from all over Turkey sent assistance. The mili-

Closure and Innovation in a Military Colony

tary forces in Ankara sent an emergency hospital, twenty medical people, and helped to airlift tons of hospital supplies. Many medical people in Ankara had to work overtime to fill the vacancies of those gone and to also aid in the necessary logistical support for the emergency units. Their efforts, according to medical service officers, were not recognized by either Turkish or American authorities.[32] Several medical officers expressed disgruntlement at the entire affair:

> One day they try to kill us, the next we're trying to help them.

> Americans are stupid. We're stoned on Friday, and Saturday we send medical support for a local disaster.

One of the usual approaches toward the improvement of intergroup relations at overseas posts has been that of the military units sponsoring a local orphanage, school, or some charitable organization. However, in Ankara none of the units seemed to be involved in this sort of program. As one high-ranking officer told me:

> No, we've been rather remiss with this. But there are many difficulties involved. For instance, we can't buy toys or candy from the PX because it is against Turkish customs laws.[33] Several times we have wanted to give ambulances— brand new ones—to the Turks. But they insisted we pay the customs, and we couldn't afford to do that.

Apparently, the only military unit as a group that had close relations with a Turkish group was the medical unit. They helped supply some of the Turkish hospitals with drugs; and there was a great deal of visiting and inspecting back and forth between administrators and doctors. There were particularly close relations between some of the American doctors and those Turkish doctors who had been trained in the United States.

228

Because of the lack of success in other areas, the primary official effort, I was told, became concentrated on encouraging friendships between Americans and Turks. The military orientations for newcomers and the periodic discussions by commanding officers, stressing respect for Turkish customs, religious holidays, and Ataturk, were expected to stimulate these friendships. "Counterpart programs" were seen as one of the most effective means toward this end: for example, a Turkish band and the Air Force band would be scheduled to play together; Turkish and American Boy Scout troops occasionally camped together; and it was hoped that the Host Nation Program in the schools would initiate exchange visits between Turkish and American classes.

Such organizations as the Turkish American Lawyers Association, Turkish-American Graduates of American Universities, the Turkish-American Association, and the Turkish-American Women's Cultural Association were also believed to provide the opportunities for making personal friendships.

Nonofficial Extra-Community Innovation

When all was said and done, there just wasn't a great deal of extra-community participation on the interpersonal level. The counterpart program took place pretty much between American groups and Turkish groups without a great deal of mingling between individuals. Turkish and American occupational counterparts would officially get together, such as the Turkish mayor and the American military base commander, but this usually occurred at the highest rank levels and seldom at the middle or lower rank levels. Even with the higher levels, it was an official relationship, infrequently becoming the basis for personal friendship. Officers and their wives were usually the only rank groups that participated in Turkish-American associations; enlisted men and their wives were seldom members. A few people taught English and English conversation to Turks, sometimes inviting students to their homes. There were instances of enlisted people playing cards or going on picnics with their landlords. The case of a sergeant who had organized a baseball team with Turkish teen-agers in an apartment complex in 1965 was still spoken of with wonderment in 1967. Nonetheless, it was generally believed in the military community that very few Americans and Turks had formed truly warm friendships. As one military authority said:

> The only Americans who do participate with Turks are those who have either been here from four to seven years, or those who were here four to seven years ago and have returned. They either had old Turkish friends or renewed old Turkish friendships and acquaintances. One thing I know, they made friends before, when diplomatic relationships were more cordial, and the Turks were more cordial to Americans as individuals.

The big thing for American military members was not to participate in the Turkish milieu but to get along in the American community. It was usually here, and here only, that status and personal friendships were sought.

Because of the highly noticeable enclaving tendencies of the American military community, little cultural acquisition of majority values and patterns occurred. Whatever acculturation did take place in the American military community was a highly selective process within the framework of community definitions of what was "acceptable." A few

GARRISON COMMUNITY

Turkish words penetrated into the vocabularies of community members, but most of these became so Americanized that they were almost unrecognizable as Turkish to a Turk. A Turkish gesture of disdain—a sharp lift of the head, coinciding with a click of the tongue and the rapid closing and opening of the eyes—was acquired by many Americans. American children, in particular, became proficient in this. A few kinds of foods, such as shish kebab, made their way onto American tables. Some Turkish items were bought: Turkish rugs were popular; brass and copper items were bought and used as decorative items, rather than for the purposes intended; the sharpened handmade dog collars that Turkish sheepherders used to protect their working dogs from wolves became an American rage for a time. Americans bought three or four of them, then draped them together as an abstract metal work of art.

In summary, truncated attempts at good intercommunity relations seemed to ineffectually drone on. But genuinely friendly intergroup or interpersonal relationships were the exception, rather than the rule. And hostility in either area tended to vitiate relationships in the other.

CLOSURE AND INNOVATION: AN ANALYTICAL SURVEY

In the first chapter a general hypothesis was posed, as follows:

Closure and innovation as community processes are related to community structure: differential patterns of closure and innovation are manifested by structural groups.

Six structural variables were considered relevant in the analytical survey and were examined in relation to extra-community participation. These were rank, education, marital status, age, time spent in the community, and career commitment. It was further hypothesized that extra-community innovation was related to inner-community innovation.

In this analysis two facets of the same problem were recognized as salient: not only the relationship between the structural position of the individual in the community and his attitudes toward participation, but also in a more general sense his relative centrality or peripherality of position in regard to the community structure as a whole. Thus it was hypothesized that core areas of extra-community participation in this overseas military community would be composed of those who had the highest ranks, were oldest, had the most years of formal education, were married with their families in Turkey with them, had lived in the community for the longest period of time, and who were committed to the military occupation as a lifetime career. The converse was proposed regarding marginal groups.

Throughout this study, rank was implicitly believed to be the primary antecedent or independent variable and innovation and closure the consequent or dependent variables. As noted previously, it was thought possible that rank would predominate as an indicator of structural effect, being directly derived from the central institution of the community. However, all of the structural variables were treated singly in order to more aptly discriminate relative effect and more accurately to ascertain theoretically relevant variables for future study.[34]

Rank Position and Innovation

A test for the possible relationship between rank position and extra-community participation was made, as presented in Table 18, yielding a chi-square of 36.76, significant

TABLE 18

DISTRIBUTION (PERCENT) OF EXTRA-
COMMUNITY PARTICIPATION TYPE
BY RANK OF RESPONDENT (N = 166)

RANK	High Participation		Medium Participation		Low Participation	
	No.	%	No.	%	No.	%
E.M.	12	14.8	26	32.1	43	53.1
W.O.–03	18	43.9	16	39.0	7	17.1
04–above	25	56.8	14	31.8	5	11.4

Chi-square (rank/extra-community participation) = 36.76   4 d.f. $p < .0001$.

TABLE 19

DISTRIBUTION (PERCENT) OF INNER-
COMMUNITY PARTICIPATION TYPE BY
RANK OF RESPONDENT (N = 166)

RANK	High Participation		Medium Participation		Low Participation	
	No.	%	No.	%	No.	%
E.M.	15	18.5	28	34.6	38	46.9
W.O.–03	15	36.6	15	36.6	11	26.8
04–above	25	56.8	12	27.3	7	15.9

Chi-square (rank/inner-community participation) = 22.18   4 d.f. $p < .001$.

233

with four degrees of freedom at <.0001. Apparently, as rank increases the amount of extra-community participation also increases, as indicated by the percentile distributions.

Because the structural variable of rank was considered highly important, it was also tested for its relationship to inner-community participation and found to be significant at <.001, having a chi-square of 22.18 with four degrees of freedom. The rank distribution of percentages indicates here, also, that the higher the rank, the more inner-community participation likely.

On the basis of observation, it is possible to tentatively suggest a few social factors contributing to these results. Role expectations for intragroup and intergroup innovation differ according to rank strata; and the higher the rank, the more extensive the role prescriptions for responsibility in these areas. In this overseas military milieu, higher-ranking personnel were obliged to affirm the need for intergroup participation; and, since intercommunity participation was stressed as an organizational goal (i.e., "duty"), cultural support was provided for certain efforts in this direction. Thus in some respects upper social strata were further legitimized in their positions by both Turks and Americans by acting as ethnic representatives to the Turkish community; and access to more and various channels of intergroup participation consequently existed for those in higher-ranking groups. Even where such participation did not offer individual satisfaction, most members of rank groups participated to the extent of acknowledged obligation. Those for whom neither extensive access nor obligations was operative —that is, the lower-ranking groups—participation was lim-

234

ited, more or less, to that which was defined as pleasurable. Hence, the more confined community members were to the narrow ethnic community and its set of standards and definitions, the fewer opportunities perceived for extra-community participation and the more overwhelming the pressure for conformity to these definitions.

Not only did the role obligations for external and internal participation differ between upper and lower rank groups, but in regard to extra-community participation the kinds and conditions of intergroup contacts also differed. For lower rank groups, intergroup contacts were far more frequently restricted to certain segments of the native population and to certain situational opportunities for interaction. It was possible that in more "Westernized" cultural settings (that is, in more technologically oriented and developed societies) these differences would not have had the importance that they had in Turkey, for the dissimilarities between equivalent cross-cultural strata would not have been so great. Upper strata Turks, those with whom higher-ranking American officers were likely to interact, were usually educated, spoke some English, and were knowledgeable, even sympathetic, in regard to Western technology and ideas. Whereas, lower strata Turks, those with whom lower-ranking American servicemen and their dependents were more likely to interact, were tied more often than not to the old traditions, less likely to speak English, far less knowledgeable in regard to Western ideas and technology, and possibly illiterate (Turkey's literacy rate was between 41 percent and 42 percent). Put differently, upper-ranking Americans and their Turkish counterparts were much more

Closure and Innovation in a Military Colony

similar than lower-ranking Americans and their Turkish counterparts; and at times the gap between the latter two groups was thought to be almost unbridgeable.

Conditions of intergroup contact were also likely to vary as to rank groups. In a military community where the relationships between people were often seen in the narrowly conceived terms of command and obedience, these power perspectives were sometimes adjusted to include the external milieu. Since lower-ranking American groups were more likely to see Turks doing what they considered to be lower-status jobs, working as janitors, servants, taxi drivers, or office subordinates, they often generalized their observations on the characteristics of and status relationships to these people to include all Turks. And, of course, when one was at the bottom of the hierarchical heap it was of no small psychological moment to feel superior to or "better than" somebody. On the other hand, higher-ranking American personnel, who were more likely to see and know higher-strata Turks, were more forcibly made aware that power relations were not one-sided. Suffice it to say, that the amount, the kinds, and the conditions of intergroup contact with the external milieu differed for the various American military strata.

To sum up, those of lower-ranking strata in the American military community had limited access to many segments of the Turkish population, and because of the gap in cultural understanding between themselves and those Turks with whom they were likely to interact and because of the lack of pleasure seen to be likely in these encounters, restriction to the American military community was more likely. This meant in effect that social space, as well as intergroup ties, was limited and that greater dependence upon the narrow community definitions possibly occurred; that is, social pressure for conformity to these definitions remained relatively unalleviated. In these respects, therefore, higher rank provided a degree of emancipation from the constrictions of the narrow ethnic-military world.

Inner-Community Participation and Extra-Community Participation

A comparison of test categories in the areas of inner-community participation and extra-community participation revealed that they were significantly associated at $<.01$ with 4 degrees of freedom and a chi-square of 17.18. It is apparent that those groups that participate most outside of the community also participate most inside the community (Table 20).

TABLE 20

DISTRIBUTION (PERCENT) OF EXTRA-COMMUNITY PARTICIPATION TYPE BY INNER-COMMUNITY PARTICIPATION TYPE ($N = 166$)

INNER-COMMUNITY PARTICIPATION TYPE	EXTRA-COMMUNITY PARTICIPATION TYPE					
	High Participation		Medium Participation		Low Participation	
	No.	%	No.	%	No.	%
High	22	40.0	23	41.8	10	18.2
Medium	19	34.5	21	38.2	15	27.3
Low	14	25.0	12	21.4	30	53.6

Chi-square (inner/extra-community participation) = 17.18   4 d.f. $p < .01$.

237

TABLE 21 ──────────────────────────────

DISTRIBUTION (PERCENT) OF EXTRA-
COMMUNITY PARTICIPATION TYPE BY
EDUCATION GROUPS ($N = 166$)

EDUCATION	High Participation		Medium Participation		Low Participation	
	No.	%	No.	%	No.	%
1–12 years	13	19.4	19	28.4	35	52.2
13–16 years	30	38.5	31	39.7	17	21.8
Graduate school	12	57.1	6	28.6	3	14.3

Chi-square (education/extra-community participation) = 22.31   4 d.f. $p < .001$.

Education and Extra-Community Participation

When the data are viewed from the perspective of
education, the relationship between years of education
achieved and extra-community participation appears. In a
comparison of the percentile distributions, it seems that
the more education the more extra-community participation
likely; or, conversely, the less education, the more closure
manifested toward participation likely.

Age and Extra-Community Participation

Age does not appear to be as clear-cut in its relationship to extra-community participation as does rank or education. However, the chi-square test of significance of difference between groups yielded 11.77, significant at the
.05 level with four degrees of freedom. It appears that the
youngest community members participated less than the
older members (Table 22).

TABLE 22

DISTRIBUTION (PERCENT) OF EXTRA-
COMMUNITY PARTICIPATION TYPE BY
AGE GROUPS (N = 166)

AGE	High Participation		Medium Participation		Low Participation	
	No.	%	No.	%	No.	%
17–25 years	9	19.1	15	31.9	23	49.0
26–39 years	29	34.5	29	34.5	26	31.0
40 and over	17	48.55	12	34.3	6	17.15

Chi-square (age/extra-community participation) = 11.77   4 d.f. $p < .05$.

Marital Status and Extra-Community Participation

The hypothesis that the structural variable of marital status was related to extra-community participation proved to be significant at the .01 level with a chi-square of 14.99 at four degrees of freedom. It should be noted, though, that it was further hypothesized that single individuals would participate the least. This was not the case. The marital status group most disaffected toward extra-community participation was that composed of married men stationed for a tour in Ankara *without* their families with them. Importantly, this group included not only those who had come to Turkey without their families, but also those who had come to Turkey with their families and for one reason or another had sent them back to the United States. As indicated by the percentage distributions, those who were married and had their families with them participated in the external community the most (Table 23).

239

TABLE 23

DISTRIBUTION (PERCENT) OF EXTRA-
COMMUNITY PARTICIPATION TYPE BY
MARITAL STATUS OF RESPONDENT ($N = 166$)

MARITAL STATUS	High Participation		Medium Participation		Low Participation	
	No.	%	No.	%	No.	%
Married w/o family	0	0	2	20.0	8	80.0
Single	11	27.5	12	30.0	17	42.5
Married w. family	44	38.0	42	36.2	30	25.8

Chi-square (marital status/extra-community participation) = 14.99   4 d.f. $p < .01$.

Military Career Commitment and Extra-Community Participation

Military career commitment was hypothesized to be related to extra-community participation. However, this variable was not found to be significantly related. Perhaps when

TABLE 24

DISTRIBUTION (PERCENT) OF EXTRA-
COMMUNITY PARTICIPATION TYPE BY
MILITARY CAREER COMMITMENT GROUPS ($N = 166$)

MILITARY CAREER COMMITMENT	High Participation		Medium Participation		Low Participation	
	No.	%	No.	%	No.	%
Committed	38	34.9	38	34.9	33	30.2
Undecided	8	36.4	9	40.9	5	22.7
Not committed	9	25.7	9	25.7	17	48.6

Chi-square (military career commitment/extra-community participation) = 5.30; 4 d.f.; not significant.

240

one reviews the results of Table 6 in Chapter 4 and notes that career commitment did not seem to be a particular property of any one rank group, it is not too surprising (Table 24).

Time in the Community and Participation

"Old timers," apparently, participated more in the external Turkish community than did newcomers. Whereas the dimension of time seemed to increasingly affect military community members in regard to extra-community participation, it did not seem to affect them to any significant degree in regard to inner-community participation. It is possible that as length of time of residence increased more avenues of approach to the foreign culture and external community opened up or became apparent to the individual; and he also, possibly, became more emancipated as time went on

TABLE 25

DISTRIBUTION (PERCENT) OF EXTRA-COMMUNITY PARTICIPATION TYPE BY TIME-IN-COMMUNITY GROUPS ($N = 166$)

TIME IN COMMUNITY	High Participation		Medium Participation		Low Participation	
	No.	%	No.	%	No.	%
New[a]	7	18.9	9	24.3	21	56.8
Middle[b]	27	30.4	28	34.2	24	35.4
Old[c]	21	42.0	19	38.0	10	20.0

Chi-square (time-in-community/extra-community participation) = 13.76   4 d.f. $p < .01$.
[a] Less than six months in the community.
[b] From six to eighteen months in the community.
[c] Over eighteen months in the community.

TABLE 26

DISTRIBUTION (PERCENT) OF INNER-
COMMUNITY PARTICIPATION TYPE BY
TIME-IN-COMMUNITY GROUPS (N = 166)

TIME IN COMMUNITY	High Participation		Medium Participation		Low Participation	
	No.	%	No.	%	No.	%
New[a]	7	18.9	15	40.55	15	40.55
Middle[b]	24	30.4	28	35.4	27	34.2
Old[c]	24	48.0	12	24.0	14	33.7

Chi-square (time-in-community/inner-community participation) = 8.79   4 d.f.   not significant.
[a] Less than six months in the community.
[b] From six to eighteen months in the community.
[c] Over eighteen months in the community.

from inner-community strictures. Whereas with inner-community participation, one may conjecture, the person's level of participation did not vary greatly from military post to military post (Tables 25, 26).

Summary of Findings

It can be concluded from the preceding analyses that the hypothesis is tenable in regard to the American military community in Ankara: certain structural variables, those of rank, education, marital status, age, and time spent in the community are related to community innovation and, by implication, to community closure. Career commitment in this overseas context was not significantly related to extra-community participation.

On the basis of these findings, it appears that the core areas of extra-community participation were composed of those groups which had the highest rank, the most education, were married with their families in Turkey, were older and had spent the longest time in the community. Marginal areas of extra-community participation were composed of those groups which had the lowest ranks, the fewest years of formal education, were married without their families in Ankara with them, were younger, and had spent the least time in the overseas community.

It should be restated that in higher rank the interaction of such variables as more education, older age, and accompanied overseas tours is more likely to occur. Of course, career commitment appeared not to be necessarily an attribute of any one rank group; and time spent in the community was an internal variant of all the structural groups. It is suggested, therefore, that rank might be considered a key variable in this context; while the other structural variables found to be significantly related to innovation and closure—education, age, marital status, and time in the community—might tend to determine the *kinds* of innovation engaged in. On the basis of the frequency distributions, it appeared that the direction of closure was as follows: closure increased as rank became lower; closure increased with less education; closure increased with youthfulness; and the less time spent in the community, the more closure manifested. The converse appears to be the case with innovation.

A Comparison of the Highest and the Lowest Extra-Community Participators

A comparison of several of the characteristics and attitudes of the five highest and the five lowest extra-community participators was made in order to ascertain distinctive differences or similarities between these two groups of "deviants." (See Table 27.)

TABLE 27

COMPARISON OF THE CHARACTERISTICS OF HIGHEST AND LOWEST EXTRA-COMMUNITY PARTICIPATORS

CHARACTERISTICS	Highest Participators (N = 5) (Score Range: 89–78)		Lowest Participators (N = 5) (Score Range: 22–20)	
Rank	04 and above =	4 (80%)	E.M.	5 (100%)
	W.O.–03	1 (20%)		
Education	Graduate school	3 (60%)	9–12 years	5 (100%)
	13–16 years	2 (40%)		
Age	26–39 years	4 (80%)	17–25 years	3 (60%)
	40 and over	1 (20%)	26–39 years	2 (40%)
Marital status	Married with family in Turkey	5 (100%)	Married with family in Turkey	3 (60%)
			Married without family in Turkey	2 (40%)
Career commitment	Committed	4 (80%)	Committed	1 (20%)
	Not committed	1 (20%)	Undecided	2 (40%)
			Not committed	2 (40%)
Religion	Protestant	4 (80%)	Protestant	4 (80%)
	Jewish	1 (20%)	Catholic	1 (20%)
Length of time in Turkey	Less than 6 months[a]	1 (20%)	Less than 6 months	2 (40%)
	6–18 months	2 (40%)	6–18 months	3 (60%)
	Over 18 months	1 (20%)		

244

TABLE 27 (continued)

COMPARISON OF THE CHARACTERISTICS OF HIGHEST AND LOWEST
EXTRA-COMMUNITY PARTICIPATORS

CHARACTERISTICS	Highest Participators (N = 5) (Score Range: 89–78)		Lowest Participators (N = 5) (Score Range: 22–20)	
Had had other overseas assignments	Yes	4 (80%)	Yes	3 (60%)
	No	1 (20%)	No	2 (40%)
Previously visited or assigned to Turkey	Yes	3 (60%)	No	5 (100%)
	No	2 (40%)		
Requested Turkey for assignment	Yes	3 (60%)	No	5 (100%)
	No	2 (40%)		
Self-judged Turkish language ability	Fluent	2 (40%)	"Kitchen"	1 (20%)
	Good	2 (40%)	A few words	1 (20%)
	"Kitchen"	1 (20%)	Not a word	3 (60%)
Interest in learning more Turkish	Yes	3 (60%)	No	5 (100%)
	No answer[b]	2 (40%)		

[a] This was the man's third tour in Turkey.
[b] These two men judged they spoke Turkish fluently.

Closure and Innovation in a Military Colony

It is apparent in perusing the following paired characteristics that the two groups differed greatly in the areas of education and rank. It is interesting to note that three of the five highest participators had had previous assignments in Turkey and that three of the five had requested Turkey for assignment. None of the five lowest participators had been to Turkey previously, nor had they requested assignment there. The self-judged language abilities and the interest evinced in learning more Turkish differed greatly between the highest and the lowest extra-community participators.

NOTES

1. According to the *Ankara Daily News* (August 31, 1966), in 65 percent of the cases of American military personnel offenses in foreign nations from November, 1964, to November, 1965, the governments waived jurisdiction. This, however, was not the case in Turkey, according to various American official sources. One official said: "Never have we been able to get American personnel involved in an incident released to the American military jurisdiction for punishment. Always they have to go through Turkish legal processes, ending up in Turkish court about 99 percent of the time." However, this was true only when the incidents involved Turkish nationals or occurred on Turkish property. "When there are problems between Americans, the Turks usually dislike handling them, feeling that Americans

should clean up their own messes." According to the Air Police officer, it was the general philosophy of the Air Police "to keep Americans out of Turkish courts, if at all possible."

2. Ataturk furnished Turkey with a new legal system, taking civil law almost in its entirety from France and criminal law from Italy.

3. The chances of getting into an automobile accident in Turkey were greater than in many countries. "Turkey has thirteen times more traffic accidents annually than the United States, it was disclosed this week in the traffic seminar held by the Communications Ministry. The figures further show that Turkey is the leading country in the world in traffic accident rates" (*Ankara Daily News,* April 5, 1967).

4. Almost all of the young military legal officers who were directly involved in the American legal cases were extremely bitter about the Turkish court system, its rules of evidence, and its frequent "miscarriages of justice" when it came to American military personnel. Most of these young men had just graduated from law school before going into the military service.

5. Rarely did an American military person live in an ostentatious fashion according to American standards, but when it did occur it was rather embarrassing to other Americans. At the extremely lush apartment of one American general, a colonel was asked by two Turkish generals: "Do American generals live this way even in the United States?"

6. The account of this riot is based on the reports from the several Turkish English-language newspapers and on information given to me by military members. I have attempted to eliminate emotional interpretations and hearsay from the account. However, while I was in Ankara American military authorities had classified all information about it as a military secret; and, consequently, there was no official American version extant.

7. *Ankara Daily News,* November 14, 1966, p. 1; *The Week,* November 18, 1966, p. 7.

8. *London Times,* November 15, 1966, p. 1.

9. *Stars and Stripes,* November 15, 1966, p. 1.

10. Don Martindale, *Institutions, Organizations, and Mass Society* (Boston: Houghton Mifflin Company, 1965), p. xv.

11. I do not know how many American secret units were stationed in Ankara or for what purposes. These units were extremely resistant to probing. However, during the course of study, I kept stumbling on agents from Detachment X or Y or Z. It is interesting or appalling, depending on one's turn of mind, that "watchers," hardly a modern phenomenon, were historically felt to be sufficiently dangerous as to merit watching themselves, or as Juvenal put it: "Who will watch the watchers? (*Quis custodiet ipsos custodes?*)"

12. In trying to carry out this study, several agents applied all of the latter set of labels to me. After gaining approval from Washington, D.C., for this study, I ran into one agent, seemingly nonplused, who said: "I wish my Russian counterpart would give me a questionnaire, just like what you're doing against the Americans. That's the trouble with a democracy."

13. *TUSLOG Daily Bulletin,* May 24, 1967.

14. There is a branch-wide Air Force prohibition against "nonauthorized surveys" which this might have come under: "A commander will *not* permit private individuals or private organizations to conduct surveys, polls, or opinion studies within his command without HQ USAF authorization" ("Air Force Sample Surveys," *Air Force Regulation,* 171–172, 25 May 1966, Section A, Paragraph 1, d.).

15. Apparently, to ask questions about chapel activities seemed to him to be either a sign of subversion or of madness.

16. "The Psychology of Punitive Justice," in *Sociological Theory,* 2nd ed., ed. Lewis Coser and Bernard Rosenberg (New York: Macmillan Company, 1964), pp. 596–597.

248

17. "Anti-Americanism," *Outlook,* November 28, 1966, p. 5.

18. American Ambassador to Turkey, the Honorable Parker T. Hart, "Americans in Turkey," speech given to an AID Orientation Meeting, October 31, 1966.

19. Even those who were best informed by the *Stars and Stripes* and by the military air network might have been shaken in the last year or so on *how well* they were informed. Commencing, I believe, in March, 1967, articles entitled as follows might have made them doubt: "Pentagon Admits Censoring Paper," *New York Times,* International Edition, March 6, 1967, p. 1; "Military Super-Censor," ibid., March 8, 1967, Editorial; "Armed Forces Net News Curb Denied," *Denver Post,* November 26, 1967, p. 13; etc.

20. The need for a community press was felt by several military professionals. In response to their request, military authorities permitted *Ankara TUSLOG,* the official weekly newspaper of TUSLOG, to be given a new name, *Anatolian Times.* However, other than the facade, the substance seemed to remain unchanged: *esprit de corps* and unit type of articles, official pronouncements, precautionary warnings, and public relations work for higher-ranking officers.

21. These agencies were as follows: Mutual Security Branch of the Embassy, Air Police, Security and Law Enforcement Agency, and Office of Information.

22. *Ankara Daily News,* February 15, 1967, p. 1.

23. *TUSLOG Daily Bulletin,* No. 188, October 19, 1966.

24. *TUSLOG Daily Bulletin,* Nos. 193 and 194, October 26 and 27, 1966.

25. An example of this was mentioned earlier: information about the station-wagon riot in Ankara was classified as a military secret. So people read Turkish, British, and American newspaper

accounts; and the gap between knowledge and fear was bridged by fabrication.

26. Gardner Murphy's concept of "socially shared autism" would be particularly germane in an analysis of this situation. The term refers to social circumstances in which members of a social group develop considerable confidence in their beliefs about something with which they no longer have any contact (*Personality: A Biosocial Approach to Origin and Structure* [New York: Harper & Brothers, 1947]).

27. It is believed that differential conditions and types of contact with the external group were also important in this regard.

28. An example of what was considered a mixed or equivocal comment is as follows: "A basic, hardworking, resourceful group of people. They are loyal to friends, eager to learn, and receptive in most cases. Majority are juvenile and childish in actions and basic development."

29. Included in this group were those who said that there was no such person as an "average Turk."

30. This type of program, commenced in 1956 by the military establishment, has gone under other names, as well: such as troop-community relations, civil-action programs, and civic-action programs. Stipulations for the community relations program in the Air Force have been codified into a regulation (AFR 190–20) and are further supplemented on the theater and local levels.

31. This emergency relief program cost the United States government approximately one million dollars.

32. However, TUSLOG and its public relations section did receive commendation: "TUSLOG was recognized as the best world-wide in the military group for its emergency public relations program in coverage of the Turkish earthquake (by the

250

Public Relations Society of America in New York City on May 18, 1966)." *Anatolian Times,* May 19, 1967, pp. 1–3.

33. It should be noted that both candy and toys can be bought on the Turkish market.

34. The appendix on methods may be consulted for a discussion of the design and methods used in this analytical survey.

6

PROBLEMS AND PROSPECTS OF THE GARRISON COMMUNITY: A SUMMARY

This study has been concerned with an overseas ethnic-military community and its processes of closure and innovation. The argument has been that patterns of closure and innovation are community-mediated, and that the effect of this mediation is internally differentiated in respect to structural groups. Viewed from within the context of community theory, this subcommunity was believed to manifest certain peculiarities derived from its predominant military institutions and from its ethnic situation in a foreign milieu.

In some respects it appeared that tendencies of resistance to extra-community innovation were endemic to the military system, and that these tendencies were even further intensified in the overseas ethnic-community situation.

THE MILITARY COMMUNITY

The corporative quality of the military organization, engendered and reinforced by the occupational mystique and ideology, the unique mission, the military way of life, in itself implies that certain boundaries exist between the corporative group and the external milieu.[1] Such boundaries, it is believed, became even more sharply delineated when the military organization formed into a community of its own in Ankara, and when, as a consequence, group ties were narrowed and rotation policies and rank structure made for a highly controlled transient population, socially and psychologically dependent upon the main institution.

The history of the community was one of growing numbers, of expanding facilities, of ever greater self-sufficiency, and of increasing isolation from Turkish life. It would seem that a cycle was instituted: the less extra-community participation necessary, the more cultural isolation, and the increasing dependence on narrowed community interpretations of the external situation, and so on. The mechanisms of community socialization served to reproduce attitudes that became increasingly solipsistic. And with isola-

Problems and Prospects of the Garrison Community: A Summary

tion, relations with the outer community tended to become more externalized and antagonistic. The military organization responded to this developing situation by reducing the possibilities of contact between community members and Turks. In a way, perhaps, the consequent inability of many community members[2] to join in activities outside of the community was seen, at least in principle, as a virtue of solidarity in the military community. And in some cases acts of closure became covertly translated in the community idiom into moral acts.

It is possible that the community members, who were more or less dependent on and restricted to the narrow military-ethnic community, barred from the diversity and interest of the wider milieu by walls of ethnocentrism, pejorative generalizations, and anxiety, were responding in part to the tensions and frustrations generated in this social climate by feeling hostile toward the outside group.[3] Feelings of hostility seemed to be more frequently in evidence in lower-ranking groups, but pressures for conformity and restriction to the community, it is believed, were also greater here.

As sociologists have pointed out, people are always the prisoners of established social systems, but the degree of imprisonment or, conversely, emancipation varies with the society—or, in this case, with the community. When the social frame of reference was further contracted by the totalization and pressures of military requirements within and by conflictual relations without, the community way of life became one of intense provincialism. Lacking the rich diversity of the wider American culture and entrance to the Turkish culture, the community with its government

254

stores and facilities, its "command performance" type of social life, its occupational limitations could perhaps be best characterized by the terms of homogeneity, rigidity, conformism, and intense closure against the penetration of external definitions.[4]

SITUATIONAL FORCES

Although the situational context was treated in a rather cursory fashion, it must be noted that the international situation and the diplomatic relations between the United States and Turkey set the stage upon which the community drama was played out. On the basis of national interpretations of such relationships, individual Americans in Turkey were often judged by Turks (and vice versa) as representatives of these policies and treated accordingly.[5]

It should also be stressed that certain aspects of the cultural milieu such as the extent of cultural differences between the two groups contributed to the general tenor of intergroup relations. The importance of the cultural gap should not be underestimated. The relative incongruence of the two cultures and the extent of extra-community closure were to some degree related. Moreover, most of the military Americans going overseas had been neither educated for nor interested in the development of broad and deep contacts and sympathies with the host nationals and their culture. Sentiments which might have taken them past the surface im-

Problems and Prospects of the Garrison Community: A Summary

pressions had not been encouraged. Negative evaluations are, perhaps, more likely in a "developing" country, with few of the material amenities of highly industrialized countries. Furthermore, differences in culture, particularly religious culture, tended to make some Americans view Turkey as a repressive and austere land, offering few pleasures or inducements to balance against the cultural difficulties of venturing out. Many of the channels that are effectively utilized in other milieus as catharsis for internally generated tensions were not seen as available in Ankara. The problem of simultaneous living in two culture worlds was solved, on the whole, by rejection of the foreign culture and subjection to the familiar culture.[6]

CLOSURE AND INNOVATION IN STRUCTURAL GROUPS

The most unequivocal findings of the study concern the relationship between structural groups and patterns of extra-community participation. The findings that certain structural groups in the community participated more than other structural groups was far from unusual and must be seen as supplementary to the numerous studies which preceded it.[7] The variables of education, occupation, income, length of residence, and age have previously been analytically demonstrated as related to participation in community affairs; and the results of many of these studies have emphasized that

256

members of higher socioeconomic classes more frequently tend to participate in voluntary associations than do members of lower socioeconomic classes. The similarities between the results of the analytical survey undertaken here and such studies are obvious, the difference primarily lying in the concern of this study with *extra*-community participation in an overseas setting,[8] rather than with internal participation in a domestic setting.

In interpreting these results in the light of participant observation experience, it appeared to me, as it has to other researchers, that role prescriptions and expectations differed for the various structural groups. It also appeared to me that the opportunities and conditions for contact with the majority community differed according to structural groups. It was interesting that although lower-ranking groups lived more frequently in areas with a higher composition of Turks than did higher-ranking groups, interpersonal relationships with these host nationals seemed, on the whole, to be more attenuated and often filled with tension. Thus, although the amount of contact possible for lower-ranking groups might well have been greater, the conditions of contact, the types of contact, and the attitudes toward contact differed somewhat from those of upper ranking groups.

Of course, only tentative conclusions can be drawn on the basis of an analytical survey, but the findings of the study suggest that so pervasive a tendency toward closure in lower-ranking groups as compared with higher-ranking groups might be primarily explained in terms of community organization, and only secondarily in terms of local conditions, differences in culture, and particular personalities.

Problems and Prospects of the Garrison Community: A Summary

Unless the international situation changes or American foreign policy changes, the likelihood of continued military assistance to Turkey and of American troops remaining there is great. Prognostications of the future are reflected in the words of Ambassador Parker T. Hart: "Our military program will be here as long as we supply military hardware to the Turks; and the Turks clearly need it for years ahead."[9] More recently, Secretary of Defense Clark M. Clifford, in reporting to the Senate Committee on Foreign Relations, declared that military aid to Turkey, Greece, and Iran must be continued because: "If the nations of Eastern Europe are beginning to feel a desire to exert greater freedom, it would be desirable not to rock our boat." He explained that we need "to present a united front in that part of the world" by helping Turkey and the other countries in order to "impress the European nations."[10]

If these statements can be considered accurate predictions of the future, then there is little reason to assume that the tenure of the American military community in Ankara will soon come to an end. Nor, based on the data, is there reason to assume that the relations between American military members and Turks will become miraculously devoid of tensions. When I left Ankara in June, 1967, there were no indications that either community was taking ameliorative measures in this direction, and it is hard to imagine that without deliberate and highly effective action the cycle will be interrupted.

Thus one can only anticipate that criticisms of these overseas Americans will continue to be warranted and forthcoming. In the past much of the criticism has had to do with the ineffectiveness and lack of success of the individuals sent overseas or, at best, of the reprehensible behavior of groups of individuals sent overseas. It is my belief that this kind of criticism has been an irrelevant nibbling on the fringes. The problem is *not* that the United States sometimes sends ill-equipped individuals overseas—but, rather, it is the *way* they are sent. The plethora of difficulties that exist between host nationals and American military people is not alone attributable to individual cross-cultural intolerance and misunderstandings. I believe that the problem is primarily *structural,* and only secondarily cultural.[11]

Viewed from this perspective, a basic question must be asked: Is it realistic to expect the military community to be politically useful in the overseas context as other than a highly organized instrument of force? The official assumption that the military community can pursue its military mission on the one hand, and yet, on the other, effectively undertake the mission of good relations with the host community and even be an adequate representative of a democratic country appears to me to be a contradiction in terms. Given the military organization as it is, it seems more likely that its response to the external community would be preponderately that of closure;[12] and to expect an organization which is characterized by authoritarianism, barracks neatness, and hierarchical order to represent other than just that seems dangerously naive and quixotic.

Seymour Martin Lipset once said: "If the influence of the military becomes predominant, America will be a different nation. Under such conditions the American Demo-

Problems and Prospects of the Garrison Community: A Summary

cratic experiment could very well end."[13] It is my belief that *where* this influence is the predominant one in American communities overseas, it must appear to the host country that the democratic experiment has indeed already ended. The plurality of ideas and of influences, the argument and the dissent, the air of freedom and of civil liberty known in the United States do not prevail in the Garrison Community.

NOTES

1. For a discussion of the "corporate group," see Max Weber, *The Theory of Social and Economic Organization,* trans. A. M. Henderson and Talcott Parsons (New York: Oxford University Press, 1947), pp. 145–146.

2. The so-called "language barrier" was believed to be a "sufficient" but far from "necessary cause" for intergroup misunderstandings. American military people were in Ankara for a long enough period to learn the language and overcome the barrier if they had so desired. As with any foreign language, Turkish is difficult but not impossible to learn.

3. Leon Festinger and Harold H. Kelley (*Changing Attitudes Through Social Contact* [Ann Arbor, Michigan: Research Center for Group Dynamics, Institute for Social Research, University of Michigan, September, 1951]) did an extremely interesting study of the relations between people in a housing project and in the central town, suggesting that such relations had developed

into a pattern, which they called the "hostile-isolation syndrome." Some of their conclusions, I believe, are applicable to this study. If anything, in Ankara a kind of community paranoia, if I might use the term, had evolved, on the basis of which fear and hostility toward what was seen as organized outer-group persecution was, perhaps, appropriate.

4. R. A. Nisbet once observed that one of the most underrated social forces in history was sheer boredom. Although located in the middle of a rather exciting foreign country, surely few modern communities could have been as intellectually dull as this one was, and boredom might well have contributed to the general climate of irritation and ill will.

5. Naturally, closure toward the out-group was not a phenomenon unique to the American military community. As it was occasionally and briefly illustrated in the foregoing pages, closure against the penetration of certain American cultural traits was also evinced by the Turkish community.

6. John Gillen's study of "Parallel Cultures and the Inhibitions to Acculturation in a Guatamalan Community" (*Sociological Analysis*, ed. Logan Wilson and William L. Kolb [New York: Harcourt, Brace and Company, 1949], pp. 95–100), is illuminating in this regard. He suggests that two groups of people "can live side by side in the same community for centuries without achieving cultural amalgamation. Unless the *conditions* of the learning and performance of customs in this community are significantly changed, this situation will persist indefinitely" (p. 110).

7. William Kornhauser (*The Politics of Mass Society* [New York: Free Press, 1959], pp. 70–72), summarizes fourteen studies which demonstrated that social participation was related to socioeconomic status. James E. Teele ("An Appraisal of Research on Social Participation," *Sociological Quarterly* 6 [Summer, 1965]:257–267), has also listed a number of studies in this area. These lists, of course, are by no means exhaustive.

261

For example, the following are helpful in indicating the general design such studies have used: Leonard Reissman, "Class, Leisure, and Social Participation," *American Sociological Review* 19 (February, 1954):76–84; Charles M. Bonjean, "Mass, Class, and the Industrial Community: A Comparative Analysis of Managers, Businessmen, and Workers," *American Journal of Sociology* 72 (September, 1966):149–162; Wendell Bell and Maryanne T. Force, "Social Structure and Participation in Different Types of Formal Associations," *American Sociological Review* 21 (February, 1956):25–34; Morris Axelrod, "Urban Structure and Social Participation," *American Sociological Review* 21 (February, 1956): 13–18; John Foskett, "Social Structure and Social Participation," *American Sociological Review* 20 (August, 1955):431–438; Peter M. Blau, "Structural Effects," *American Sociological Review* 25 (April, 1960):178–193; Robert C. Angell, "The Moral Integration of American Cities," *American Journal of Sociology* (July, 1951):94–100; C. R. Wright and H. H. Human, "Voluntary Association Memberships of American Adults; Evidence from National Sample Surveys," *American Sociological Review* 23 (June, 1958):284–294; B. G. Zimmer, "Participation of Migrants in Urban Structures," *American Sociological Review* 20 (April, 1955):218–224.

8. Charles C. Moskos, Jr. ("Racial Integration in the Armed Forces," *American Journal of Sociology* 72 [September, 1966]: 132–148), stated that observers of overseas American personnel had told him that Negro soldiers were more likely than whites to learn the local language. In Germany, for example, his data revealed "that there is an inverse correlation between formal education (as ascertained from battalion personnel records) and likelihood of learning German! This reflects the greater likelihood of Negro soldiers, compared to whites, to learn German while averaging fewer years of formal education." This was one of the very few studies that indicated an inverse relationship between education and the participation necessary to informally learn the language of a foreign country.

262

9. Ambassador Parker T. Hart, "Americans in Turkey," speech given to an AID Orientation Meeting, October 31, 1966.

10. "Mr. Clark Clifford Out in the Open," *The New Republic,* June 1, 1968, pp. 9–10.

11. At last, voices from sociology are suggesting that societies of the "Third World" be conceived primarily as structural and institutional systems differing from those that have prevailed from anthropology. See, for example, the following: Norman Jacobs, *The Sociology of Development: Iran as an Asian Case Study* (New York: Frederick A. Praeger, 1966); Gunnar Myrdal, *Asian Drama* (New York: Pantheon Books, 1967); Charles C. Moskos, Jr., "Research in the 'Third World,' " *Trans-action* 5 (June, 1968) :2–3.

12. Of course, secondary adjustments and adaptations are possible. Perhaps manipulated changes of extra-community perceptions might be undertaken by several means. An extensive and well-planned educational program could be presented prior to leaving for an overseas post and during the entire tour overseas for each military member. Also "targets for change" might be carefully selected from the contemporary community and given intensive courses. Programs for regular intergroup contacts providing conducive conditions for intergroup friendship and respect might be set up. And so on and on. How truly effective these would be I do not know. Surely some of these ideas have been tried elsewhere, and yet reports of American military and local population problems continue to resound from almost every place the American military forces have gone.

13. Seymour Martin Lipset and Irving Louis Horowitz, "The Birth and Meaning of America: A Discussion of *The First New Nation,*" *Sociological Quarterly* 7 (Winter, 1966) :5.

Problems and Prospects of the Garrison Community: A Summary

APPENDIXES

APPENDIX 1

METHODS
OF STUDY

Three methods of procuring data were utilized in this study: participant observation, interviewing, and an analytical survey. It was believed that by accumulating data in these ways, three sources would be tapped which would not only tend to complement one another but also would serve as mutual checks upon one another. It was thought that the first two means would provide insight into the processes operative in many facets of community life; the third, or statistical means, would enable the researcher to ascertain with much greater certainty the location and the incidence of the processes. Together, it was hoped, they would do the following: first, indicate variables which were theoretically relevant in the ethnic community context; and second, help to portray an overseas community within the narrowed perspective of openness and closure.

PARTICIPANT OBSERVATION

As a participant observer, using noncontrolled or non-structured observation as a methodological tool,[1] I lived in the military community in Ankara for two years. Entering the community or explaining my presence posed no special difficulty, since I was there as a military dependent. The second year of this kind of observation, however, was somewhat more difficult, since by that time I had become known as an observer, due to the problems I had encountered in procuring official approval for the survey. In some ways, however, this "ill wind" did blow some good, because as a consequence some information was given to me that probably would not have been.

On the whole, the data that I collected by using this method came from observation of overt behavior and from verbal interaction and inference of meaning. I participated in any and all community activities as time and circumstances allowed. Every evening I recorded the notes I had jotted down in odd places and at odd times during the day. I attempted to systematize these somewhat by dividing the factual details of the observation—who, what, when, where —from my interpretations of these situations. Frequent analyses of these notes seemed to be quite necessary in order to see where weak points and gaps lay and to see where the information seemed to be taking me.

There are a plethora of problems involved in immersing oneself in a community of one's own kind. The core of these problems lies in the ever-present struggle to maintain

268

detachment and in the limits situationally imposed on one, delineating the spectrum of potential data. The range of observation possible for me tended at times to become restricted in this highly structured community: military people wanted to know not only who I was and what I did, but most important where I fitted in—that is, the precise rank category of my husband.

The twin difficulties of time and involvement tended to blunt perception. It is a truism to mention, but nonetheless essential, that the longer I remained in the community the more usual became the unusual, the freshness of the first-seen tended to stale with continual contact. Furthermore, one is likely to make friends, to feel sympathetic with those whom one meets and talks to. So there was the never-ending problem of how to skirt the quagmire of distance and imputation on the one hand and involvement which dulls perception with intimacy and identification on the other. It was curious but at times the force of the prevailing way of seeing events became so overwhelming that only in leaving the community for a few days or spending time in the old section of town by myself could this be overcome. If nothing else, it made me aware of how difficult it was to live in a tight little community and remain independent and aloof from the climate of opinion.

There are the further ethical considerations of reconciling one's role as investigator or observer with the role of participant: Do research considerations justify the disregard of personal obligations of secrecy and trust? Do they justify doing things as an observer that one would not ordinarily do? I felt they did not. In some ways, this limited my data, but it was my belief that an expedient attitude was dangerous in the long run, unethical both professionally and personally. The words of William F. Whyte served me well, I think:

> [One] cannot afford to think only of learning to live with others in the field. He has to continue living with himself. If the participant observer finds himself engaged in behavior that he has learned to think of as immoral, then he is likely to begin to wonder what sort of a person he is after all.[2]

This brings me to a final problem, which in a way encompasses many of the foregoing. Participant observation in one's own milieu has highly subjective implications for oneself. The weighing and reweighing of each event, the striving for emotional and intellectual honesty, the summing up make for an intense awareness of self, bringing up questions of one's own identity, one's own place in the community setting.

However, with all the disadvantages, participant observation did give insight, did give access to sources for intimate, detailed material that would not ordinarily have been available; and, perhaps most important, it helped to give the dimension of time that would not have been possible in a cross-sectional study.

INTERVIEWS

A number of interviews were undertaken during the course of study in Ankara, primarily in order to fill in the gaps of information regarding certain segments of community life. On the whole, they were carefully planned interviews with individuals especially qualified to give information on particular phases of the community. The schedules utilized differed, depending on the person with whom I planned to talk and the information I wished to elicit. From the interviews were gained, for example, detailed data on official patterns of action, on rumors, on events, and on how these were seen, rationalized, and discussed.

ANALYTICAL SURVEY

The Research Design

The design[3] of the study was cross-sectional, resting on a comparison of structural groups, delineated by means of the questionnaire, and the variable of extra-community participation, which was determined by individual and group scalar scores.

The sample design chosen to be used was a stratified random sample. Basically, two groups were distinguished: enlisted men and officers. The rationale for this choice was grounded in the belief that rank was of the utmost importance in a study of this kind, and it was thought to be associated with (or equivalent to) socioeconomic status. Since one hundred officers and one hundred enlisted men were selected for the sample, it is apparent that officers, in comparison with their representation in the community, made up a disproportionate number in the sample. This was the case because particular interest was attached to the difference between the two groups in terms of their social participation. Officers were further stratified into two groups: a W.O. to 03 rank group $(N = 50)$; an 04 and above rank group $(N = 50)$.

The population from which the sample was drawn in the autumn of 1966 was that of all the American military men and women stationed in Ankara at that time. The exact size of the adult population was unknown, even though the total population, including children, I believe, was estimated to be 5,126 people. The sample, therefore, was thought to be roughly 5 percent of the total adult population. It was randomly selected from the only available complete list of all military personnel: the Emergency Area Wardens' List. Each adult name listed was given a number; then a Table of Random Numbers was employed as the basis of selection. The only problem encountered was, of course, that a larger number of enlisted men's names than needed was drawn before the requisite number of officers. Therefore a sub-sample of one hundred names was subsequently drawn from the original sample of enlisted men. This was also necessary for the 04 and above rank group, since it took much sampling before arriving at the designated number of fifty names for the W.O.–03 rank group.

Chi-square (χ^2) was selected as the statistical tool to test the significance of the relationship between the structural variables and the variable of participation. It was chosen because it would permit statistical manipulation of nonparametric data and would also weigh each case in the distribution proportionately to every other case. The 5 percent level of probability was adopted as the criterion of significance.

The Research Instrument

The research instrument,[4] a precoded questionnaire, consisted of basically three parts: (1) a partially or completely structured set of questions and a few open-ended questions from which demographic, ecological, and other descriptive information were derived; (2) an extra-community participation scale; (3) an inner-community participation scale. The development of these scales was based on the work of some of the pioneers in this field.[5] These scales were constructed to operationally represent the variables of extra-community participation and inner-community participation. The scales were precoded by scores of one to five in an attempt to disperse individuals along a continuum—that is, in a rank order of positions.

The two sets of scales are primarily of the ordinal type. However, in addition to ordinal scales, the instruments contain some partially ordered scales of the nominal type. The extra-community participation scale contains two nominal scales out of a total of twenty-two items (questions 39 and 41); the inner-community participation scale contains one nominal scale (question 37) from a total of fifteen items. In scales of the ordinal type the relative position of individuals is defined with respect "to a characteristic, with no implication as to distance between positions."[6] Whereas, with nominal scales there is no implication, of course, that responses indicate more or less of the characteristic being measured, consisting only of "two or more named categories, into which objects or individuals or responses are classified."[7]

The scaled questions were designed to be representative of most phases of social participation available for military personnel in Ankara. The extra-community participation scale is composed of twenty-two items, designed to assess the amount and type of participation and attitudes toward participation, as follows:

1. Associations: membership
2. Associations: positions
3. Associations: volunteer or committee work
4. Associations: time spent in committee or volunteer work
5. Turkish language: study of the language
6. Turkish language: self-judged ability to speak Turkish
7. Turkish language: self-judged ability to read and write
8. Knowledge about Turkey: newspapers and magazines read
9. Knowledge about Turkey: books read
10. Participation: cultural events
11. Participation: sport events
12. Participation: night clubs
13. Participation Preferences: Turkish restaurants
14. Participation Preferences: Turkish guests
15. Commensalism: being invited by Turks to their homes

274

16. Commensalism: inviting Turks to the home
17. Neighboring patterns: frequency of visits to homes of Turkish neighbors
18. Friendship patterns: number of Turkish friends
19. Friendship patterns: circumstances of association
20. Friendship Patterns: frequency of contact
21. Attitudes: toward Turkey
22. Attitudes: toward Turks

(Maximum Score: 110; Minimum Score: 18)

The inner-community participation scale is composed of fifteen items, which assess the extant and kind of inner-community participation:

1. Associations: membership
2. Associations: positions
3. Associations: frequency of attendance
4. Associations: committee and volunteer work
5. Associations: time spent on committee and volunteer work
6. Informal social activities: number
7. Informal social activities: time spent
8. Formal social activities: frequency
9. Neighboring patterns: frequency of visits to American neighbors
10. Neighboring patterns: frequency of American neighbors visiting
11. Friendship patterns: number
12. Friendship patterns: circumstances of association
13. Friendship patterns: frequency of contact

14. Participation preferences: American restaurants
15. Participation preferences: American guests

(Maximum Score: 75; Minimum Score: 15)

Validity of the scales. "A scale possesses validity when it actually measures what it claims to measure."[8] In order to assure the validity of the two scales (if one can ever be assured of this most important but nebulous characteristic), such measures as the following were taken: logical validation or "face validity"; jury opinion; and "known groups." Since it was believed that the scales measured a relatively unambiguous dimension, social participation, the scale items were judged valid on their own strength—that is, on the basis of "face validity." Nonetheless, the answers of *known* participators were compared with those of *known* nonparticipators. In this the scales distinguished between the two groups with great clarity. The knowledge of who was or was not a participator was gained from participant observation and interview data.[9] The third measure, that of jury opinion, was carried out by locating five people from the officer group and five from the enlisted group who were considered to be "knowledgeables" in some circles of the community. These ten evaluated certain people on the basis of high and low participation. Here again, based on their judgments, the scales distinguished accurately.

Reliability of the scales. According to Goode and Hatt: "A scale is reliable when it will consistently produce the same results when applied to the same sample."[10] The test-retest method was chosen as the measure of reliability; the degree

276

of association between the two sets of scores for each scale was tested by the Spearman Rank Order (or Rank Difference) Correlation. Ten people were randomly selected from the sample for retest six months after the original test, then the scores of both sets of test questions were compared. The Spearman Rank Correlation Coefficient, demonstrating the degree of association between the two sets of scores, was .98. However, I have considerable reservations as to the meaningfulness of this correlation coefficient. Due to the difficulties of testing at all, because of restrictions imposed when the survey was approved by Air Force Headquarters in Washington, D.C., and by local headquarters, a retest had to be given, by necessity, to a very small group of people. Furthermore, it was necessary that only a six-month period of time was allowed to elapse between the first test and the second, since due to rapid rotation policies my sample might well have disappeared in a longer interim. Given these two restrictions, it was difficult to see how correction could have been made, except by using a different method.

Administration of the Questionnaire

The questionnaire was self-administered. It was taken to the homes of the selected people during their off-duty hours. Of the selected sample of 200, a total of 166 questionnaires were successfully completed. The shrinkage in the number of respondents was due to the following reasons:

Refusal to cooperate	13
Unable to locate	5
Rotation out of Turkey	10
Uncompleted questionnaires	6
Total	34

Of the questionnaires used in this study, 81 or 48.8 percent of the total were completed by enlisted personnel; 41 or 24.7 percent of the total were completed by people of the W.O.–03 group; 44 or 26.5 percent of the total were completed by members of the 04 and above group.

Data Analysis

On the basis of the scores made on the participation scales, three groups from each were yielded: high, medium, and low participators.

EXTRA-COMMUNITY PARTICIPATION
(Range of Scale Scores: 89–20)

Type of Participant	Range of Scale Scores
High	89–53
Medium	52–39
Low	38–20

INNER-COMMUNITY PARTICIPATION
(Range of Scale Scores: 61–21)

Type of Participant	Range of Scale Scores
High	61–47
Medium	46–41
Low	40–21

It is apparent that the cutting points were not based on the absolute range of scores possible. This did not seem defensible with what was more or less an ordinal scale. Furthermore, the extremes of the scale score continuum could hardly be interpreted as real opposites in regard to meaning. Quinn McNemar, in discussing attitude scales, states: "If one end indicates a favorable attitude, does the other end represent unfavorableness or something else? . . .

278

Are we dealing here with one or two dimensions?"[11] Consequently it was considered more feasible to divide the respondents into three groups on the basis of relative scores.

A Note on the Asking of Questions in a Military Community

One military man told me: "Opinions and attitudes are dangerous." And indeed this seemed to be a highly prevalent attitude among military men. Even after receiving official approval from Air Force Headquarters in Washington, D.C., acceptance by local authorities was far from overwhelming. For that matter, in receiving approval from the Department of the Air Force, I was required to delete three questions from the questionnaire. These questions had to do with attitudes toward cross-cultural marriages; and they were considered by the Air Force representative to be "too personal and possibly offensive to the respondents." I was also required to delete the word "cocktail" from another question, as this could "possibly restrict the scope and acceptability of the question." I thought that this evangelical defense of the Spartan virtues of military members was particularly interesting in view of the military style of life. Before completing the study I was told that a complete OSI (Office of Special Investigation) investigation of me had been undertaken and a dossier now existed.

For those who might contemplate studies of the military organization, I can only say that to do so comfortably one would have to either work with easily accessible data or within the narrowed scope of that which is militarily considered appropriate or as immediately applicable, under the hovering auspices, of course, of the military establishment.

For those who might wish to test more daring and original hypotheses, I can give little encouragement as to the conditions of study they might very well encounter.

NOTES

1. Numerous books were consulted before undertaking this aspect of the study, but those I found most helpful were the following: Nels Anderson, *The Hobo* (Chicago: University of Chicago Press, 1923); Howard S. Becker and Blanche Geer, "Participant Observation: The Analysis of Qualitative Field Data," in *Field Relations and Techniques,* ed. Richard N. Adams and Jack J. Preiss (Homewood, Ill.: Dorsey Press, 1960), pp. 267–289; Florence R. Kluckhohn, "The Participant-Observer Technique in Small Communities," *American Journal of Sociology* 45 (1940):331–343; Arthur J. Vidich and Joseph Bensman, *Small Town in Mass Society* (Garden City, N.Y.: Anchor Books, 1958); William Foote Whyte, *Street Corner Society* (Chicago: University of Chicago Press, 1964).

2. Ibid., p. 317.

3. The books which were referred to continually in designing and carrying out this study were as follows: William J. Goode and Paul K. Hatt, *Methods in Social Research* (New York: McGraw-Hill Book Company, 1952); Claire Selltiz et al., *Research Methods in Social Relations,* rev. ed. (New York: Holt, Rinehart and Winston, 1963); Mildred Parten, *Surveys, Polls, and Samples; Practical Procedures* (New York: Harper & Brothers, Publishers, 1950); Sidney Siegel, *Nonparametric Statistics*

for the Behavioral Sciences (New York: McGraw-Hill Book Company, 1956); F. Stuart Chapin, *Experimental Designs in Sociological Research* (New York: Harper & Brothers, 1947).

4. The questionnaire is reproduced later in this section.

5. For example: August B. Hollingshead, *Elmtown's Youth: The Impact of Social Classes on Adolescence* (New York: John Wiley & Sons, 1949); Samuel A. Stouffer et al., *The American Soldier: Measurement and Prediction,* Vol. IV (Princeton, N.J.: Princeton University Press, 1950); W. Lloyd Warner and Paul S. Lunt, *The Social Life of a Modern Community,* Yankee City Series, Vol. 1 (New Haven: Yale University Press, 1941); W. Lloyd Warner, Murchia Meaker, and Kenneth Eels, *Social Class in America: A Manual of Procedure for the Measurement of Social Status* (Chicago: Science Research Association, 1949).

6. Selltiz et al., *Research Methods in Social Relations,* p. 191.

7. Ibid., p. 189.

8. Goode and Hatt, *Methods in Social Research,* p. 237.

9. Reuben Hill, *Families Under Stress* (New York: Harper & Brothers, 1949), used case narrative materials in this way.

10. Goode and Hatt, *Methods in Social Research,* p. 235.

11. Quinn McNemar as quoted by Stouffer et al., *The American Soldier,* pp. 213–214.

APPENDIX 2

AMERICAN MILITARY COMMUNITY STUDY QUESTIONNAIRE

GENERAL INSTRUCTIONS

1. Please, <u>do not</u> put your name on this questionnaire. All answers remain anonymous.

2. Be frank in your answers. We all have our own beliefs and opinions.

3. Your reactions and attitudes are most important.

4. Please answer each question. Use (X) wherever possible.

DATE_____

1. Code number_____

2. Sex:
   ( ) 1. Male
   ( ) 2. Female

3. Marital status:
   ( ) 1. Single
   ( ) 2. Married with wife (or husband) and family in Turkey
   ( ) 3. Married without wife and family in Turkey
   ( ) 4. Other (divorced, widowed, separated, etc.)

4. Your rank (or that of your spouse):
   ( ) 1. Enlisted
   ( ) 2. Noncommissioned Officer
   ( ) 3. Warrant Officer
   ( ) 4. Officer Rank of 01-03
   ( ) 5. Officer Rank of 04 and above

5. Your birthplace:

   _____

   Town or City   State   Country

6. Birthplace of spouse (if applicable):

   _____

   Town or City   State   Country

7. Your age:
   ( ) 1. 17-25 years of age
   ( ) 2. 26-32 years of age
   ( ) 3. 33-39 years of age
   ( ) 4. 40 years of age or over

8. Age of spouse (if applicable):
   ( ) 1. 17-25 years of age
   ( ) 2. 26-32 years of age
   ( ) 3. 33-39 years of age
   ( ) 4. 40 years of age or over

9. Please give the following information about your children if they are living

284

in Turkey with you at this time:
a. Number of children of school age:____
b. Number of children of preschool age:____
c. Number of children attending American schools in Ankara (e.g. Kindergarten, Elementary School, High School):____
d. Number of children attending Non-American schools in Ankara (e.g. Turkish schools, the French School, the British School, etc.):____

10. Your formal education:
( ) 1. 1-4 years
( ) 2. 5-8 years
( ) 3. 9-12 years
( ) 4. 13-16 years
( ) 5. Graduate School

Graduated from _____

Degree held _____

11. Formal education of spouse (if applicable):
( ) 1. 1-4 years
( ) 2. 5-8 years
( ) 3. 9-12 years
( ) 4. 13-16 years
( ) 5. Graduate School

Graduated from _____

Degree held _____

12. Your religion:
( ) 1. Protestant
( ) 2. Catholic
( ) 3. Jewish
( ) 4. None
( ) 5. Other (please specify) _____

13. Religion of spouse (if applicable):
    ( ) 1. Protestant
    ( ) 2. Catholic
    ( ) 3. Jewish
    ( ) 4. None
    ( ) 5. Other (please specify) _____

14. How frequently do you attend church
    services at the Military Chapel here in
    Turkey?
    ( ) 1. Never
    ( ) 2. Rarely (1-4 times per year)
    ( ) 3. Occasionally (5-11 times per year)
    ( ) 4. Frequently (once a month or
             oftener)
    ( ) 5. Every Sunday

15. How frequently do your children attend
    Sunday School?
    ( ) 1. Never
    ( ) 2. Rarely (1-4 times per year)
    ( ) 3. Occasionally (5-11 times per year)
    ( ) 4. Frequently (once a month or
             oftener)
    ( ) 5. Every Sunday

16. How long have you (or your spouse) been in
    the Service?
    ( ) 1. 1 year or less
    ( ) 2. Over 1 year up to 5 years
    ( ) 3. Over 5 years up to 10 years
    ( ) 4. Over 10 years up to 15 years
    ( ) 5. Over 15 years up to 20 years
    ( ) 6. Over 20 years

17. Do you plan to make the military profes-
    sion your lifetime career (in other words,
    do you plan to spend, or have you spent,

at least 20 years in the military service)?
( ) 1. Yes
( ) 2. No
( ) 3. Undecided

18. Is this tour of duty in Turkey your first
    overseas military assignment?
    ( ) 1. Yes
    ( ) 2. No

19. If you have had other overseas assign-
    ments, please give the following in-
    formation:
             Length of Tour: With Dependents
Place of Town From   To   (Yes or No)

_____

_____

_____

_____

_____

20. Did you ever visit Turkey before this tour?
    ( ) 1. No
    ( ) 2. Yes
        If so, what was the purpose of the

        visit? _____

        _____

        and the duration of the stay? _____

        _____

21. Before being assigned here, did you re-
    quest that Turkey be your next duty
    station?
    ( ) 1. No
    ( ) 2. Yes

22. How long have you currently been in
    Turkey?
    ( ) 1. 1 month or less
    ( ) 2. Over 1 month up to 3 months
    ( ) 3. Over 3 months up to 6 months
    ( ) 4. Over 6 months up to 18 months
    ( ) 5. 19 months and over

23. What is the total length of your tour of
    duty in Turkey? Check the nearest number.
    ( ) 1. 1 year
    ( ) 2. 18 months
    ( ) 3. 2 years
    ( ) 4. 30 months
    ( ) 5. 3 years
    ( ) 6. Indefinite

24. When you first arrived in Ankara, did
    you feel that you were adequately wel-
    comed into the American military commu-
    nity, or did you feel isolated and lost
    for a time?
    ( ) 1. I felt that I was warmly welcomed.
    ( ) 2. The welcome was not as warm as I
           would have liked it to be.
    ( ) 3. I felt ignored and lonely for a
           while.
    ( ) 4. Undecided

25. Before you arrived in Turkey, did any
    Americans who were living in Turkey at
    the time (such as your sponsor) write
    to you and tell you what you might expect
    when you got here (for example: the liv-
    ing conditions in Turkey, what the Turks
    were like, what the other Americans in
    Turkey were like, etc.)?
    ( ) 1. No
    ( ) 2. Yes
           If yes, please tell in a few sen-

288

tences what they wrote to you and whether
you thought their comments were favorable or unfavorable.

_____

_____

_____

_____

26. After you arrived in Turkey, did any
Americans tell you in conversation what
you could expect now that you were here
(for example: the living conditions here,
what the Turks were like, what the other
Americans in Turkey or at your place of
work were like, etc.)?
( ) 1. No
( ) 2. Yes
    If yes, please tell in a few sentences,
as exactly as possible, what they told
you in conversation and whether you
thought their comments were favorable or
unfavorable.

_____

_____

_____

_____

27. Do you think that American military facilities, such as the commissary, post
or base exchange, schools, hospital,
recreational facilities, etc. are an absolute necessity for overseas American
military life, or do you think that
American military personnel should get

along without them and manage on the
local economy?
( ) 1. I think American facilities are
a necessity for American military
personnel overseas.
( ) 2. I think American military personnel overseas should manage to
get along on the local economy,
without American facilities.
( ) 3. Undecided
Why do you believe as you do? _____

_____

_____

_____

28. Which of the following facilities would
be the hardest to do without in an over-
seas assignment? Please rank as follows:
1—the hardest to do without; 2—the
next hardest; 3—not quite so hard; 4,
5, 6, 7—fairly easy; 8—the easiest to
do without.
( ) Commissary
( ) Library
( ) Post or Base Exchange
( ) Military Chapel
( ) Schools
( ) Hospital
( ) Recreational Facilities (e.g. movies,
bowling alleys, swimming pools,
roller skating rinks, etc.
( ) Club Facilities (NCO Club, Officers'
Club, Teen-Clubs, etc.)

29. Are you a member of any local American
clubs or associations? (Please include
NCO Club or Officers' Club membership

and membership in any hunting, sporting,
card clubs, etc.)
( ) 1. None
( ) 2. One
( ) 3. Two
( ) 4. Three
( ) 5. Four or more
Please list all the local American clubs
or associations to which you belong:

_____   _____

_____   _____

_____   _____

30. Do you hold, or have you held, any posi-
    tion(s) in these local American clubs
    or associations?
    ( ) 1. No
    ( ) 2. One position
    ( ) 3. Two positions
    ( ) 4. Three positions
    ( ) 5. Four or more positions

31. How frequently do you go to the Ameri-
    ican NCO Club or the American Officers'
    Club?
    ( ) 1. Never
    ( ) 2. Rarely (1-6 times per year)
    ( ) 3. Occasionally (7-15 times per year)
    ( ) 4. Frequently (16-24 times per year)
    ( ) 5. Very frequently (more than 24
              times per year)

32. Besides club or association membership,
    do you engage in any social activities
    or hobbies with Americans (nonfamily
    members)—such as bowling, card playing,

playing billiards, etc.?
( ) 1. None
( ) 2. One social activity or hobby
( ) 3. Two-three social activities or hobbies
( ) 4. Four-five social activities or hobbies
( ) 5. Six or more social activities or hobbies
Please list what your social activities or social hobbies are:

_____   _____

_____   _____

_____   _____

33. If you do enjoy social activities or hobbies with other Americans, how much time, on the average, do you spend on these per week?
( ) 1. Two hours or less
( ) 2. Three to four hours
( ) 3. Five to six hours
( ) 4. Seven to nine hours
( ) 5. More than nine hours

34. How many American parties do you attend or give, on the average, per month?
( ) 1. None
( ) 2. One
( ) 3. Two or three
( ) 4. Four or five
( ) 5. More than five

35. Are you a member of any local Turkish or Turkish-American clubs or associations?
( ) 1. None
( ) 3. One or two
( ) 5. More than two. Please specify the number:____

GARRISON COMMUNITY

Please list all the local <u>Turkish</u> or <u>Turkish-American</u> clubs or associations to which you belong:

_____   _____

_____   _____

_____   _____

36. Do you hold, or have you held, any position(s) in these <u>Turkish</u> or <u>Turkish-American</u> clubs or associations?
( ) 1. No
( ) 2. One position
( ) 3. Two positions
( ) 4. Three positions
( ) 5. Four or more positions

37. Do you do any volunteer work or committee work for <u>American</u> organizations (for example: the American Red Cross, the Scouts, the AYA or other teen-age groups, church groups, charity or fund-raising groups, Little League, etc.)?
( ) 1. No
( ) 5. Yes
Please list the organizations for which you have done volunteer work or committee work:

_____   _____

_____   _____

_____   _____

38. If you do, or have done, volunteer work or committee work for <u>American</u> organizations, how much time, on the average, do

293
_____

you spend on these per month?
( ) 1. Two hours or less
( ) 2. Three to four hours
( ) 3. Five to six hours
( ) 4. Seven to ten hours
( ) 5. More than ten hours

39. Do you do any volunteer work or committee work for any Turkish or Turkish-American organizations (for example: Turkish orphanages, Turkish hospitals, Turkish community projects or Turkish social-welfare groups, or donating time to teach English language classes to Turks)?
( ) 1. No
( ) 5. Yes

40. If you do volunteer work or committee work for Turkish or Turkish-American organizations, how much time, on the average, do you spend on this per month?
( ) 1. Two hours or less
( ) 2. Three to four hours
( ) 3. Five to six hours
( ) 4. Seven to ten hours
( ) 5. More than ten hours

41. Since coming to Turkey (or just prior to coming to Turkey) have you studied the Turkish language?
( ) 1. No
( ) 5. Yes
      If yes, where did you study: _____

      _____

      How long did you study: _____

42. How well do you think you speak Turkish?
    ( ) 1. Not a word
    ( ) 2. A few words
    ( ) 3. "Kitchen Turkish"—enough
           Turkish to shop and get around
           with
    ( ) 4. Fairly good Turkish
    ( ) 5. Fluently

43. How well do you read and write Turkish?
    ( ) 1. Not a word
    ( ) 2. A few words
    ( ) 3. Enough Turkish so that store or
           hotel signs, road signs, adver-
           tisements, etc., are understood
    ( ) 4. I can read a Turkish newspaper or
           magazine and understand much of
           what is read
    ( ) 5. I can read and write Turkish
           fluently

44. If you are not fluent, are you interested
    in learning more Turkish?
    ( ) 1. No
    ( ) 2. Yes
        If yes, how and when do you plan to
    improve your Turkish?

    _____

45. Do you read any Turkish newspaper (in
    either English or Turkish) regularly?
    ( ) 1. No
    ( ) 3. Yes, in English
    ( ) 5. Yes, in Turkish

46. Since you have been in Turkey, have you
    read a book (or books) about travel in

295
___

Appendixes

Turkey or about Turkish life or history?
( ) 1. No, and I don't plan to
( ) 2. No, but I plan to
( ) 3. Yes, one or two books
( ) 4. Yes, three to five books
( ) 5. Yes, more than five books
    If yes, please list those books you
have read which you remember best?

_____   _____

_____   _____

47. How frequently do you attend such Turk-
    ish cultural events as the ballet, sym-
    phony concerts, opera, art exhibitions,
    plays, etc.?
    ( ) 1. Never
    ( ) 3. Occasionally (1-3 times per year)
    ( ) 5. Frequently (4 or more times per
           year)

48. How frequently do you attend Turkish
    sporting events, such as soccer games,
    wrestling matches, horse shows, horse
    races, etc.?
    ( ) 1. Never
    ( ) 3. Occasionally (1-3 times per year)
    ( ) 5. Frequently (4 or more times per
           year)

49. How frequently do you go to a Turkish
    nightclub?
    ( ) 1. Never
    ( ) 2. Rarely (1-2 times per year)
    ( ) 3. Occasionally (3-6 times per year)
    ( ) 4. Frequently (7-12 times per year)
    ( ) 5. Very frequently (more than 12
           times per year)

296

50. When you go out for dinner and you have a choice between going to an American restaurant or to a Turkish restaurant, which do you choose?
   ( ) 1. Always an American restaurant
   ( ) 2. More frequently than not an American restaurant
   ( ) 3. Go to each about evenly
   ( ) 4. More frequently than not a Turkish restaurant
   ( ) 5. Always a Turkish restaurant

51. When you go to or give a party, do you prefer the guests to be:
   ( ) 1. All Americans
   ( ) 2. Mostly Americans
   ( ) 3. About half Americans and half Turks
   ( ) 4. Mostly Turks
   ( ) 5. All Turks

52. How often do you visit in the homes (house, apartment, or room) of your American neighbors?
   ( ) 1. Never
   ( ) 2. Less often than once a month
   ( ) 3. At least once a month
   ( ) 4. At least once a week
   ( ) 5. Daily

53. How often do you casually and informally invite your American neighbors or American friends into your home (or out to a restaurant or bar) for a cup of coffee, or for a drink, or for a dinner?
   ( ) 1. Never
   ( ) 2. Less often than once a month
   ( ) 3. At least once a month
   ( ) 4. At least once a week
   ( ) 5. Daily

54. How often do you visit in the homes of
    your Turkish neighbors?
    ( ) 1. Never
    ( ) 2. Less often than once a month
    ( ) 3. At least once a month
    ( ) 4. At least once a week
    ( ) 5. Daily

55. Have you invited a Turk into your home
    or to a restaurant for something to eat
    or drink?
    ( ) 1. Never
    ( ) 2. Once or twice
    ( ) 3. Three to five times
    ( ) 4. Six to ten times
    ( ) 5. More than ten times

56. Have you been invited by a Turk to come
    into his (or her) home for something to
    eat or drink?
    ( ) 1. Never
    ( ) 2. Once or twice
    ( ) 3. Three to five times
    ( ) 4. Six to ten times
    ( ) 5. More than ten times

57. Have you made any good American friends
    since you have come to Turkey?
    ( ) 1. None
    ( ) 2. One
    ( ) 3. Two or three
    ( ) 4. Four or five
    ( ) 5. Six or more

58. If you have good American friends here,
    under what circumstances do you usually
    associate?
    ( ) 1. Most casually at parties or sport-
           ing or cultural events, or see
           around the apartment house or

298

place I live, or associate with
for business reasons
( ) 3. Go out to dinner, parties, picnics, or cultural or sporting
events with
( ) 5. Entertain in each other's homes

59. How often on the average do you get together?
( ) 1. Less than once a month
( ) 3. Once or twice a month
( ) 5. More than twice a month

60. How many good Turkish friends do you have?
( ) 1. None
( ) 2. One
( ) 3. Two or three
( ) 4. Four or five
( ) 5. Six or more

61. If you have good Turkish friends, under
what circumstances do you usually associate?
( ) 1. Meet casually at parties or sporting or cultural events, or see
around the apartment house or place
I live, or associate with for
business reasons
( ) 3. Go out to dinner, parties, or
cultural or sporting events with
( ) 5. Entertain in each other's homes

62. How often on the average do you get together?
( ) 1. Less than once a month
( ) 3. Once or twice a month
( ) 5. More than twice a month

63. During which part of your tour here do
you believe that you participated the
most in Turkish life (that is, tried to

get to know Turks and to learn their
language and to learn about their
country)?
( ) 1. I have never participated in Turk-
       ish life.
( ) 2. During the first three months I
       was here I participated the most.
( ) 3. When I had been here for 3 to 6
       months, I participated the most.
( ) 4. After I had been here 6 months I
       participated the most.
( ) 5. There has been no change. I have
       participated the same amount
       throughout the tour.

64. When you first arrived in Turkey, did you
    expect to like the Turks and to enjoy
    your tour in Turkey?
    ( ) 1. Yes
    ( ) 2. No
    ( ) 3. I had no opinion

65. Do you think that when you leave Turkey
    you will return to the United States with
    a favorable or unfavorable attitude
    toward Turkey and its people?
    ( ) 1. Very unfavorable
    ( ) 2. Fairly unfavorable
    ( ) 3. About 50-50
    ( ) 4. Fairly favorable
    ( ) 5. Very favorable

66. How much have you personally liked Turks?
    ( ) 1. Not at all
    ( ) 2. No so much
    ( ) 3. Don't care either way
    ( ) 4. Pretty much
    ( ) 5. Very much

300
——

67. If you had to describe the "average
Turk" or "average Turks" in a few
words, how would you do so?

_____

_____

_____

_____

68. Please describe in a few sentences how
you feel about living in Turkey. Also,
please describe any pleasant or unpleasant experiences you have had while
living here.

_____

_____

_____

_____

_____

BIBLIOGRAPHY

Anderson, Nels. *The Hobo*. Chicago: University of Chicago Press, 1923.

———. *The Urban Community*. New York: Holt, Rinehart and Winston, 1959.

Andrzejewski, Stanislaw. *Military Organization and Society*. London: Routledge & Kegan Paul, 1954.

Angell, Robert C. "The Moral Integration of American Cities." *American Journal of Sociology* 57 (July, 1951):93–100.

Anonymous. "Informal Social Organization in the Army." *American Journal of Sociology,* Vol. 51 (March, 1946).

Arensberg, Conrad M. "The Community-Study Method." *American Journal of Sociology* 60 (September, 1954):109–124.

Axelrod, Morris. "Urban Structure and Social Participation." *American Sociological Review* 21 (February, 1956):13–18.

Becker, Howard S., and Geer, Blanche. "Participant Observation: The Analysis of Qualitative Field Data." In *Human Organiza-*

tion Research. Field Relations and Techniques, edited by Richard N. Adams and Jack J. Preiss, pp. 267–289. Homewood, Ill.: Dorsey Press, 1960.

Bell, Wendell, and Force, Maryanne T. "Social Structure and Participation in Different Types of Formal Associations." *American Sociological Review* 21 (February, 1956):25–34.

Bernardo, C. Joseph, and Bacon, Eugene H. *American Military Policy.* Harrisburg, Pa.: The Military Service Publishing Co., 1957.

Biderman, Albert D. "Sequels to a Military Career: The Retired Military Professional." In *The New Military,* edited by Morris Janowitz, pp. 287–336. New York: Russell Sage Foundation, 1964.

Bidwell, Charles E. "The Young Professional in the Army: A Study of Occupational Identity." *American Sociological Review* 26 (June, 1961):360–372.

Blau, Peter M. "Structural Effects." *American Sociological Review* 25 (April, 1960):178–193.

Bonjean, Charles M. "Mass, Class, and the Industrial Community: A Comparative Analysis of Managers, Businessmen, and Workers." *American Journal of Sociology* 72 (September, 1966):149–162.

Brotz, Howard, and Wilson, Everett. "Characteristics of Military Society." *American Journal of Sociology* 51 (March, 1946): 371–375.

Brownell, Baker. *The Human Community.* New York: Harper & Brothers, 1950.

Campbell, D. T., and McCormac, T. H. "Military Experience and Attitudes toward Authority." *American Journal of Sociology* 62 (March, 1957):482–490.

Campbell, Ernest Q., and Alexander, C. Norman. "Structural Effects and Interpersonal Relationships." *American Journal of Sociology* 71 (November, 1965):284–289.

304

Campbell, John C. *Defense of the Middle East.* New York: Frederick A. Praeger, 1960.

Cantril, Hadley. "Perception and Interpersonal Relations." In *Current Perspectives in Social Psychology,* edited by E. P. Hollander and Raymond G. Hunt. New York: Oxford University Press, 1963.

Chapin, F. Stuart. *Experimental Designs in Sociological Research.* New York: Harper & Brothers, 1955.

Cleveland, Harland, and Mangone, Gerald J., eds. *The Art of Overseasmanship.* Syracuse, N. Y.: Syracuse University Press, 1957.

———— and Adams, John Clarke. *The Overseas Americans.* New York: McGraw-Hill Book Company, 1960.

Coates, Charles H., and Pellegrin, Roland J. (with contributions by Norman A. Hilmar). *Military Sociology. A Study of American Military Institutions and Military Life.* University Park, Md.: Social Science Press, 1965.

Coleman, James S. "Community Disorganization." In *Contemporary Social Problems,* edited by Robert K. Merton and Robert A. Nisbet, pp. 553–604. New York: Harcourt, Brace & World, 1961.

————. "Relational Analysis: The Study of Social Organizations with Survey Methods." In *Complex Organizations: A Sociological Reader,* edited by Amitai Etzioni, pp. 441–453. New York: Holt, Rinehart and Winston, 1964.

Davis, Arthur K. "Bureaucratic Patterns in the Navy Officer Corps." *Social Forces* 27 (December, 1948):143–153.

Davis, Paul C., and Fox, William T. R. "American Military Representation Abroad." In *The Representation of the United States Abroad,* edited by Vincent M. Barnett, Jr., pp. 129–183. New York: Frederick A. Praeger, 1965.

Elias, Norbert, and Scotson, John L. *The Established and the Outsiders: A Sociological Enquiry into Community Problems.* London: Frank Cass & Co., 1965.

Elkin, Frederick. "The Soldier's Language." *American Journal of Sociology* 51 (March, 1946):414–422.

Feld, Maury D. "The Military Self-Image in a Technological Environment." In *The New Military,* edited by Morris Janowitz, pp. 159–193. New York: Russell Sage Foundation, 1964.

Festinger, Leon, and Kelley, Harold H. *Changing Attitudes Through Social Contact.* Ann Arbor, Mich.: Research Center for Group Dynamics, Institute for Social Research, University of Michigan, September, 1951.

Finer, S. E. *The Man on Horseback.* London: Pall Mall Press, 1962.

Foskett, John. "Social Structure and Social Participation." *American Sociological Review* 20 (August, 1955):431–438.

Freeman, Felton D. "The Army as a Social Structure." *Social Forces* 27 (October, 1948):78–83.

Gerth, Hans, and Mills, C. Wright. *Character and Social Structure.* New York: Harcourt, Brace & World, 1964.

Glaser, Daniel. "The Sentiments of American Soldiers Abroad Toward Europeans." *American Journal of Sociology* 51 (March, 1946):433–438.

Goffman, Erving. "The Characteristics of Total Institutions." In *Complex Organizations,* edited by Amitai Etzioni, pp. 312–340. New York: Holt, Rinehart and Winston, 1964.

Gold, Raymond. "Roles in Sociological Field Observations." *Social Forces* 36 (1958):217–223.

Goode, William J., and Hatt, Paul K. *Methods in Social Research.* New York: McGraw-Hill Book Company, 1952.

Gordon, C. Wayne, and Babchuk, Nicholas. "A Typology of Voluntary Associations." *American Sociological Review* 24 (February, 1959):22–29.

Greer, Scott. "The Social Structure and Political Process of Suburbia." *American Sociological Review* 25 (August, 1960):514–526.

Grusky, Oscar. "The Effects of Succession: A Comparative Study of Military and Business Organization." In *The New Military,* edited by Morris Janowitz, pp. 83–111. New York: Russell Sage Foundation, 1964.

Hadden, Jeffrey K., and Rymph, Raymond C. "Social Structure and Civil Rights Involvement: A Case Study of Protestant Ministers." *Social Forces* 45 (September, 1966):51–61.

Hall, Edward T. *The Silent Language.* Greenwich, Conn.: Fawcett Publications, 1963.

Hawley, Amos H. *Human Ecology.* New York: Ronald Press Company, 1950.

Hiller, E. T. *Social Relations and Structures.* New York: Harper & Brothers, 1947.

Hillman, Arthur. *Community Organization and Planning.* New York: Macmillan Company, 1950.

Hollingshead, August. "Adjustment to Military Life." *American Journal of Sociology* 51 (March, 1946):439–447.

————. "Community Research: Development and Present Condition." *American Sociological Review* 13 (April, 1948):136–139, 144, 145.

————. *Elmtown's Youth. The Impact of Social Classes on Adolescents.* New York: John Wiley & Sons, 1949.

Hovey, Harold A. *United States Military Assistance. A Study of Policies and Practices.* New York: Frederick A. Praeger, 1965.

Huntington, Samuel P. *The Soldier and the State.* Cambridge, Mass.: Harvard University Press, Belknap Press, 1964.

Iverson, Noel. *Germania, U.S.A.* St. Paul: University of Minnesota Press, 1966.

Jacobs, Milton, and Louis Schatz. *Some Effects of Overseas Duty on the Attitudes of American Troops toward Host Populations.* Washington, D.C.: Human Resources Office, George Washington University, 1954.

Janowitz, Morris. "Hierarchy and Authority in the Military Establishment." In *Complex Organizations,* edited by Amitai Etzioni, pp. 198–212. New York: Holt, Rinehart and Winston, 1964.

————. *Sociology and the Military Establishment.* New York: Russell Sage Foundation, 1959.

————. *The Community Press.* 2nd ed. Chicago: University of Chicago Press, 1967.

————. "The Military Establishment: Organization and Disorganization." In *Contemporary Social Problems,* edited by Robert K. Merton and Robert A. Nisbet, pp. 515–552. New York: Harcourt, Brace & World, 1961.

————. *The Military in the Political Development of New Nations.* Chicago: University of Chicago Press, 1964.

————. *The Professional Soldier.* New York: Free Press, 1960.

Jonassen, Christen D. "Community Typology." In *Community Structure and Analysis,* edited by Marvin B. Sussman, pp. 15–34. New York: Thomas Y. Crowell Co., 1959.

Kahl, Joseph A. *The American Class Structure.* New York: Holt, Rinehart and Winston, 1961.

———— and Davis, James A. "A Comparison of Indexes of Socio-Economic Status." *American Sociological Review* 20 (June, 1955):317–325.

Katz, Daniel. "The Functional Approach to the Study of Attitudes." In *Information, Influence and Communication,* edited by Otto Lerbinger and Albert J. Sullivan, pp. 277–300. New York: Basic Books, 1964.

———— and Braly, Kenneth W. "Verbal Stereotypes and Racial Prejudice." In *Readings in Social Psychology,* 3rd ed., edited by Eleanor E. Maccoby, Theodore M. Newcomb, and Eugene L. Hartley. London: Methuen & Co., 1958.

Key, William. "Urbanism and Neighboring." *Sociological Quarterly* (Autumn, 1965), pp. 379–385.

Kluckhohn, Florence R. "The Participant-Observer Technique in Small Communities." *American Journal of Sociology* 46 (1940):331–343.

Korpi, Walter. *Social Pressures and Attitudes in Military Training.* Stockholm: Almquist & Wiksell, 1964.

Lambert, Richard D. "Some Minor Pathologies in the American Presence in India." *The Annals* 368 (November, 1966): 157–170.

Lang, Kurt. "Technology and Career Management in the Military Establishment." In *The New Military,* edited by Morris Janowitz, pp. 39–81. New York: Russell Sage Foundation, 1964.

Lasswell, Harold D. "The Garrison-State Hypothesis Today." In *Changing Patterns of Military Politics,* edited by Samuel P. Huntington, pp. 51–70. New York: Free Press, 1962.

Lazarsfeld, Paul F., and Menzel, Herbert. "On the Relation between Individual and Collective Properties." In *Complex Organizations,* edited by Amitai Etzioni, pp. 422–440. New York: Holt, Rinehart and Winston, 1964.

Lederer, William J., and Burdick, Eugene. *The Ugly American.* New York: W. W. Norton & Company, 1958.

Lindeman, E. C. "Community." In *Encyclopedia of the Social Sciences* 3–4:102–105. New York: Macmillan Company, 1935.

Lindquist, Ruth. *Marriage and Family Life of Officers and Airmen in a Strategic Air Command Wing.* Technical Report No. 5, Air Force Base Project, sponsored by Human Resources Research Institute, U. S. Air Force and executed by the Institute for Research in Social Science, University of North Carolina, October, 1952.

Lowie, Robert H. *Social Organization.* New York: Holt, Rinehart & Company, 1948.

Lynd, Robert S., and Lynd, Helen Merrell. *Middletown.* New York: Harcourt, Brace and Company, 1929.

————. *Middletown in Transition.* New York: Harcourt, Brace and Company, 1937.

MacIver, Robert M. *Community.* New York: Macmillan Company, 1928.

———— and Page, Charles H. "Society: Primary Concepts." In *Society Today and Tomorrow,* edited by Elgin F. Hunt and Jules Karlin, pp. 24–32. New York: Macmillan Company, 1961.

Mack, Raymond W. *Social Stratification on a U. S. Air Force Base.* Technical Report No. 4, Air Force Base Project, sponsored by Human Resources Research Institute in Social Science, University of North Carolina, n.d.

Maine, Sir Henry Sumner. *Ancient Law.* Boston: Beacon Press, 1963.

————. *Village Communities in the East and West.* New York: Henry Holt and Co., 1889, pp. 131–171.

Martindale, Don. *American Social Structure.* New York: Appleton-Century-Crofts, 1960.

————. *American Society.* Princeton, N.J.: D. Van Nostrand Company, 1960.

————. *Community, Character and Civilization.* New York: Free Press, 1963.

————. "The Formation and Destruction of Communities." In *Explorations in Social Change,* edited by George K. Zollschan and Walter Hirsch, pp. 61–87. Boston: Houghton Mifflin Co., 1964.

————. *Institutions, Organizations, and Mass Society.* Boston: Houghton Mifflin Company, 1965.

————. "Prefatory Remarks: The Theory of the City." In Max Weber, *The City,* translated and edited by Don Martindale and Gertrud Neuwirth, pp. 9–67. New York: Collier Books, 1962.

————. *Social Life and Cultural Change.* Princeton, N.J.: D. Van Nostrand Company, 1962.

————. "The Sociology of National Character." *The Annals* 370 (March, 1967):30–35.

McCreary, Edward A. *The Americanization of Europe*. Garden City, N.Y.: Doubleday & Company, 1964.

Merton, Robert K. "Selected Problems of Field Work in the Planned Community." *American Sociological Review* 12 (June, 1947):304–312.

———— and Lazarsfeld, Paul. *Continuities in Social Research: Studies in the Scope and Method of the American Soldier*. New York: Free Press, 1950.

Military Assistance Institute, The Department of Defense. *Country Study. Republic of Turkey*. American Institute for Research, February, 1963.

Mills, C. Wright. *The Power Elite*. New York: Oxford University Press, 1956.

Morgan, Arthur E. *The Community of the Future and the Future of the Community*. Sevagram, Wardha, Bombay State: Hindustani Talimi Sangh, 1958.

Morris, Richard T. "National Status and Attitudes of Foreign Students." *Journal of Social Issues* 12 (1956):20–25.

Moser, C. A. *Survey Methods in Social Investigation*. London: William Heinemann, 1958.

O'Neill, Ralph C. "Attitudes and Experiences of High School Students Living in Turkey." *The Personnel and Guidance Journal* 45 (September, 1966):43–46.

Owen, John E. "The Community." In *Contemporary Sociology*, edited by Joseph S. Roucek, pp. 29–43. New York: Philosophical Library, 1958.

Page, Charles H. "Bureaucracy's Other Face." *Social Forces* 25 (October, 1946):88–94.

Paige, Ralph F., and Zagorski, Frank J. "Preparation for the Cross-Cultural Relationships." Thesis, Graduate School of Public and International Affairs, University of Pittsburgh, 1960.

311

Bibliography

Parsons, Talcott. *The Social System.* New York: Free Press, 1951.

Parten, Mildred. *Surveys, Polls, and Samples: Practical Procedures.* New York: Harper & Brothers, 1950.

Presad, J. "The Psychology of Rumor: A Study Relating to the Great Indian Earthquake of 1934." *British Journal of Psychology* 26 (1935–1936):1–15.

Public Relations Office, JUSMMAT. "The Joint Military Mission for Aid to Turkey. 1947–30 June 1950. History." Mimeographed, n.d.

Reissman, Leonard. "Class, Leisure, and Social Participation." *American Sociological Review* 19 (February, 1954):76–84.

Riddlesberger, Alice B., and Motz, Annabelle B. "Prejudice and Perception." *American Journal of Sociology* 62 (March, 1957):498–503.

Riesman, David. "Some Questions about the Study of American Character in the Twentieth Century." *The Annals* 370 (March, 1967):36–47.

Rose, Arnold M. "The Social Structure of the Army." *American Journal of Sociology* 51 (March, 1946):361–364.

————. *Theory and Method in the Social Sciences.* Minneapolis: University of Minnesota Press, 1954.

Roscow, Irving. "Forms and Functions of Adult Socialization." *Social Forces* 44 (September, 1965):35–45.

Ross, Murray G. *Community Organization.* New York: Harper & Row, 1955.

Sanders, Irwin T. *The Community. An Introduction to a Social System.* New York: Ronald Press Company, 1958.

Seeley, J. R.; Sim, R. A.; and Loosley, C. W. *Crestwood Heights. A Study of the Culture of Suburban Life.* New York: John Wiley & Sons, 1963.

Selltiz, Claire; Jahoda, Marie; Deutsch, Morton; and Cook, Stuart W. *Research Methods in Social Relations*. New York: Holt, Rinehart and Winston, 1963.

Shank, Donald J. "The American Goes Abroad." *The Annals* 335 (May, 1961):99–111.

Siegal, Sidney. *Nonparametric Statistics for the Behavioral Sciences*. New York: McGraw-Hill Book Company, 1956.

Simirenko, Alex. *Pilgrims, Colonists, and Frontiersmen: An Ethnic Comunity in Transition*. New York: Free Press, 1954.

Sims, N. L. *The Rural Community*. New York: D. Appleton-Century Company, 1920.

Snedden, David. "Communities, Associate and Federate." *American Journal of Sociology* 28 (May, 1923):681–693.

Spindler, G. Dearborn. "The Military—A Systematic Analysis." *Social Forces* 27 (October, 1948):83–88.

Stebbins, Robert A. "Class, Status, and Power Among Jazz and Commercial Musicians." *The Sociological Quarterly* (Spring, 1966), pp. 197–213.

Stein, Maurice R. *The Eclipse of Community*. New York: Harper Torch Books, 1960.

Steiner, Jesse Frederick. *Community Organization*. New York: D. Appleton-Century Company, 1930.

Stouffer, S. A.; Suchman, E. A.; Devinney, L. C.; Star, S. A.; and Williams, R. M., Jr. *The American Soldier*. Princeton, N.J.: Princeton University Press, 1950.

Swomley, John M., Jr. *The Military Establishment*. Boston: Beacon Press, 1964.

Tarr, David. "The Military Abroad." *The Annals* 368 (November, 1966):31–42.

Teele, James E. "An Appraisal of Research on Social Participation." *The Sociological Quarterly* (Summer, 1965), pp. 257–267.

Teele, James E. "Measures of Social Participation." *Social Problems* 10 (Summer, 1962):31–39.

Thomas, Lewis V., and Frye, Richard N. *The United States and Turkey and Iran*. Cambridge, Mass.: Harvard University Press, 1951.

Thomas, William T., and Znaniecki, Florian. *The Polish Peasant in Europe and America*. Boston: Gorham Press, 1920.

Tönnies, Ferdinand. *Community & Society* [Gemeinschaft und Gesellschaft]. Translated and edited by Charles P. Loomis. New York: Harper Torchbooks, 1957.

Vagts, Alfred. *A History of Militarism*. 2nd ed. New York: Meridian Books, 1959.

————. *Defense and Diplomacy. The Soldier and the Conduct of Foreign Relations*. New York: King's Crown Press, 1956.

Vidich, Arthur J., and Bensman, Joseph. *Small Town in Mass Society*. Garden City, N.Y.: Anchor Books, 1960.

———— and Stein, Maurice, eds. *Reflections on Community Studies*. New York: John Wiley & Sons, 1964.

Vidich, Arthur J., and Stein, Maurice R. "The Dissolved Identity in Military Life." In *Identity and Anxiety,* edited by Maurice R. Stein, Arthur J. Vidich, and David Manning White. New York: Free Press, 1960.

Wallis, W. Allen, and Roberts, Harry V. *Statistics. A New Appoach*. New York: Free Press, 1956.

Walter, Paul, Jr. "Military Sociology." In *Contemporary Sociology,* edited by Joseph S. Roucak, pp. 655–672. New York: Philosophical Library, 1958.

Warner, W. Lloyd; Meeker, Marchia; and Eels, Kenneth. *Social Class in America*. Chicago: Social Research Association, 1949.

Warner, W. Lloyd, and Srole, Leo. *The Social Systems of Ameri-*

314

can Ethnic Groups. Yankee City Series, Vol. 3. New Haven: Yale University Press, 1945.

Warren, Roland L. *The Community in America.* Chicago: Rand McNally & Company, 1963.

Weber, Max. "Ethnic Groups." In *Theories in Society,* Vol. 1, edited by Talcott Parsons, Edward Shils, Kaspar D. Naegele, and Jesse R. Pitts. New York: Free Press, 1961.

————. *From Max Weber: Essays in Sociology.* Translated, edited, and with an introduction by H. H. Gerth and C. Wright Mills. New York: Oxford University Press, 1958.

————. *The Theory of Social and Economic Organization.* Translated by A. M. Henderson and Talcott Parsons. New York: Oxford University Press, 1947.

West, James. *Plainville, U.S.A.* New York: Columbia University Press, 1945.

Whyte, William Foote. *Street Corner Society.* Chicago: University of Chicago Press, 1964.

Whyte, William H., Jr. *The Organization Man.* Garden City, N.Y.: Doubleday Anchor Books, 1956.

Wirth, Louis. *The Ghetto.* Chicago: University of Chicago Press, 1962.

Wright, C. R., and Human, H. H. "Voluntary Association Memberships of American Adults: Evidence from National Sample Surveys." *American Sociological Review* 23 (June, 1958): 284–294.

Young, Pauline V. *Scientific Social Surveys and Research.* 3rd ed. Englewood Cliffs, N. J.: Prentice-Hall, 1956.

Zald, Mayer N., and Simon, William. "Career Opportunities and Commitments among Officers." In *The New Military,* edited by Morris Janowitz, pp. 257–285. New York: Russell Sage Foundation, 1964.

Zenner, Walter P. "Ethnic Assimilation and Corporate Group." *The Sociological Quarterly* 8 (Summer, 1967):340–348.

Zimmer, B. C. "Participation of Migrants in Urban Structures." *American Sociological Review* 20 (April, 1955):218–224.

Zimmerman, Carl C. *The Changing Community.* New York: Harper & Brothers, 1938.

Znaniecki, Florian. *Social Relations and Social Roles.* San Francisco: Chandler Publishing Company, 1965.

INDEX

Adams, Sidney, 85
adult education, 150–153
age: extra-community participation and, 238; rank group and, 114–115
Air Force Family Services, 99
Althusius, Johannes, 6
American behavior, Turkish judgment and stereotyping of, 89–90
American cars, restrictions on, 95
American community, "blending in" of, 47; see also community; military community
American culture, evaluations of, 89
American forces, first demonstration against, 53
American image, U.S. military bulletins and, 91–92
American Jews, 166–168
American military colony, socio-structural properties of, 113–189; see also military colony

American "nonimage," 94–96
American personnel, postarrival opinions of, 147–148
American products, vis-à-vis Turkish, 126–127
American road equipment, Turkish use of, 48
Americans: "discrimination" against, 101; free mingling of with Turks, 46; "good image" of, 92–93; restrictions on movements of, 95–96; rioting against, 94, 204–205
"American way of life," 65
American wives, attitudes of, 172–173
American work ethic, 198
analytic study, design of, 271–280
Ankara: American Military Mission in, 42–54; Americans outside military community, 97–102; census of, 113–120; changing conditions in, 46–54; community members in, 80–81; demo-

graphic factors in, 113–189; demonstrations against American forces in, 53, 94, 204–205; general conditions in, 33–35; housing problems in, 50; medical facilities in, 49; military community in, 17, 42–54, 78–88, 253–254; nationalism in, 78–79; political background in, 35–42, 87–88; recreational facilities in, 51–52, 169–172; religion in, 51, 162–168; riots in, 94, 204–205; schools in, 50; size of military community in, 211–224; social environment of, 24; Turkish judgment and stereotyping in, 89–97; Westernized areas of, 35; see also military community

Ankara Community Center, 125
Ankara Daily News, 40
anti-American demonstrations, 53, 94, 204–205
apartment buildings, 51
Arensberg, Conrad, 10
Aristotle, 4, 5
Ataturk (mustafa Kemal), 34, 229
authority, in military organization, 72–73
automobiles, restrictions on, 95

babies, delivery of, 49
Baghdad Pact, 38
Balgat Air Station, 48, 51, 94–96, 125, 153
Becker, Howard, 8
behavior, stereotypes of, 89–97
Bilateral Agreements of Cooperation, 38
black market, 101
blood ties, community of, 7
boredom, 173
Brotz, Howard, 70, 73
Brownell, Baker, 9
bureaucracy, 71–75; elite and, 134; ideal, 74
Burgess, Ernest, 7–8

campanilismo, 9
Cankaya hill, 123
census studies, 113–120
Central Treaty Organization (CENTO), 38, 45
children: education of, 153–159; recreation for, 171–174
churches and church attendance, 124, 164; see also religion
Clifford, Clark M., 258
closure: analytical survey of, 231–246; in Ankara community, 17; community structure and, 232; ethnic force and, 206; extra-community, 19–20; implements of, 206–210; innovation and, 190–251, 255; in military community, 255, 259; military organization and, 206; participation and, 237; reciprocal relationship with innovation, 22; secrecy and, 209; social behavior and, 14–15; in structural groups, 256–257
clubs, 125, 169–170
Coates, Charles H., 73–74
Cole, G. D. H., 6
Coleman, James, 10
command concept, in military mission, 80
communication: channels of, 87–88; conspiracy and, 214; emergency and, 213; information and, 217; lack of, 81; news and, 213; radio and, 213; rumor and, 212–218
communism, fear of, 209
Communists, vs. democrats, 78–79
community: analytic approaches to, 4; biological bases of, 5–7; blood ties and, 6–7; definitions of, 9–11; economic life of, 159–162; ethnic, see ethnic community; family membership and, 8; garrison, 252–280; group attitudes in, 78; institutions as core of, 14; as local territorial group, 11; mediation of, 24; as mind or soul, 5;

318

319

facilities and services, military, 123–129
family life: conveniences in, 177–179; dependent actions in, 172; domiciles available for, 177; furniture in, 180; juvenile delinquency and, 174; manners in, 180; military life and, 172–183; recreation and, 174–175; servants and, 179; and single man, 175–177; style of, 177–180; tenancy and, 177
family membership, 8
Family Services, 148
Freeman, Felton D., 68

Galpin, C. J., 12
garrison community: military community as, 68; prospects and problems of, 252–280; see also military community
Gemeinschaft und Gesellschaft (Tönnies), 8
generalists, vs. specialists, 70
good-bad dichotomy, 78, 207
Goode, William J., 276
Goodenough, W. H., 10
"good relations," organization man and, 135
government groups, and military community, 98–101
Greece, U.S. aid to, 37
Green, Arnold, 11
Grotius, Hugo, 5

Hart, Parker T., 211, 258
Harvard Law School, 75
Hatt, Paul K., 276
health, sanitation and, 181–183
hierarchy: community structure and, 130–138; in military organization, 71–72
Hobbes, Thomas, 5–6
horseback riding, 52
hospital facilities, 49
Host Nation Program, 157, 224

hotel rooms, 50
housing, 50–51
Hughes, E. C., 7
Hume, David, 6

ideology: attitudes and, 219; community, 218–224; counterstereotypes and, 223–224; culture and, 219; justification of, 225; prejudice and, 219
"Inbound Briefings," 148
inner-community innovation, 21
inner-community participation, 237
innovation, 17; closure and, 190–251; core areas of, 19; extra-community, 19–20, 226–231; group contacts and, 234–236; inner-community, 21; marginal areas of, 19; rank position and, 233–237; reciprocal relationship with closure, 22; social behavior and, 14–15
interchangeability policy, 82–83
interviews, 270–271

JAMMAT (Joint American Military Mission for Aid to Turkey), 42
Janowitz, Morris, 68, 73, 77
Jewish synagogue, 51
Jews: American, 166–168; Turkish, 167
Johnson, Lyndon B., 39, 41
Joint American Military Mission for Aid to Turkey (JAMMAT), 42
JUSMMAT (Joint United States Military Mission for Aid to Turkey), 43, 47, 142, 162, 176, 212

Kavaklidere Tennis Club, 169
Kayla, Ziya, 40
Kemal, Yashar, 40
kindergarten, 155
Kocas, Sadi, 40
Korean War, 44

laws: customs and, 193; NATO and, 191; Turkish, 191–195

320

legal problems: customs and, 193; punishment and, 192; Turkish law and, 191–195
Lindeman, E. C., 12
Lipset, Seymour Martin, 259
living standards: disparities in, 199–201; marketing and, 199; poverty and, 200; style of life and, 199
Livy (Titus Livius), 5
loneliness, 173
Lowie, Robert H., 9–10

McDougal, Myres S., 5
MacIver, Robert M., 5, 12
McKenzie, Roderick, 7
McNemar, Quinn, 278
Maine, Sir Henry, 8, 10
marginal structural areas, 21
marital status: participation and, 239; rank and, 115
Martindale, Don, 3, 13, 16, 110
Marx, Karl, 227
MDAP (Military Defense Assistance Program), 43
Mead, G. H., 210
medical facilities, 49
mental health, 181–183
Mercer, B. E., 10
military age, 114
military base, U.S., 67
military bulletins, on neatness and dress, 91–92
military code, fairness and violations in, 75–76
military community: administration in, 125–126; asking questions in, 279–280; closure and innovation in, 190–251, 255, 259; communication and, 212–218; cultural impact on, 212; density of habitation in, 123; education in, 116, 138–159; facility concentration of, 120; family life in, 172–183; fringe benefits in, 99; as garrison community, 68; government

groups and, 98–101; history of in Ankara, 253–255; ideology and stereotypes in, 218–224; intereffects of other groups with, 102–103; isolation and, 253–254; law enforcement in, 124; medical facilities in, 124; mental attitudes in, 127–129; modal age in, 114; nongovernment groups and, 101–102; overseas problems and concepts of, 1–24; programs in, 98–99; recreational facilities of, 125; relations with Turks in, 201–206; religious facilities in, 124; school facilities in, 123–124; size of, 211–224; socio-structural properties of, 113–189; status in, 103; tenure of, 258; transportation facilities in, 124; see also community; military organization
military construction, U.S., 44
Military Defense Assistance Program (MDAP), 43
military ethnic community, 64–112
military facilities, American comments on, 127–129
military institution: characteristics of, 66–68; dominance of, 66–67
military life: ethnic community and, 64–112; temporal sequences in, 129–130
military man, bureaucratic role of, 71–73
military mission: command conception of, 80–82; military units and, 42–46
military organization, 68–88; authority in, 72–73; bureaucracy of, 68; closure and, 206; democracy and, 69; expertise in, 69–70; individual in, 69–70; and organization man, 71–72; secrecy in, 206–210
military personnel: interchangeability of, 70–74; prearrival orientation of, 139–150

GARRISON COMMUNITY

research design, 271–273
research instrument, 273–277
riots, 1966, 94, 204–205
Rose, Arnold, 75
rotation policy, 83; status and, 86–87
Rousseau, Jean Jacques, 6
rumor, communication and, 212–213

Sanders, Irwin T., 10
sanitation, health and, 181
Sapir, Edward, 88
Schaffle, Albert E., 5
school buses, painting of, 94–95
school children, parents' attitudes toward, 158–159
schools: discipline in, 156–157; problems connected with, 50; segregation in, 155; see also education
secrecy, 206–210
segregation, in schools, 155
services and facilities, 123–129
settlement patterns, 121–123
Sherman, Edward F., 75
short-term perspectives, of community personnel, 85
situational forces, 255–256
social contract, community and, 6
social environment, structural and social variables in, 24
socialization, defined, 13
social organism, community as, 5
Soviet bloc, Turkish relations with, 41
Spencer, Herbert, 5, 8
stabilization, 13
Stars and Stripes, 213
State Department: legal problems and, 193–194; as "select group," 100
status: desire for, 103; ethnic, 88–97; marital, 239; rank and, 103
Stein, Maurice R., 73
Steiner, Jesse Frederick, 10
stereotypes, 89–90; ideology and, 218–223

structural variables, social environment and, 24
Sunay, Cevdet, 41
suspicion, 209–210
Sussman, Marvin B., 10

technical knowledge, 70–72
teen-agers, recreation for, 174–175
tension, intergroup, 190–206
Tönnies, Ferdinand, 8, 10
tour of duty, time perspectives in, 83–85
Truman, Harry S., 36
Truman Doctrine, 36–37
Turk(s): attitudes toward vs. rank, 220–221; "average," 219–220; prejudices against, 219–223
Turkey, U.S. relations with, 1947–1963, 37–38
Turkish-American Associations, 229
Turkish-American Community Council, 227
Turkish-American country club, 51–52
Turkish-American friendship, deterioration of, 39
Turkish children, education of, 154
Turkish "conspiracy," 214
Turkish culture: American evaluations of, 89; as "inferior," 225; postarrival opinions of, 147–148
Turkish food, American views on, 149
Turkish foreign policy, 41
Turkish Jews, 167
Turkish language, courses in, 150–152, 157–158
Turkish law: problems of, 191–192; religion and, 166
Turkish markets, American shopping in, 47–48
Turkish people: "good relations" with, 135; see also Turk(s)
Turkish products, as "inferior," 79, 126–129

Turkish "resentment," American view of, 211
Turkish Revolution of 1960, 226
Turkish schools, 50
TUSEG (The United States Engineer Group), 43
TUSLOG (The United States Logistics Group), 44–45, 50, 53, 95, 207–209, 212
TUSLOG Daily Bulletin, 202, 217

uniform, psychological effect of, 101
Uniform Code of Military Justice, 76
United States: aid to Turkey and Greece, 36–37; as "Big PX," 79; "get tough" policy against, 39; idealization of, 79–80; military community in, 65; relations with Turkey, 1947–1963, 38–39
United States Aid Mission to Turkey, 97
United States Embassy, demonstrations outside, 53
United States Engineer Group (TUSEG), 43
United States Information Service, 97, 101
United States Logistics Group, *see* TUSLOG

"unpleasant incidents," 203
value systems, cultural differences in, 197–199
"victim" psychology, opinions based on, 200–201
Vidich, Arthur J., 73
visitors, U.S., 97
voluntary services, in military establishment, 66–67

Wadsworth, George, 52
Warren, Roland L., 10
water supply, 48–49
Weber, Max, 69
"Whiskey Hill," 123
Whyte, William F., 270
Wilson, Everett, 70, 73
Wirth, Louis, 8
work ethic, violation of, 198
World War II: U.S. military commitments following, 1; U.S. role during, 35–36

Yashar, Kemal, 40

Zimmerman, Carl C., 10
Znaniecki, Florian, 11
Zorro, "mark" of, 214–215